Dedication

This book is lovingly dedicated to my grandchildren:
Roxanne,
Rebecca,
Jason,
Kimberly,
Kevin,
Caitlin,
Anneliese
Sarah,
and Nicholas.

Other books by Elaine Egbert:
The Edge of Eternity

To order, call 1-800-765-6955.
Visit us at www.reviewandherald.com for information on other
Review and Herald® products.

Daily Devotions for **Juniors**

Nature
in a
Nutshell

Elaine
Egbert

REVIEW AND HERALD® PUBLISHING ASSOCIATION
HAGERSTOWN, MD 21740

The author assumes full responsibility for the accuracy of all facts and quotations as cited in this book.

This book was
Edited by Lori Peckham
Copyedited by Delma Miller and James Cavil
Designed by square1studio
Cover art by Ron J. Pride / Photos.com
Typeset: ITC Officina Serif 11.5/14

PRINTED IN U.S.A.

07 06 05 04 03   5 4 3 2 1

R&H Cataloging Service
Egbert, Anita Elaine, 1938-
    Nature in a Nutshell

    1. Teenagers—Prayer—books and devotions—English. 2. Devotional calendars—Juvenile literature.
3. Natural history—Juvenile literature. I. Title

                    242.6

ISBN 0-8280-1669-0

A Note of Thanks

Many grateful thanks go to the following individuals, who directly or indirectly helped with the making of this book: Robert Egbert for his subject and Try It ideas, research, and constant moral support; Dennis Negrōn for his long-term loan of excellent resource books; Janelle Wahlman and Janet Qualls for their theme ideas, preview, and advisement; Alberta Oliver, Chris Hansen, Carl Swafford, Frances Egbert, Henry Kuhlman, Gene Swanson, and John Baker for sharing ideas and information; Lloyd Speers for continual encouragement to keep on writing; and to all the others who quietly inspired me as I wrote.

Dear Reader,

It's amazing how we can see the caring hand of God, our Creator, in nature. In love God has provided for each of His creatures—including you!

Of course, sometimes we see sad moments, such as when one animal preys upon another. But it wasn't that way in the beginning. When sin invaded our world not only human beings suffered—animals did, too.

But we can learn something from everything that happens in nature. Most of all, nature teaches us that God cares about even minor details of our lives. And someday He'll end all killing, sorrow, and pain and make everything new. Now, that's something to look forward to!

I encourage you to use the Talk Back sections to discuss the day's lesson with your parents or an adult you trust. And don't forget the activities or thoughts after the readings. They'll help you learn about the world you live in and the God who loves you more than you can imagine!

—Elaine Egbert

Look Often!

Our dog, Molly, loves to run free when we hike in the mountains. She's a springer spaniel, a hunting dog with a superb sense of smell. So she'll race back and forth across the path and up and down the hillsides with her nose to the ground, following every interesting scent.

Sometimes she'll stop to roll in the leaves. Other times she'll poke her nose into a hole and sniff loudly.

There's one thing, though, that Molly doesn't forget. No matter how fast and hard she plays, she stops often to check on where we are.

If she's separated from us for too long, just a glimpse of us isn't enough—she must return for petting and reassurance. She understands that she needs us, and that without us she'd be lost.

Daniel knew the importance of looking often to God. The king had issued a decree that anyone who prayed to any god or human other than himself would be thrown into the lions' den. But this is what Daniel did: *"Three times a day he got down on his knees and prayed, giving thanks to his God, just as he had done before."*

Daniel wanted to make sure he stayed on the pathway that God wanted him to walk. We need God just as much as Daniel did. So this year let's look to Him often.

MISSION: Several times each day—wherever you are—pray silently to God. Tell Him what's on your heart. Then watch for the ways He'll guide and encourage you.

Arctic Tundra

The part of our earth north of the Arctic Circle is called tundra. It looks like a desert, except it gets very cold there. The tundra receives only about 10 inches of rain in a year.

Considering how dry and cold it is, you'd think nothing could survive there. But many plants, animals, and birds actually thrive. Why? Because of the permafrost. Permafrost is permanently frozen subsoil, or dirt.

Even during the summer, when the sun never sets, the subsoil stays frozen. So water that hits it doesn't sink into the dirt. Instead, the water gets trapped in shallow ponds and marshy areas for the plants and animals to use.

There's one problem, though. When water freezes, it swells. So in the winter the frozen subsoil creates lumps called frost heaves. When these heaves thaw the soil slips away, leaving only rocks where plants can't grow. These bare spots become permanent wounds.

Words we say in anger can also make wounds. Even though we might apologize afterward, the effects of what we say can last forever. That's why the apostle James said, *"The tongue is a small thing, but what enormous damage it can do"* (TLB).

Why not dedicate your tongue and your words to Jesus? With His help, determine to say only positive things.

TRY IT: Mix dirt, pebbles, and water into mud. Put the mud in a bowl and freeze it. Later remove the frozen dirt from the bowl and drip water on it. What happens?

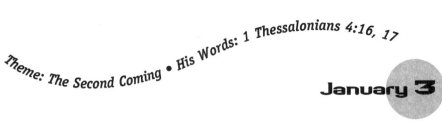

Lemmings

Home: Northern alpine and tundra areas
Size: 4-6 inches

Lemmings are rodents that look like mice. Except lemmings have short tails and furry little feet. Also, their ears are hidden beneath their fur. That helps them to conserve heat, because they live on the cold tundra.

In the summer lemmings burrow under stumps or rocks. But before the winter sets in, they head for a meadow and build cozy nests under branches or snow.

Lemmings eat grasses, tender shoots, moss, and even bark when food is scarce. They hunt for food both day and night, alternating eating and sleeping every couple hours.

By the time lemmings are 16 days old they begin to mate. Three weeks later they have their babies. Populations grow quickly, and food soon becomes scarce.

So lemmings have to migrate in search of new food sources. When they come to rivers or lakes, they try to cross them. But many drown trying to get across.

Someday we as God's children will need to "migrate" in order to escape this sinful world. But unlike lemmings, we'll have Someone to rescue us. The Bible promises, *"For the Lord himself will come down from heaven, with a loud command. . . . After that, we . . . will be caught up . . . to meet the Lord in the air. And so we will be with the Lord forever."* What a wonderful day!

MISSION: Read Mark 13. What signs can you see that Christ will come soon? How can you be ready?

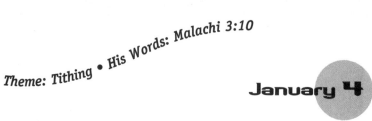

Potter Wasps

Home: Many temperate areas
Size: To .75 inch

Potter wasps are black insects with yellow or white markings. They have long, strong mandibles, or biting jaws.

In preparation for laying her eggs, the female finds a puddle or creek where there's plenty of dirt. First she mixes the dirt with water until it's just the right consistency. Then she carries mouthfuls of the mud in her mandibles. She hunts for vegetation or a rock and uses the mud to build her pot-shaped nest. (That's how the potter wasp got its name.)

Next she finds some caterpillars and stings them. She carefully puts them in the nest. Only then does she lay her eggs. Once the eggs hatch, the babies have food to eat until they're large enough to find their own.

Now, if the mother didn't provide so well for her babies, they wouldn't survive. That's because once she lays the eggs, it's time for her to fly away.

When God set up His church, He knew that pastors and missionaries would need to be provided for so they could spend their time preaching the gospel. So He said, *"Bring the whole tithe into the storehouse, that there may be food in my house. Test me in this."*

Tithe is a tenth of whatever you gain. Actually, everything you have belongs to God. And God has promised that when you're faithful in returning your tithe to His storehouse, you'll receive a wonderful blessing. Try it.

TALK BACK: What Bible characters tithed? What happened?

The One That Got Away

At one time I was in charge of the girls' dormitory at Blue Mountain Academy, a Christian high school. That's when my husband, Bob, began collecting nonpoisonous snakes.

One of Bob's snakes was a six-foot boa constrictor named Stretch. Stretch was particularly active, and one day he disappeared. The dorm girls and I looked everywhere but couldn't find him.

Then the following summer during camp meeting, families stayed in the dorm. One night while a woman slept in her bunk, something touched her cheek. She brushed at it and turned over.

A little later something began to slide across her face. Panicked, she flung it away, sprang out of bed, and turned on the light. To her horror, a snake slithered beneath the bed!

"Snake!" she screamed, racing down the hallway in her nightgown.

Everybody woke up, and Bob and I went to see what had happened. When we heard, I tried to calm the woman, and Bob brought Stretch back home!

Have you ever gossiped about someone, only to have your words repeated to the one you talked about? Did your unwise chatter cause problems? The Bible says, *"Without gossip, quarreling will stop" (ICB).*

The trouble with words is that once you let them loose, like Stretch, you no longer have control over where they go. So determine that the words you say today won't make you or anyone else uncomfortable tomorrow.

TALK BACK: What kinds of feelings do people have when they gossip?

Nature's Slinky

Home: Worldwide forests and meadows
Size: To 26 inches, including tail

Maybe you've seen a Slinky, the coiled toy that "walks" down stairs. The animal world has its own Slinky. It's called a ferret—a long, slender mammal in the weasel family.

Ferrets have short legs and a bushy tail. While their coats might differ in color, all ferrets have one thing in common: a flexible backbone that allows them to twist, turn, and move through tight, curved spaces impossible for other animals their size to manage.

Many farmers consider ferrets pests because they kill chickens and small mammals. But some people make good use of this little animal's skills.

For instance, electricians sometimes place a harness on a ferret and attach wires to the harness. Then they put the ferret by a hole. The animal's inborn curiosity will prod it to investigate. When it does, it pulls the wires through tight, curvy conduits, coming out the other end happy for the chance to explore!

The apostle Paul said, *"Be devoted to one another in brotherly love. Honor one another above yourselves."* To be a true friend, you'll need to learn to be flexible. That means taking turns in choosing activities, letting others be first most of the time, and not insisting on always having your way,

TALK BACK: There's one area in which we shouldn't be flexible—in doing what Jesus asks us to do. So how can we be flexible with our friends if they want to do wrong things?

14

The Double-humped Camel

Home: Gobi Desert, Mongolia
Size: To 1,500 pounds

One day I watched a two-humped Bactrian camel have her calf. First she made a loud groan. Then the calf dropped out and landed on the ground on its head! Fortunately, it seemed unhurt and soon tried to stand up on its wobbly little legs.

Bactrian camels have long woolly coats that shield them from summer sunburns and icy winters on the Gobi Desert. Their double eyelashes and nostrils that close help protect them from blowing sand. Also, to make walking on shifting terrain easier, their feet expand. And they can drink 25 gallons of water at once, which allows them to go many days without drinking again.

These camels eat tough desert scrub bushes, which they chew as cud to make it digestible. Their two humps store excess food and water as fat for times when they must go without.

Domesticated Bactrian camels work hard, but if they feel mistreated, they hold a grudge. To get even, they'll spit a foul-smelling substance into their handler's face. This trait has given them the reputation of being bad-tempered. Have you noticed how miserable you feel when you hold a grudge? And have you seen how the situation usually gets worse if you blow up? The Bible says, *"A wise man restrains his anger and overlooks insults"* (TLB).

Being wise means realizing that things won't always go your way. It also means learning to face problems in a calm way and forgiving wrongs—and forgetting them.

CONTACT: Father, help me to be able to forgive others as You forgive me.

Shoebill Stork

Home: Africa
Size: Wingspan to 6.5 feet

Shoebill storks have huge shoe-shaped bills with a hook on the end. These hooks help them hold on to the slippery fish they catch.

The storks stand quietly on their long legs, waiting for a fish to come to the water's surface. When they spot one, they pounce at it, scooping it up with their beaks.

Shoebill storks use reeds from swamps to build thick, eight-foot nests. In this nest by the waterside the mother stork incubates up to three eggs. The father often roosts beside her at night. In the daytime when it's hot, these careful parents use their beaks to scoop water onto the eggs—and later the chicks—in order to keep them cool. Instinct tells them that if their babies get too hot they'll die.

Sometimes people get angry at each other and let things get too hot. When this happens, do you know how to cool things off? The Bible says, *"A gentle answer turns away wrath, but a harsh word stirs up anger."*

When someone's tormenting you, it's hard to keep your cool. You want to strike back. But the quickest way to cool a situation like that is to pray for help, and then say or do something nice. Wait until things have calmed down to explain your actions or prove your innocence.

TALK BACK: Why do some people want everyone to think that they're always right?

Squirting Cucumber

Home: Europe, Britain

When Jesus was a child, He might have played with an amusing plant that grows wild in Israel. It's called the squirting cucumber.

Squirting cucumbers grow on a spreading vine much like the cucumbers you eat in salads. Only these tough-skinned cucumbers, which look oval like a kiwi, are poisonous.

After the cucumber vine blossoms, small green gourdlike objects appear. These cucumbers are covered with triangular prickles. As the cucumber matures, pressure builds up inside it.

Then, when an animal or desert grasses brush against it, the cucumber blows away from the vine with a loud *pshwittt!* Seeds and a sticky juice spray from the fruit, sending the cucumber sailing 10 feet or more. The juice makes the seeds stick to whatever they touch, enabling the plant to set up new colonies of vines.

The Bible tells stories of people who became angry and took hasty action. But it warns, *"Don't get angry. Don't be upset; it only leads to trouble"* (ICB).

When you spout off with hot words or let your fists fly, it just brings more trouble. That's why God expects you to manage your temper, and He promises to help you stay cool.

TRY IT: When anger starts building up, step away from the situation. Ask God to help you calm down and understand what's really upsetting you. After you're calm, talk to the person involved. Following God's leading, find a way to make peace.

Orion's Fuzzy Sword

My favorite constellation is Orion. You can see it from anywhere on the earth, and it's even mentioned in the Bible!

Look in a star book to see an illustration of it. Imagined to be a hunter, Orion moves sideways across the sky.

Notice his "sword." The center star of the sword is actually M42, a nebula made of glowing gas and dust particles. When examined through a telescope, the M42 looks like a bright, hazy cloud. It seems tiny, yet its diameter is 100,000 light-years—and it's 1,500 light-years away!

Something really excites me about the M42. After having a vision, the apostle John said, *"And I saw the holy city coming down out of heaven from God. This holy city is the new Jerusalem"* (ICB).

Many years later Ellen White also had a vision of the end of the world. She wrote, "The atmosphere parted and rolled back; then we could look up through the open space in Orion, whence came the voice of God. The Holy City will come down through that open space" (*Early Writings,* p. 41).

I wonder if heaven's behind that nebula. Some people think so. What I do know is that after we spend a millennium in heaven with Jesus, He'll bring the New Jerusalem to earth. I want to ride in the Holy City as it passes through the nebula, don't you?

TRY IT: On a clear moonless night, use your binoculars to view M42 in Orion's sword. What colors do you see?

Bushbuck

Home: Africa
Size: 3.5-5 feet in length

The bushbuck is an antelope with a special coat. Slower than most other antelopes, it leaps in a zigzag manner. Then it freezes, and its markings completely blend with the background.

The doe chooses a secluded thicket in which to give birth. After her baby is born, she must leave it each day in order to graze for food. To keep predators from catching the baby's scent, the mother gets rid of its dung by eating it!

Left by itself for the day, the baby must remain quiet. Otherwise it could be found by leopards or pythons. If the baby doesn't cooperate, it might not survive.

Sometimes you'll find yourself without adult supervision. At those times, do you still follow your parents' instructions? Sometimes it's hard to understand why parents make certain rules. Yet you must trust that they're for your good and might even save your life!

When you think that no one will see what you do, that's when your real character shows. Your character is the only thing you'll take with you to heaven. So let God form your character. Then you'll be able to say with Paul, I *"have done everything with an honest and pure heart from God"* (ICB).

TALK BACK: Why are people tempted to do wrong things when not supervised?

Wild Sheep or Wild Goat?

Home: World wilderness areas

How can you tell the difference between a wild sheep and a wild goat? Both animals live in mountainous, craggy places. Both are good runners and jumpers. Both chew their cuds and are covered with warm fur.

But the male goat has a beard. He also has long horns that curve up and back in a V above his head. The male sheep, on the other hand, has thick curved horns that grow in a spiral back and down around his ears. Female sheep and goats have shorter horns.

In Bible times people drove goats into town and milked them. They also used their fur and meat. Independent, the goats wanted things their own way.

Sheep acted more gentle and cooperative. They didn't have to be driven but stayed near their shepherd, depending on him to care for them. They often became pets, prized more for their wool than for their meat.

The Bible speaks of people resembling sheep and goats. While goats want to go their own way, sheep love to follow Jesus. When Jesus comes again He *"will separate the people one from another as a shepherd separates the sheep from the goats."*

You need to give your heart and your will to Him now, so when that exciting day comes you'll find yourself in the right flock!

TALK BACK: How do you think the lost sheep (Luke 15: 3-7) felt when it was lost? when the shepherd rescued it? Tell about a time you needed to be rescued. How did you feel?

20

The Bat-eared Fox

Home: Africa
Size: 6-12 pounds

The bat-eared fox is a small grayish-yellow animal. It gets its name from its large oval ears, which can get as big as five inches.

A member of the dog family, this fox lives in dry, grassy areas or brushlands. For protection it digs a deep den or takes one from another animal. The den usually has several entrances, which helps the fox duck for cover from predators, such as large birds, jackals, and leopards.

The bat-eared fox has two daily goals: to find food, and to avoid *being* food. It eats mostly insects, which it hears moving beneath the ground. The fox considers scorpions a delicacy, eating the poison sac, stinger, and all.

The bat-eared fox is smart. To confuse predators trying to follow its trail, it goes one way and then another. Sometimes it even retraces its steps to make its scent harder to follow. It must plan ahead in order to stay alive.

You also must plan ahead in order to keep out of trouble. Lying, for instance, is a trap that some people get caught in. After telling one lie, they find themselves telling more lies to avoid getting caught. Unlike the fox that plans many ways of escape, liars box themselves in with their tongues. Solomon was right when he said, *"He who pours out lies will not go free."*

TALK BACK: How can I prepare a safety net that will keep me from lying? If I do slip and tell a lie, what must I do?

Why Do Animals Kill?

A shiny-backed beetle crawled beneath the rosebushes looking for a meal. Suddenly it spied a ladybug. With a pounce, the beetle captured the ladybug. It was about to satisfy its hunger when a robin spied the beetle and snatched it for dinner.

After eating the beetle, the robin was about to look for another when something big pounced on it. It hadn't remembered the flower garden's cat!

Three lives were lost. And if we continued the story, we might see another predator catch the cat, and so on.

If God is love, why did He create animals to kill each other? He didn't! The Bible tells us that God said, *"To all the beasts of the earth and all the birds of the air and all the creatures that move on the ground—everything that has the breath of life in it—I give every green plant for food."*

When God created our world, all the animals got along. They enjoyed eating the plants that God had provided. But when Satan brought sin to our world, it not only affected human beings—the animals suffered, too.

God has allowed nature to take its sinful course. But someday He'll return and make things right again. Observing how nature works has made me even more eager for Jesus to come again. How about you?

CONTACT: Dear God, help me understand the lessons You have for me in nature. And help me remember that You're always a God of love.

The "Big Doggie"

Three-year-old Derry went winter camping with his parents. But he wandered off from the campsite and got lost. As evening neared, his parents became frantic. They knew that the temperature in the mountains normally dropped to well below freezing at night.

For three days Derry's parents and rescue workers looked for him. Finally, on a warmer than normal day, a rescue dog picked up Derry's scent. The dog led them to Derry, who was sleeping in a sunny place on a hillside. Other than being very hungry, Derry was fine.

Puzzled that he hadn't died from the cold, the searchers asked him, "Where did you sleep?"

"With the big doggie," Derry answered, pointing to a sheltered cove.

The rescue workers saw big pawprints in the snow and the body indentations of both a bear and little Derry. Strange as it seemed, the bear had cuddled up to the child at night, keeping him warm and saving his life.

God has many unexpected ways to protect and care for His children. He says, *"Was my arm too short to ransom you? Do I lack the strength to rescue you? By a mere rebuke I dry up the sea."*

We don't have to understand how God works His miracles. Our part is to live as He's asked us to and to thank Him for His warm care.

TALK BACK: Tell about a time God used you to help someone. How did you know you were to help?

23

When the Difference Makes a Difference

Home: Madagascar
Size: To 5 feet long, including tail, and 13 pounds

The fossa is a catlike animal related to the mongoose. Living in dense forests, it's at home either in the trees or on the ground.

Madagascar's largest carnivore, it hunts at night. Though it's chunkier than a cat, it behaves like one, feeding on chickens and wild prey.

The strangest thing about the fossa is that females and males look identical in every way. They both have reddish-brown fur, short faces, rounded ears, long back legs, ropy tails, and retractable claws. So it's hard to tell the difference between them.

Many people profess to love and follow Jesus. They talk about Him and seem to do all the right things. Some are sincere, but others live this way as a cover-up to keep from getting into trouble.

As with the fossa's gender, it's sometimes hard to tell the difference between people who truly love God and those who don't. But there's a solution. The Bible says, *"By their fruit you will recognize them."* That means that eventually their activities and words will tell on them.

If you love God, know your Bible, and live by what it says, you'll be a genuine Christian. And if you ask God to help you, you'll be able to choose friends who truly love Him, too.

CONTACT: Dear God, lead me to know the truth so I can better serve You.

24

The Best Door

When I was little I was playing in a vacant lot by my house. I spotted some round disks on the ground that looked like dirty bottle caps. Then I noticed one standing on its end.

Curious, I squatted to peek into the hole beside the cap. Suddenly the cap closed. I waited quietly, and in a while it reopened. That's when I saw a black spider peeking out of the hole. It was a trap-door spider.

These spiders build tunnels about an inch wide and a foot deep, lining them with silk. At the tunnel entrance they construct a hinged door by alternating layers of dirt and silk.

When they're hungry they push open the door and crouch just inside their hole, watching for an insect to wander by. When one does, they dart out to capture it, then return to their hole, pulling the door shut. The closed door traps prey inside.

Doors protect what's inside and also keep unwanted guests out. But doors also serve another purpose. They're meant to open so things can pass through.

Jesus said, *"I am the door: by me if any man enter in, he shall be saved, and shall go in and out, and find pasture"* *(KJV)*. If you wish to enter heaven, it must be through the door of Jesus. When you accept His sacrifice for your sins and claim Him as your Savior, you go through that door.

MISSION: Jesus called Himself the door. What other names did He call Himself? Look in a concordance to find the texts.

Asian Elephant

Home: Asia
Size: To 11,000 pounds

Asian elephants have smaller bodies and ears than African elephants. But their smaller size doesn't mean they can't work effectively. In fact, these huge, thick-skinned animals are used in Asian forests to fell trees and transport logs. In their late teens they begin doing light work and can handle heavy loads by about age 25.

Elephants are sensitive, gentle, and loyal. Loving owners bathe their elephants each day and even polish their tusks with sand. In return, the elephants break off overhead branches so their riders won't be scraped off their backs.

Elephants and their riders often remain devoted to each other, staying together until one of them dies. Like humans do, elephants cry when they're sad. Caring riders know this and treat them like family, doing all they can to keep them happy.

In Bible times when a loved one died, the family members would save their tears of sorrow in tiny bottles. Then they buried the bottles with the body to show how much they loved and respected the loved one.

King David said to God, *"You have recorded my troubles. You have kept a list of my tears" (ICB)*. Only a God who loves us would keep such a list. He cares about our problems, big or small. When we're sad He feels it. And through His Holy Spirit He's always nearby.

CONTACT: Loving God, help me to always sense Your presence.

26

Animal Watching

If you want to observe animals in the wild, you must follow these rules: don't move quickly, be quiet, dress to blend with the surroundings, and give them plenty of room. Keep in mind that you're in *their* living room, and they hear better than you do.

Don't startle animals to make them run or fly. And don't rescue babies that seem to be lost. (Their mother is probably watching from a distance.) Stay far from nests. Your approach could alert a predator to the presence of the nest. And don't touch eggs or chicks, because your scent could scare off the mother from returning.

To find animals think like one. What does it eat? Where is that food? Watch the landscape for motion. Look above and below. Check for horizontal shapes in forests (animals' backs) or textures in leaves or branches (fur or feathers). Learn to use binoculars. You'll see animals "up close" without alarming them.

If you unexpectedly encounter a wild animal, don't stare directly at it. Animals stare at each other when about to attack, and your behavior could be taken as a threat.

The Bible says of God, *"Marvellous are thy works" (KJV)*. By observing nature, you can learn about how God provides for His creatures. That will help you understand how He cares for you.

TRY IT: Go outside and listen for a faint sound. Facing the sound, cup your hands around your ears to form "mule ears." Notice how God created animal ears to amplify sound.

Molly O'Dog

Size: To 50 pounds

Molly, our springer spaniel, was badly abused during her first year of life. After having several owners, she spent a few months in an animal shelter.

By the time we got her, she desperately wanted to belong to *someone*. Eager to be close, she worshiped us with worried brown eyes, wildly greeted us, flung herself into our laps when we sat down, and viciously warned off other dogs that approached us.

She wouldn't eat if we weren't present and became frantic and destructive when we left for work. She was so out of control that we wondered if we should keep her. But how could we disrupt her life again?

I began walking her, reassuring her, and gradually teaching her to obey. She joyfully learned tricks to earn dog biscuits. Now, three years later, she's usually polite, always devoted, and no longer insecure if we pet another dog. She's gained a very important thing—trust.

Maybe you know people whose behavior keeps them from fitting in. A hard start or insecurity has made them bullies, whiners, or clingy. How can you help them become happier, more reasonable people? Jesus said, *"Trust in the Lord and do good."*

As you prayerfully befriend them, God can heal their hurts. Trust, after all, can make all the difference in the world.

CONTACT: Dear God, help me to care enough to help others who have a hard time making friends.

28

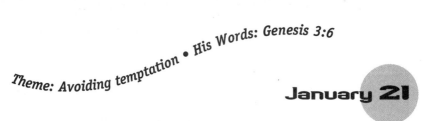

"Just Looking"

After Molly learned several tricks, I decided to teach her to be patient. So I put a dog biscuit by my foot. When she rushed toward it, I covered it and said, "Wait!"

She nudged my foot with her nose. Then, watching my face, she learned to leave the biscuit alone until I said "OK."

Then I asked her to perform for my husband, Bob.

"Wait!" I told Molly, placing the biscuit about five feet away.

Molly waited, but this time she stared at the biscuit instead of at me. Finally she could bear it no longer. Drooling, she snatched it.

Keeping her eyes on the biscuit had been her undoing. If she'd watched only me, she'd have passed the test.

Have you noticed that the more you look at something, the more you want it? That's what happened to Eve. *"When the woman saw that the fruit of the tree was good for food and pleasing to the eye . . . she took some and ate it."* If Eve had refused to linger and gaze at the tree, she wouldn't have given in to temptation.

When you're tempted to do something wrong, it's best to put the idea out of your mind immediately. "Just looking" only makes your desire grow stronger, providing a foothold for the devil's temptations. Learn to say, "Get thee behind me, Satan," and turn away fast!

TALK BACK: If something you want isn't good for you, how can you use your mind instead of following your desires?

He Wears His Foot!

Home: Intertidal ocean areas
Size: From 3-4 inches across

If you walk on the beach, you might find a moon snail shell. These brownish-colored spirals have an unusually large opening. Through this space the moon snail extends its enormous mantle, or foot.

This slippery mantle is actually the membrane the snail uses to burrow through the sand in search of clams. Once it covers its prey with its mantle, the snail drills a little hole into the clam's valve and sucks the juices out it.

Another meaning for the word "mantle" is cloak, or robe, and the snail uses its mantle for this as well. Starfish try to capture the snail using their suction cups. But if the snail moves quickly enough, it can wrap its huge mantle completely around itself. This makes it too slippery for the starfish to grasp.

Satan is a predator who wants to devour us. But Jesus can foil his wicked plans. David said, *"He hath covered me with the robe of righteousness"* (KJV).

Wouldn't you like to be covered with Christ's protective robe of righteousness? If so, faithfully study the Bible and follow its teachings. Pray to God. And accept Jesus as your Savior. Then He can protect you from Satan's attacks.

CONTACT: Dear Father, help me choose to stay beneath Jesus' robe of righteousness today.

30

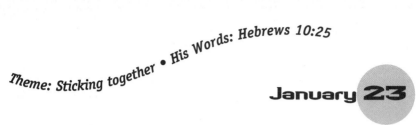

Living Collar

Home: Intertidal ocean areas
Size: From 3-4 inches

Moon snails have both male and female products within them. So when it's time to reproduce, the snail spreads its foot out wide. Then it oozes an egg-filled jellylike substance on its top.

As the secretion gets covered with grains of sand, the eggs and sand form a thin, collar-shaped egg case. This quickly hardens. Then the moon snail pulls its foot out from beneath the case and secures the open end of the collar into the sand.

For several weeks the ocean tides pound the hard case. But because the sand, jelly, and eggs are so well mixed, it takes a lot to make it disintegrate. When it finally does, the baby moon snails are ready to go their way.

God's love is like the jelly. Your home, your church, and the people inside are like the sand. Combined, they make a strong place for you to grow.

Paul said, *"Don't give up the habit of worshiping together as some have already done, but encourage each other"* (Clear Word). When you're firmly embedded in this protective Christian atmosphere, problems and questions may batter you. But with the help of God and your "big family," you'll be able to weather any storm.

TALK BACK: How can I help make my school a strong and safe place for others to grow?

Standing Tall

I keep a block of suet (beef fat) outside my window. The suet sits in a mesh box fastened to a crossarm on a tall pole. Placed that way, two birds can eat from it at once.

Most birds sit on the crossarm and peck through the sides of the container. But not Stretchy. This sparrow perches on the crossarm, then stands as tall as he can and pecks his food out of the top of the container.

"Good enough" isn't his style. He makes himself work for his treat, and he seems to enjoy the task.

Are you like Stretchy, setting high goals for yourself and doing more than required? Or do you choose the easy way out? If Dad asks you to mow the lawn, do you also trim it, then carefully put things away? If Mom asks you to do the dishes, do you wipe the counters and clean under the toaster as well? At school, do you learn more about a subject than you have to?

While working in Egypt Joseph always did his best. We're told that *"the Lord gave him success in everything he did."*

Remember that everything you do is for Jesus. So stretch yourself mentally and physically. He'll bless your efforts.

MISSION: Choose something that's hard or unpleasant to do. Then do it in the best way possible. You'll find that it's not so unpleasant when you do your best.

The Little Brumby

Home: Semiarid Australia
Size: To 4 feet high

Early settlers introduced horses to Australia. They used the horses to work their farms and provide transportation.

Eventually some horses escaped, and others were abandoned when people moved away. Left to fend for themselves, the horses became wild and bred.

The result was the brumby, which means "wild." These small wily horses live in hot sandy areas. They feed on sparse scrub grass, acacias, and shrub leaves, thriving in hostile conditions that most other horses can't tolerate.

Brumby horses don't like humans. If captured, they're stubborn and nearly impossible to train, even though domestic life would be easier for them. Left to themselves, they wreck fences, overgraze the land, stir up water holes, and become a nuisance to people. In Australia, if you're called a "brumby," you're considered unruly and disorderly.

Maybe you've experienced feelings of rebellion. You wanted to do things your own way and resented being told what to do or where to go.

Everyone experiences these feelings, but if you're wise, you'll learn to control them. The Bible says, *"Whoever heeds correction gains understanding."* Don't make your life harder by being a brumby!

TALK BACK: Consider Samson. In what ways was he like a brumby? What could he have done to avoid the problems he experienced?

33

Tangled Kitten Tales

The two cats batted Grandma's ball of yarn across the bedroom floor. They leaped and rolled as they caught the strands. Before long there was yarn everywhere, including around Mifty's tail.

Then Grandma came in. Quick as a blink, Tommycat jumped onto the rocker and began to clean his paw. Even though he'd started it all, he looked at Grandma as if to say, "What? I'm innocent! It's all *her* fault."

This blame-shifting thing all started when God came to the garden and asked Adam, *"Have you eaten from the tree that I commanded you not to eat from?"* Adam told God that Eve had given him the fruit, and then Eve blamed the serpent for tempting her.

When people get in trouble, they often say such things as, "Brad started it!" or "Dina told us it was OK." People don't want to accept blame for their mistakes.

All of us do unwise and sinful things sometimes. Why, then, is it so hard to admit our guilt? Maybe we want people to think we're perfect. Or maybe we're scared of being caught. Whatever the reason, it takes guts to admit we're wrong. Let's have the guts!

TRY IT: Ask Jesus to help you have the courage to take responsibility for your mistakes.

Vines

In the South flowering vines grow in the woods, climbing up trees and fences. These vines fill the air with sweet perfume.

One day I decided that I wanted one in my yard. So I bought a vine with fragrant yellow flowers. It didn't take long to plant it and to "show" the tendrils where to go by pointing them upward. But though the vine flourished, it wouldn't climb. Instead, it spread along the ground.

Finally, I used twine to tie the vine to a tree trunk. By the end of the summer it had climbed six feet. The next summer it had climbed 20 more. It now covers one tree and is reaching for the next tree.

It's growing so fast that I'll have to dig it out before it chokes and kills the trees. What seemed harmless has turned into an uncontrollable and deadly monster.

That's what happens when you tell a lie. You might fib to cover up something you don't want anyone to know. Then suddenly you have a new problem. You have to cover old lies with new ones and can't even remember the truth!

That's why the apostle Paul said, *"Do not lie to each other."* God's commandments tell you the same thing. Lying might seem harmless at first, but it becomes a monster that turns deadly.

CONTACT: Father, please give me the courage to be truthful in everything. Help me find honest ways to deal with problems.

35

Dancing Night Lights

Home: North and South polar regions
Size: 40-600 miles above earth

Imagine you're winter camping. You've had your supper and climbed into your sleeping bag. Now you lie there, watching the stars twinkling in the blackness overhead.

Then suddenly the sky toward the polar region begins to brighten. A glowing arc appears, quickly getting lighter. Holding your breath, you wonder what's happening. Soon the glow becomes a shimmering green or red, flowing like drapes rippling in a breeze.

Wondering if your eyes are playing tricks on you, you awaken your buddy. When he sees the same thing, you decide it's true. You're watching an aurora.

The aurora borealis (northern lights) and the aurora australis (southern lights) occur when the earth's magnetic field meets charged particles being blown away from the sun. The particles interact with gas molecules in our upper atmosphere, causing them to glow.

The color of the aurora depends on which gases are present. Auroras are usually seen in the far northern or southern latitudes, but have actually been seen at the equator!

The psalmist wrote, *"The heavens declare the glory of God; the skies proclaim the work of his hands."* How great is the God who made our earth and the heavens! I believe He delights in giving us glimpses of the beauties we'll someday experience in the new earth.

CONTACT: God, thank You for the beautiful things You let me see. Help me realize that You're God over all.

36

Empty Promises

Food growers need to receive the right amount of rain at the right time. Otherwise, their crops won't develop properly. Especially in areas where irrigation isn't practiced, growers must rely on rain to do the job.

Some years the rains come at the right times, and bountiful crops result. But when little or no rain falls, the plants begin to wither. That's when growers keep an eye on the sky, hoping and praying that every tiny wisp of cloud will develop into a thunderhead. If the clouds darken and roll in, joy spreads through the farming community.

Sometimes those promising clouds just pass over, and rain doesn't fall. That brings disappointment, for the growers want to deliver good produce to merchants.

Have you ever promised to give something to a friend? It's exciting to think of how happy they'll be. But what if you fail to carry out your promise?

The Bible says, *"People who brag about gifts they never give are like clouds and wind that give no rain" (ICB.)* Don't be an empty boaster, promising to give or do something but then not following through. That's disappointing! Give people showers of blessings!

CONTACT: Lord, help me to make only wise promises, and then to follow up on them, even when it's not convenient.

Longing for Light

Long ago people's homes were made of logs or sod and usually consisted of only one room. Within that space families worked and ate by firelight. Many homes had no windows, for glass was expensive and often broke during shipping.

Even in the daytime the interior would look dark and gloomy. Longing for light, resourceful pioneers sometimes spread lard on butcher paper and used that to make a window. But it wasn't much good.

Then someone noticed the rock-forming mineral called mica lying on the ground. Mica's smooth, shiny surface easily reflects sunlight. The pioneers learned that mica can easily be peeled into thin sheets that are quite clear. This was just what they needed!

Soon they were using sheets of mica to make windows. The windows were called isinglass. (Isinglass was also made out of fish air bladders.)

Sunlight is very important in people's lives. Without it, health deteriorates. People often refer to light in a spiritual sense, too. David wrote, *"The Lord is my light and my salvation."*

In order to receive light, though, you must provide a window. The window is the Bible and the Spirit of Prophecy. As you open your heart to their messages from God, He'll help you live up to the light that shines through.

TALK BACK: In your busy life, how can you make more time to gather God's valuable light into your heart?

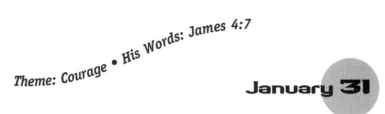

January **31**

The Little Destroyer

Home: Europe
Size: 15-18 inches long

Polecats aren't really cats but weasel-like mammals. They're about four times longer than they are tall. They have creamy fur tipped with dark hair. Before it became illegal, people trapped them to make coats from their fur.

Polecats live in many habitats. Nighttime hunters, they eat rodents, frogs, snakes, insects, birds, eggs, and fish. Because of their size and flexible vertebrae, they can squeeze through very small spaces.

Ruthless, they hunt whether they're hungry or not. And when they find a den of rabbits or mice or chickens in their coop, they often kill them all rather than just enough to eat. This and the unpleasant odor they emit when frightened have made them unpopular. (However, the Forest Service appreciates their ability to destroy rodents that chew bark off young trees.)

There's another hunter who destroys everything he touches. He ruins purity, looks, health, relationships, morals, and happiness. He uses trickery and lies to camouflage his activities. He can make bad things look good. His name is Satan, and it takes real courage to fight against him.

But James advised, *"Submit yourselves, then, to God. Resist the devil, and he will flee from you."* You're not in this fight alone! When tempted to do something wrong, immediately ask God to help you. He will.

TALK BACK: What are some tricks Satan uses to destroy people's lives? How can you foil him?

Habitats That Attract

I love to watch the wild creatures that visit our yard. Turtles amble between the flower beds to hunt tasty grasses. Tiny green and brown frogs live in the ivy and perch under the porch light at night to catch insects. Brightly colored lizards sun on our stone walls that provide cracks for them to hide in.

Chipmunks live beneath our back stairs, and squirrels nest in the trees. These animals feed on seeds or tender shoots near our bird feeder. Rabbits dine on lawn clover by our thicket. And our flowers—butterfly bush, cornflowers, violets, marigolds, and daisies—attract butterflies, bees, and hummingbirds.

Goldfinches snatch up seeds from certain weeds we allow to grow for them. And the wide, shallow bowl of water we leave out provides drink and bath for both birds and animals.

Each one needs the right habitat in order to make our place their home.

How can you make your heart an inviting habitat for Jesus? The Bible says, *"You shall fear the Lord your God; you shall serve Him and cling to Him" (NASB)*. That means keeping your thoughts on God, obeying His Word, and inviting Him into your heart. Then you can live in His love and protection. And that's a *wonderful* habitat!

TRY IT: Create an inviting habitat in your yard for wildlife. Then when you see creatures, remain quiet and don't try to catch them. Soon they'll feel safe, and you can observe some of the nature lessons God has for you.

My Laughing Dog

Home: Siberia
Size: 45-65 pounds

The Samoyed is a dog that lives in Siberia and other cold arctic countries. Stocky and strong, it herds reindeer and pulls sleds. Its large hairy feet provide good traction on snow.

Especially adapted for frigid weather, Samoyeds have double coats. Thick fur grows next to their skin to keep them warm. Then another layer of long, coarse hair helps them shed snow and keep dry. They even have a protective growth of hair between their toes!

As a child I had a pet Samoyed named Buck. He was snow white, except for his black nose and lips. Buck always appeared to be smiling and ready for play. He had furry, erect ears and a bushy tail that curled over his back.

Twice a year he shed great amounts of hair. I'd brush it out and fill large bags with it. Then I gave it to a woman who spun it into yarn for knitting soft, warm sweaters.

Samoyeds are friendly and reliable. They're happiest when kept busy. So their breed has earned a good reputation as hard workers and good pets.

Your reputation means the quality of character for which you're known. Each person develops a reputation or "name." Such traits as loyalty, kindness, honesty, and purity help you create a good reputation. The Bible says, *"A good name is more desirable than great riches."*

What kind of reputation are you earning for yourself? for your family? for your God?

TALK BACK: What earns people bad reputations? Name three ways you can guard against these things.

Buck and the "Lie"

When I was 11 Buck got me into trouble. In our garage my mom kept a big bag of unshelled walnuts for us to snack on. One day she reminded me not to leave the broken shells on the lawn.

"I didn't," I explained. "Buck did." Then I told her how he bit the walnuts into perfect halves and dug the meat out with his canines.

Mother looked doubtful, so I handed Buck a walnut so he could demonstrate. But he dropped it and seemed to laugh at me.

"Elaine, how ridiculous to lie by blaming your dog!" my mom scolded.

After the same thing happened two more times, I got grounded for lying and disobedience. Alone in my room, I sobbed. I hated to have to stay inside!

Maybe I should say that I fibbed, I thought. *But then I really would be a liar!* Brokenhearted, I asked Jesus to help me stick to the truth and to politely obey.

Later that week my mom met me after school and apologized. She'd seen Buck helping himself to the walnuts and leaving the shells on the lawn.

Solomon declared, *"Everything I say is honest"* (ICB). That's an important goal, but what if someone still doesn't believe you?

Don't react angrily, and don't change your story. Realize that everyone—even parents and teachers—makes mistakes. Be obedient, polite, and ready to forgive. Then let God take care of your hurt feelings.

CONTACT: Father, help me have the courage to be honest and to stick to my principles, no matter what.

42

The Hairy Chair

Buck loved to sleep on my dad's chair. And Buck's fur was long and white and clung to everything.

As a physician, my dad wore dark suits to work. So a layer of white hair always ended up on the back of his pants!

"I'm sorry, but Buck must stay outside unless you can keep him off my chair," my dad finally threatened.

Leave my precious dog outside? Not a chance! So I watched Buck and scolded him every time he got near the chair. After several days I felt satisfied that he was trained.

For two weeks not one hair appeared on Dad's chair. But then one Sabbath when we returned from church, I was slipping the key into the front-door lock. *Thump!* went something inside the house.

I opened the door. Buck lay on the carpet sound asleep, his usual tail-wagging greeting absent.

Suspicious, I went to my dad's chair and felt it. It was toasty warm—and hairy! My "sleeping" dog was lying by acting as if he hadn't disobeyed!

Honesty involves more than speaking the truth. It also means not allowing your actions to cause others to believe something untrue. For instance, if I act surprised when my dad finds the wrench I left in the driveway, I'm bearing a false witness or lying.

The Bible says, *"A false witness will not go unpunished."* Resolve to be truthful, even in your actions.

TALK BACK: Are there circumstances in which a person may lie? (Read Matthew 19: 18.)

43

Beneath His Dignity

Buck had many canine friends in our neighborhood. So as we kids played after school, the dogs romped with us.

Then Growler moved into the neighborhood. One by one he bullied the other dogs, sending them off with tattered ears and drooping tails. Soon everyone left their dogs at home.

One evening as Buck and I returned from the store, Growler zeroed in on Buck. Stiff-legged, he circled us, hair bristling, teeth bared. My heart raced! Then Growler rushed Buck from the side.

But Buck simply ignored him. Growler tried again, lowering his head, aggressively stepping directly in front of Buck.

Buck was large enough to fight Growler, but he seemed to consider fighting beneath his dignity. Instead he tipped his black nose up in the air and ambled off, leaving a very puzzled Growler behind.

It's not popular to avoid fights or let someone else get the best of you. The world says, "Look after yourself first, and use force if necessary." But the Bible advises differently: *"Do not envy a violent man or choose any of his ways."*

You may need to ignore taunts, live with unfair circumstances, or walk away from a fight. You may be called "chicken" or laughed at. But we've been instructed to be peaceful (check out Matthew 5:9). With God's help you can do just that.

TALK BACK: What would you do or say if you saw somebody making fun of a classmate? picking a fight?

44

Flying High

It's part of a Samoyed's nature to enjoy pulling things. So I decided to train Buck to pull me on my bike.

After buying a harness and a long leash, I began training sessions. First I taught Buck the signals for "pull," "slow down," and "wait." Then I trained him to trot to my left when not pulling and to not stop to sniff things. He also had to learn to stay away from the bike wheels.

Then some new kids moved into the neighborhood, and we compared pets. "Buck's a sled dog," I bragged. "He's so well trained that he pulls me anywhere I want to go. Do you want to see?"

I hooked Buck's leash to the handlebars, gave the command, and Buck took off. Down the street we sped. It was a perfect run, and I knew the kids were envious.

But then a gray cat streaked across the road. Somehow Buck forgot all his training and lunged after it. The bike went with him, and I flew in the other direction. And behind me I could hear wild laughter.

The Bible says, *"Pride goes before destruction, a haughty spirit before a fall."*

When we become sure of ourselves, we can mess up quickly. Instead of trusting ourselves, we need to place our trust in Jesus, asking Him to keep us humble and to lead us each day.

TALK BACK: What's the difference between haughty pride and realizing that you can do a specific thing well?

About Those Rules

I had a terrible time teaching Buck to stay out of the street. He was so friendly that he seemed to think nothing would hurt him!

I tried to warn him about cars, but it was hopeless. He simply couldn't understand. And when he didn't understand, he didn't *obey*.

One day while we neighborhood kids were playing tag, Buck got bored and wandered off. Suddenly, far down the street, I heard screeching tires and shrill yelping. Horrified, I glanced up. Buck had been hit!

Fearing the worst, I raced toward him. At the same time, he got himself up, then ran toward me, limping and crying all the way. When we finally met, he flopped down and passed out. Luckily he was only bruised, but after that he gave cars plenty of room.

Rules are made for people's protection. Just like Buck, we don't always understand their usefulness and are sometimes tempted to ignore them. But that could be dangerous.

If you think a rule is unreasonable, what can you do? Investigate by courteously asking questions. If you still don't understand and the rule can't be adjusted, then trust the experience of reliable grown-ups. The Bible says, *"Obey your leaders and submit to their authority."*

God will help you cooperate and eventually understand, if you let Him.

TALK BACK: What are some of your family's rules? Do they help your family? Are there any you don't understand?

46

My Comforter

I flopped down behind our backyard bushes. As the sobs came, I thought back to Sabbath. During the Communion service I'd told two friends that I thought they were acting sacrilegious. They were mimicking Bugs Bunny by making faces and nibbling at their Communion bread.

At school the following Monday those friends had taunted me and nicknamed me "Sac Sac" (because I'd said they were sacrilegious). Other students eventually joined in, saying more hurtful things.

They pointed out that I had flyaway hair, wore glasses, didn't make very good grades, and worst of all, had buckteeth! I couldn't face going back to school!

Then something wet nudged my cheek. A furry head slipped beneath my arm, and a pink tongue licked my hand. Buck, my dog, gazed at me with worshipful eyes. It was obvious *he* thought I was OK. *He* didn't care about my height or rabbit teeth. And if he could talk, *he'd* agree that being sacrilegious is wrong!

Suddenly I began feeling better. Buck had been my comforter.

Isn't God good? He knew we'd face times too hard to bear alone, so He planned ways to help us—through kind words from another person, through an encouraging welcome from a pet, or through the Holy Spirit placing thoughts in our mind. After all, He's promised, *"I will not leave you."*

CONTACT: Thank You, God, for Your promise to comfort me when I'm down.

47

Three Feathers

Birds have three kinds of feathers. Contour feathers outline the wing and tail. They have a long, straight shaft with many barbs held together by tiny hooks. These provide lift and also act as a steering rudder during flight. Down feathers are soft, loose plumes that cover the bird's body and provide temperature control. Filoplumes are long and hairlike with only a few barbs. They grow at the base of the others to fill everything in.

A bird must spend time preening its feathers. It does this by pulling the pieces through its bill to zip the fringes closed. Unless it takes time to do this, its flight and warmth are affected.

Just as a bird has three kinds of feathers to support it, you have God, Jesus, and the Holy Spirit working together for your good. Saying goodbye to friends, the apostle Paul once said, *"May the grace of the Lord Jesus Christ, and the love of God, and the fellowship of the Holy Spirit be with you all."*

Three pictures of the Godhead are in that text: Jesus' example and sacrifice for you, God's love and protection, and the Holy Spirit's companionship as He speaks to your mind. Together They provide the "covering" to keep you spiritually safe and flying straight.

TRY IT: Find a contour feather. Separate its Velcro-like barbs and pass it through the air. Next zip the barbs together by pulling the feather through your fingers. Wave it through the air again. Which way does the feather have more lift? Why?

48

Mr. Stubborn?

Home: Africa
Size: Shoulder 3-4.5 feet

You've probably seen domesticated donkeys. They're big-eared horselike creatures. For thousands of years they've been used as work animals because they're surefooted and can labor in difficult situations. Donkeys even helped the Egyptians in building the Pyramids.

What about wild donkeys? These sturdy animals live in areas so hot and barren that most other animals couldn't survive. They forage up to 20 hours a day for grass or desert shrubbery, and they need water only every two to three days.

A year after the male (jack) and female (jenny) mate, their foal is born. The jenny's milk is very rich, providing all the nutrients the foal needs until it can graze with its parents.

Though a donkey is a hard worker, it can be very stubborn. If it decides it isn't going to do something, it won't budge!

Humans can be that way, too. Yet while stubbornness can be a bad trait, it can also be a good trait. We should stubbornly refuse to do wrong.

God needs people who will stand for the right regardless of the situation. Paul said, *"Stand firm. Let nothing move you."* Why not "stubbornly" stand for the right today?

TALK BACK: What makes you feel stubborn? How can you make your stubbornness work for everyone's good?

49

Glaciers

If you ever visit Alaska, you'll want to see the glaciers. These huge packs of ice have formed over many years.

Each year new snow falls on old snow in the basins between mountain peaks. Because the weather stays cold, more snow falls than melts, making the snow very deep. The weight of the new snow presses the old snow tighter, until the lower levels become solid ice or glaciers.

As the ice on the mountains gets deeper, gravity causes the glaciers to slide downhill. As they slide they push huge boulders with them.

Most glaciers slide only a little distance each day. Sometimes the toe of the glacier is on land, and it gets warm enough to melt. But if the icy toe hangs over a body of water, it breaks off and drops into the water below. This is called calving.

If you know what to look for, you can see places where glaciers once moved. Many are now lush U-shaped valleys in which forests and meadows flourish. Only the strength of a great glacier could shape such a valley.

What's shaping your life? Are you learning life lessons from your hard times? Have you chosen to keep God as your focus? The Bible says, *"In all your ways acknowledge him, and he will make your paths straight."* God knows what lies ahead, and He'll help you "slide" the right way.

MISSION: When you experience a difficult situation, consider what you can learn from it.

Theme: God's provisions • His Words: Psalm 34:9

February 12

Ice Worms

Home: Alaskan glaciers
Size: To 1 inch

I've always thought worms like nice, warm dirt. But one relative of the earthworm never touches soil. It's an ice worm.

These amazing creatures look like tiny earthworms. They crawl around using their bristle-like appendages. Brown or black, they burrow deep into Alaska's glaciers, avoiding sunlight. At dusk they emerge to feed on snow algae or pollen that's arrived on the wind. When the sun rises, they burrow deep into the glacier again.

How do the worms keep from freezing in Alaska's extreme winters? Actually, an ice worm freezes at a lower temperature than the water does. Inside the glacier the temperature is always 32 degrees Fahrenheit, which is nice and comfortable for the ice worm. If it were much warmer, the worm would die.

Isn't it interesting that even in harsh habitats some creatures manage to make a home? God has provided each animal with what it needs to withstand the temperatures. He's given each the instinct to know what to do and how to stay alive.

Just as God has provided for each animal in its habitat, He'll provide for you. After all, you're far more important to Him than the animals. King David said, *"People who belong to the Lord, fear him! Those who fear him will have everything they need"* (ICB).

CONTACT: Thank You for Your promise, Father, to provide for me when I trust You.

Century Plant

Home: Desert areas
Size: 15-foot flower spike

The century plant is a spiky desert succulent. It has sword-like leaves with sharp points. They grow to 18 inches long and three inches wide.

Rain doesn't come often in the desert, but when it does it falls in torrents, washing over the sand toward low areas. The century plant then hoards water in its huge leaves. This allows it to sustain itself for many months until it gets more water.

Though people used to believe the century plant must be 100 years old to bloom, it actually blooms sometime after it's 8 years old. By that time its flower stalk has reached 15 to 40 feet. Insects swarm to the blossoms for nectar, and birds come to feed on the insects. This is the plant's only chance to share its yellow flowers. When the blooms drop, the plant dies, leaving seeds and little "suckers" that start new plants.

Have you met people who don't know Jesus or who've turned away from Him? Maybe you plan to tell them about Him someday.

But life is uncertain. People move away or die from accidents, diseases, or old age. So if we don't share Jesus' love when we have the chance, we may never have another opportunity. Jesus said, *"Go into all the world and preach the good news to all creation."*

Where does the world start? At your fingertips. How are you going to help today?

MISSION: Brainstorm some good methods of sharing Jesus' love. Then prayerfully put your plans into action.

The Sea Horse

Home: Temperate and tropical seas
Size: 1-14 inches

The sea horse has a grasping tail like a monkey's and a face like a horse's. It lives among ocean grasses in shallow water. It usually swims and rests upright. Though its dorsal fin beats 35 times per second, this fish can't swim rapidly because its fins are so tiny.

To keep from being washed away from home, it anchors itself by wrapping its tail around a plant. Then it waits to catch plankton and other small fish that wander by. Its eyes swivel independently to watch approaching prey, so it doesn't have to move and reveal its hiding place. Also, it can change colors to match its background.

In temperate climates sea horses congregate and mate during the full moon. The female places her eggs in the male's abdominal pouch, and then he fertilizes them. He's the one that's pregnant and must carry the eggs!

When it's time for the eggs to hatch, the father turns and twists and tries to squeeze them out. Sometimes he presses his abdomen against a rock or shell to help with the process. The hatched babies look like very tiny full-grown sea horses.

Just as the sea horse holds on to something to keep from being washed away, we need to cling to the instructions and promises God has given us. The Bible and the Spirit of Prophecy direct us in the best way to live. And God's promises give us courage when things get tough.

The psalmist proclaimed, *"I will say of the Lord, 'He is my refuge and my fortress, my God, in whom I trust.'"*

TALK BACK: Tell about a time you claimed one of God's promises. How did it help you?

53

Angel in Slippery Skin

One day Kent, a 12-year-old Australian boy, went surfing with friends. Somehow he got separated from the rest of the boys and washed out with the tides. At first he didn't worry. He just lay atop his surfboard and paddled for shore.

But an hour later he wasn't any closer to shore. That's when he felt his first prickle of fear. Then he noticed a triangular fin slicing through the water a few feet away. Frantically looking around, he glimpsed another fin on his opposite side!

Terrified, he realized that sharks were circling him. Quickly he prayed to God for help. Then something bumped his leg!

Sucking in his breath, he peered into the water beneath him. There he noticed a couple dolphins. They were positioning themselves between him and the hungry sharks!

Kent paddled again but soon became exhausted. Then one of the dolphins nosed up to the rear of his surfboard and began to push him toward shore! Only when he was close enough to finish the journey on his own did the dolphins leave him.

"Those dolphins were like guardian angels to me," Kent said later.

The Bible tells us, *"The angel of the Lord encamps around those who fear him, and he delivers them."* Kent believes that God used dolphins as special-duty angels that day.

CONTACT: Dear God, help me to remember to call on You when I'm in trouble, and to have faith to believe You'll help me.

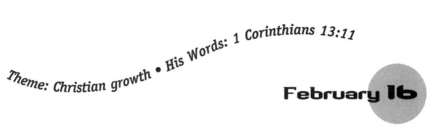

Tarantula!

Home: Warmer climates
Size: Leg span to 10 inches

Tarantulas have hairy bodies and long legs. Docile, these spiders usually won't bite humans unless provoked.

Forty of the 300 identified species of tarantulas live in the United States. They eat insects and other small creatures and can survive 30 years or more. For defense against predators they rear back and wave their hairy legs, produce an unpleasant odor, or rub hair from their bodies. If their barbed hair contacts the eyes or skin of a predator, it causes pain or even temporary blindness.

My husband, Bob, had a young tarantula his students loved to handle. One morning he found it writhing in its terrarium. The next day it appeared crisp and lifeless. Disappointed, Bob started to remove it, but then he noticed movement behind a rock. It was his tarantula, alive and sporting a new skin! Thus he learned that tarantulas periodically shed their skins so they can grow larger.

Paul said, *"When I was a child, I talked like a child, I thought like a child, I reasoned like a child. When I became a man, I put childish ways behind me."* Christianity is a growing process. True Christians can't stay the same spiritual "size," but daily must develop a more complete understanding of God's plans for them. Is it time for you to do some growing?

TALK BACK: Why does one Christian seem to never make mistakes, while another makes them all the time?

A Drop of Water

Have you ever stood on a bridge and watched a creek rush beneath you? A creek forms when droplets of water that have seeped from hillsides or fallen as rain gather together.

The creek itself heads downhill, but the exact pathway each droplet of water takes is unpredictable. A drop can't decide which rock to splash upon or which current it will follow. It may even splash upon the bank and sink into the earth. The water droplets are affected by everything around them and have no choice where they land.

Your life is like a creek. You spend time with others. Lots of outside influences try to grab your attention. There may be "rocks" beneath the surface that you don't see, yet they affect you from day to day.

You're different from that droplet of water, though, because you have the power to choose which direction you'll go. You can direct your thoughts and make decisions.

God has ultimate wisdom. He says, *"I lead in the way of righteousness, in the midst of the paths of judgment" (KJV)*. When you give your heart to Him, you can trust that He'll help you make wise choices so you can go in the right direction.

TALK BACK: What kinds of things affect your choices? How can you take control of them?

Mixed-up Cottontail

Home: Americas
Size: To 15 inches long

Cottontail rabbits hop around woodsy or brushy areas. There they dig little hollows on the ground, lining them with leaves and fur as nests for their young.

A baby cottontail weighs about three ounces at birth. It's born blind, helpless, and without fur. So the mother covers it with leaves and hair when she leaves the nest to hunt for food. If a snake or other predator threatens her baby, the normally shy mother attacks with her claws and teeth.

Last week I found our neighborhood cottontail gobbling suet (beef fat) I'd set out for the birds. Cottontails are vegetarians, but in this sinful world even an innocent rabbit can develop perverted eating habits.

How about you? Are you careful about what you eat? Or do you turn up your nose at fruit and vegetables and go for the chips, ice cream, and candy? Such things may taste good, but eating them doesn't help you develop a healthy body.

The Bible says, *"So whether you eat or drink or whatever you do, do it all for the glory of God."* You glorify God when you care for your body. Doing so makes you stronger and healthier and also helps your mind work more efficiently. And a clear mind makes it easier for you to understand what God wants you to know.

TRY IT: For one week write down everything you eat each day. Look at your list. Ask God if there are things you should change.

57

Your Tiniest Bone

The tiniest bone in your body is the stapes. It's located in your middle ear, just behind your eardrum. Shaped like a two-pronged tuning fork, it's smaller than a grain of rice!

How your ear works is an amazing process. First, vibrations get collected by the visible part of your ear. These vibrations pass into your ear canal, shaking your eardrum and making a tiny bone on the back of your eardrum move.

This tiny bone passes the vibrations through two more bones, the last being the stapes. After several more transfers through tissues and nerves, the vibrations reach your brain, which interprets them into sounds you recognize.

If any of these delicate parts are damaged or missing, loss of hearing occurs. Maybe you know someone who's hard of hearing. You might find it challenging to talk to them, because they misunderstand what you say or don't know that you're speaking at all!

Have you ever felt that God doesn't hear what you say to Him? Or that He's turned a deaf ear to you because of something you've done?

Satan's specialty is making us feel unheard. That's why we must learn to trust God by faith, not by feelings. The Bible promises that if you put God first in your life, *"You will find delight in the Almighty and will lift up your face to God. You will pray to him, and he will hear you."*

CONTACT: Thank You, God, for hearing me even when I feel as if You're not listening.

How Other Creatures Hear

God has made a variety of ways for creatures to hear or sense motion and sound.

All vertebrates (animals with backbones) have inner ears. Their inner ear transmits vibrations and pressure to their auditory nerve. This nerve communicates with their brain. A sense of hearing helps vertebrates keep their balance, too.

With fish, sound usually gets transmitted through their skin. Some fish have an organ filled with a jellylike substance. Tiny hairs inside this organ swish around, stimulating their sensory cells. Other fish hear when sounds cause their skull bones to vibrate.

Frogs wear their eardrums on the outside of their heads! You can actually see the round spots that vibrate and pass information to their brain.

Amphibians (cold-blooded vertebrates) have no eardrum or middle ear at all. Instead, they pick up vibrations through their legs. These transmit the vibrations through other bones to their inner ear.

Birds are able to hear different tones and sense the direction from which sounds come.

Often when the Bible speaks of "hearing" God's Word, it's not talking about our ability to pick up sounds with our ears. Instead, it's referring to our understanding, agreeing with, and doing God's will.

Once someone asked Jesus who His mother and brothers were. Eager for them to understand about the family of God, He explained, *"My mother and brothers are those who hear God's word and put it into practice."*

TALK BACK: What things have you "heard" God tell you to do? How can you help yourself be more willing to "hear"?

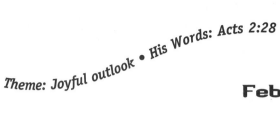

The Binturong

Home: Southeast Asia
Size: To 31 pounds

The binturong is a long, low, thickset mammal. It has dark, shaggy fur and a long, bushy tail. Waddling like a bear, it puts the entire sole of its foot on the ground as it walks.

It spends most of its time in trees, though. Its sharp claws help it grasp the branches, and its strong tail, from which it can hang, helps it keep its balance.

Binturongs sleep during the day and hunt for fruit, insects, and birds at night. With their long whiskers, they can feel their way around the dark forest. Their large eyes also provide good night vision.

Binturongs are playful with their families and enjoy tussling together. During play they somersault into the air and land on their backs. Observers say that grown binturongs smell like popcorn! Because they're so pleasant they make good pets.

How about you? Are you pleasant to have around? Do you say nice things? You can choose to bring sunshine into others' lives by being cheerful when things go wrong and not complaining about little annoyances.

David said of Jesus, *"You will teach me God's way to live. Being with you will fill me with joy"* (ICB). Ask Jesus to help you look on the bright side of life. When He fills you with joy, it will spill out and affect all your words and actions.

MISSION: Today when you feel like complaining, say something nice instead. Watch for the smiles you'll bring.

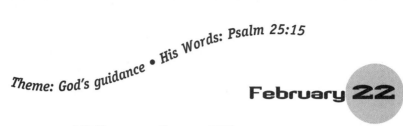

February 22

Bluefin Tuna

Home: Temperate and tropical seas
Size: To 1,800 pounds

Bluefin tunas never stop swimming. If they do, they'll die. That's because water must continually flow over their gills in order to provide the oxygen they need.

These fish have sleek, streamlined bodies. Even their fins fold into grooves, and their eyes are flush with their bodies so they don't create a drag. Their body temperature is warmer than the surrounding water, which keeps their muscles warm and ready to go.

Bluefins have been clocked going 45 miles per hour! Normally, though, they swim at about nine miles per hour.

They travel in groups called schools. In the wintertime they live in deeper waters, but during the late summer they flock to coastal areas to lay their eggs. At this time many are caught by fishing ships, which surround the schools with large fishing nets, then draw them in. Here the tuna's speed does it no good, for once in the net, it can't escape.

King David knew the danger of getting caught in a net. Speaking of God's care, he said, *"My eyes are ever on the Lord, for He shall pluck my feet out of the net" (NKJV).*

Though you can't always recognize dangerous spiritual situations, God can. If you ask for His help, He'll guide you to safety, far from the nets Satan sets to snare you.

TALK BACK: What are some traps Satan sets for us? Why don't we always notice them?

Theme: Really listening • His Words: Ephesians 4:32

The Teacher Who Drools

Synjee, our Lynxpoint Siamese cat, used to come to me only when she needed food or water. She came to my husband only when she wanted to play "Gitchoo-kitty," a bitey, scratchy game.

But now when I sit down to write, Synjee jumps into my lap. She purrs and kneads my legs with her front paws. Then she drools, spreading strings of spittle everywhere as she wipes her mouth on me.

If I keep writing, she places her paws on my chest and puts her eyes right in front of mine. "Prurrup prurrup!" she says. (Translation: "I'm here. Forget the other stuff!") Only if I give her my full attention will Synjee settle down to suck her tail and fall asleep on my lap.

The Bible says, *"Be kind and compassionate to one another."* One way to be kind is to give people your undivided attention. Forget about yourself and listen wholeheartedly when someone needs to talk. Try to understand what the other person is saying, because it shows them that you care. And with God's prompting, maybe you can encourage them.

Synjee's a pretty wise teacher, don't you think?

TRY IT: Today count how many times you hear people interrupt others. How do you think it made the interrupted person feel? How did it make you feel?

62

Just a Little Twig

You probably know that you can figure the age of a tree by counting its trunk rings. But did you know that you can tell how many seasons twigs on branches have been growing? This is easiest to do with deciduous trees (trees that lose their leaves), but it's also possible to do with conifers (trees that have needles).

Each year new leaf buds at the end of a twig leave a scar that looks like a bunch of little rings pressed together. To determine the age of a twig, first examine it from its tip to where it meets the branch. The twig looks smooth for a while, and then you'll see a bunch of rings. The distance between the groups of rings, or scars, shows how much that twig grew in a given year.

It takes time for a twig to become a branch. And you're the same way. At first you learned to crawl, then walk, then ride a bike, then do schoolwork, each thing in order. Your learning didn't happen overnight. And just as what you put into your body affects your physical growth, what you put into your mind affects your spiritual growth.

The Bible says of those who try to do what's right: *"The righteous will flourish like a palm tree, they will grow like a cedar of Lebanon."* Cedars grow straight and strong. Why don't you determine to grow straight and strong physically *and* spiritually?

TRY IT: Check several twigs on two different trees. Did they all grow at the same rate during the past few years?

The Upside-down Eater

Home: Near tropical saltwater marshes and lakes
Size: 4-5 feet high

Maybe you've noticed how a flamingo appears to hold its head upside down while eating. This is because its large beak bends sharply down in the shape of a boomerang.

Reaching into the water, it uses its beak like a backhoe, sliding the top half toward itself to scoop up mud and sand. Once the beak gets filled, the flamingo closes its mouth. Then it uses its tongue to push water and debris through the strainer-like ridges along the edges of its beak. Finally it swallows the good stuff—the crustaceans and algae that remain.

The flamingo has long legs for wading. And it has a long neck for reaching under water in shallow lagoons and lakes. Its pink or reddish color comes from chemicals in the algae it eats. People can tell what it's been eating by how it looks!

It's the same with you. Jesus said, *"Every good tree bears good fruit, but a bad tree bears bad fruit."* Your friends and your activities influence your mind, just as the flamingo's food affects its color. If you fill your mind with pure thoughts, you'll behave differently than if you feed it ungodly jokes, reading, or TV programs.

Only you can choose how you'll "look" as you grow up. You can fool others for a while, but eventually your "true colors" will show.

TALK BACK: What kinds of activities will help you bear good fruit? What activities will hinder your Christian growth?

The Flamingo's Mini-night

Most birds, including flamingos, depend on daylight to help them gather food.

Each morning flocks of flamingos fly from their island home in Bonaire to the larger island of Curaçao, off the coast of Venezuela. There they wade in the shallows to feed on brine shrimp. As evening nears, they return home to roost.

Six years ago today, at 2:15 p.m., there was a total solar eclipse over Curaçao. That afternoon darkness fell more rapidly than usual. The flamingos, certain that night had come, quickly took off for Bonaire.

But because of the eclipse, the sun peeked out again just three and a half minutes later. Confused by the quick arrival of the "morning," the birds headed back to Curaçao. They changed plans instantly based on the new information they observed.

Have you ever been absolutely certain about something and then learned new information that proved you wrong? Hopefully you changed direction because you wanted to be right.

While growing up, you'll hear many things about what's right and wrong. It's important to check out what the Bible says so you don't "fly off" at the wrong time or in the wrong direction.

King David requested God's directions. He said, *"Your word is like a lamp for my feet and a light for my way. I will do what I have promised and obey your fair laws"* (ICB). Won't you join him in that promise?

TALK BACK: If you think someone in authority is teaching error, what steps should you take?

The Perfume King

Home: Russia to Burma
Size: 15-40 pounds

The musk deer is a small, nervous animal. It keeps mostly to itself. While eating, it stops often to listen and bolts quickly at any noise.

Its back legs are longer than its front legs, and its feet have two long toes that can spread out. Another toe grows out of the deer's heel, increasing its surefootedness when running downhill. The buck's upper canines stick out over his lower lip and can inflict a nasty cut.

From a gland the buck produces a valuable secretion called musk. This musk is harvested and added to products to help fragrance last longer.

Remember how Mary poured perfume on Jesus' feet at a feast? It wasn't long before everyone in the room could smell it.

Judas complained that she'd wasted the expensive perfume, but Jesus understood. He said, *"She did what she could,"* meaning that the fragrance was nice, but her caring action was the real perfume.

When you offer your love to God, it's like a sweet odor to Him. When you're kind to those around you, it creates a pleasant smell. And when you share the gospel with others, you spread a lovely fragrance that can be far-reaching. See how you can perfume the world today!

TRY IT: Put a dab of cheap perfume on one wrist, and a dab of good perfume on the other. Sniff each wrist every half hour. Which smell lasts the longest? Which are you the most like?

You Need More Than Blossoms

Home: Temperate zones
Size: 15-25 feet tall

Long before spring arrives, tulip magnolia trees begin their yearly cycle. As the days lengthen, their sap rises. Then the tiny buds on their branches begin to swell. While other trees still look naked, the tulip magnolia bursts with large, cuplike, pink blossoms. Then as the leaves appear the flower petals drop.

Delighted with the magnolia tree's blossoms, a young girl ran to pick a bouquet from it. A moment later she returned, her nose wrinkled. "It stinks!" she exclaimed.

Most of us would like to look good. After all, beautiful people get noticed and often seem to be popular. Unfortunately, not all attractive people develop personalities to match. Some become spoiled and unkind, making unreasonable demands on those who crowd around them. They rely on their looks to get them what they want.

Looks are only temporary. A pleasant personality, a wise mind, and a caring heart are eternal. The prophet Samuel said, *"Man looks at the outward appearance, but the Lord looks at the heart."*

Peek into your mirror. Look deeper than the surface. Check your personality. What do you see?

MISSION: Make a list of good personality traits. Ask for God's help, then work on one.

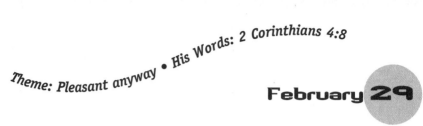

Stinkbug, the Insect Skunk

**Home: Nearly universal
Size: To 2 inches**

There are more than 5,000 kinds of stinkbugs around. So some probably live in your neighborhood!

These insects have horny, shield-shaped backs and five-segmented antennae. Through their sucking beak they draw up plant or animal juices to nourish themselves. They also use their beak as a pump to inject poison into their victims.

Insect-eating stinkbugs often appear brightly colored, and they especially enjoy caterpillars. Stinkbugs that prefer to eat tree sap hang out on tree trunks and may look like dull-colored flakes of bark.

The stinkbug gets its name because of the unpleasant smell it produces when it's frightened or disturbed. It can open the valves of two scent glands near its hind legs and release a horrible-smelling liquid. The bad odor and taste discourage predators from pursuing it.

What kind of atmosphere do you create when things don't go your way? Do you whine, grumble, and complain? Being pleasant during difficult times is an important skill to learn. With God's help, you can do it, just as Paul did when he said, *"We are troubled on every side, yet not distressed; we are perplexed, but not in despair"* *(KJV)*.

TRY IT: Hunt in a park or garden for a stinkbug. Gently touch it with a twig. Watch (and smell) its behavior.

The Feathered Hero

A firefighter went to check a forest that had recently been destroyed by fire. In the smoldering ashes he noticed a charred object shaped like a bird with outstretched wings. Curious, he tipped it over and discovered several live baby birds beneath the dead mother's scorched wings.

Generally an animal's instinct tells it to flee from fire. So this mother bird could probably have saved herself if she'd flown away. But what about her babies? Her instinct to care for them won out over her fear. Covering them, she stayed in spite of the licking flames and choking smoke. Because of her heroic act her babies survived and were eventually set free.

The psalmist, in talking about God's love for us, wrote, *"He will cover you with his feathers, and under his wings you will find refuge."*

Jesus could have stayed in heaven and let you suffer the consequences of your sins. But instead He came to earth.

When it got "hot" for Him here and He faced crucifixion on the cross, He could have saved Himself. But instead He thought of you.

He thought about how much He loves you and wants to spend eternity with you. So He willingly accepted your punishment. I guess you could say He covered *you* with His wings.

CONTACT: Thank You, Jesus, for having the courage to come and save me. Help me have the courage to be true to You.

Spring Hare

Home: Eastern and southern Africa
Size: 6-9 pounds

The spring hare isn't related to rabbits, though it's about the same size. It's a rodent, but it moves like a kangaroo. It has back legs that are about four times longer than its front legs. So it can easily cover nine to 12 feet with each leap. While hopping, its front feet don't even touch the ground.

Spring hares dig burrows in sandy ground and prepare many exits for escape. While digging they can completely close their ears to keep dirt out of them.

Most animals carefully peek out before leaving their burrows. Not the spring hare! It bursts into the air, springing beyond any waiting predator. It simply jumps over situations that might trap it.

Have you ever wanted to do something you knew was wrong? Maybe you thought about it a lot, picturing how exciting it would be. If so, you probably ended up doing it.

The apostle James said, *"It is the evil that a person wants that tempts him. His own evil desire leads him away and holds him"* (ICB).

The next time you face temptation, follow the spring hare's example and "spring away" from it instead of letting your imagination dwell on it. Then, with God's help, you'll be able to escape.

TRY IT: When you're tempted ask God to help you put the temptation out of your mind. Then get as far away from it as you can. Also, think about something good you'd like to do, and do it.

The Mighty Tongue

Your tongue contains about 10,000 taste buds. They tell you the difference between sweet, sour, salty, and bitter.

Your taste buds are grouped on the tip of your tongue, the front sides, the rear sides, and the middle back. When food touches them, they're chemically stimulated, and your brain decodes this as taste.

The tongue has a rough surface covering muscles that run along its length, width, and depth. These muscles help move your tongue in almost any direction.

Your tongue keeps food between your teeth until you're ready to swallow it. Then it helps push the food into the pharynx and esophagus. And because dry food is hard to swallow, God covered your tongue with a mucous membrane that secretes saliva to moisten the food. Saliva also aids in digestion.

Besides helping you eat food and enjoy it, your tongue helps you speak. With it you can say encouraging, funny, and truthful words. Or you can say things better left unsaid. The Bible points out, *"The tongue has the power of life and death."*

If you love Jesus, you'll want to use your tongue in the right way—to bring joy and honor to Him and encouragement to others.

TRY IT: Do two experiments in front of a mirror: 1. Try curling your tongue tip into a U-shape. A recessive gene is required to do this. 2. Discover which part of your tongue detects each of the flavors listed above.

The Sticky Lizard

Home: Wide range of habitats
Size: 1.5-14 inches

There are at least 800 species of geckos. These reptiles belong to the lizard family. The smallest gecko is the *Sphaerodactylus parthenopion,* from the British Virgin Islands. Barely one and a half inches long, it's the world's smallest reptile.

A gecko's head and eyes seem large for its body, but its acute vision helps it hunt for insects at night. Most geckos don't have closable eyelids. To keep their eyes clean, they just lick them with their long tongues.

The most unique thing about geckos is their feet. Their wide toes have thick pads that are covered with hundreds of bristles. Each bristle is tipped with a tiny suction cup. These cups allow geckos to walk on nearly any surface without falling off, even slick windowpanes and ceilings. Geckos can scamper across the ceiling as easily as you can run across the floor. They're masters at "sticking to it."

Do you need to become more like a gecko in your ability to "stick to it"? For example, when you're tired of studying but there's still more to do, do you say, "I'll finish that tomorrow"? Or, like a gecko, do you stick to the project until it's done?

The apostle Paul said, *"Test everything. Hold on to the good."* That means that even if you find a task hard or boring, you should stick to it! The results will be worth your effort.

MISSION: Next time you feel like giving up on something, think of how good it will feel to be done! Keep on track until you finish.

Leaping the Wall

Home: Decaying vegetation
Size: About 0.2 inch long

Pole vaulting is a popular sport at the Olympics. Vaulters carry a long flexible pole as they run toward a high horizontal bar. Then they jam the pole into the ground and flip their body, feet first, into the air. Their momentum and the pole's flexibility carry them up and over the bar.

An insect called the springtail also pole-vaults. Its "pole" is called a furcula. This forked appendage on the insect's abdomen tucks beneath it. When the springtail is ready to jump, it snaps its furcula straight, which tosses it several inches through the air.

Springtails live in leaf litter and decaying vegetation or logs. Their tiny legs can't climb over obstacles very well, but with the help of their "pole" they can leap amazing distances. They've even helped engineers study how to store and release energy.

Sometimes we focus on satisfying our own wants before thinking of God and others. When we do this we build up a wall called "self." It's very hard to get over the wall of self, because it goes against human nature to say no to our desires. But King David said, *"With God's help I can jump over a wall"* (ICB).

God's help is like the springtail's furcula or the vaulter's pole, giving us the strength we need to leap over obstacles and put His will first.

TALK BACK: How can you tell if a desire is selfish? What's the difference between wants and needs?

73

Built-in Umbrellas

Home: Trees and scrub areas
Size: Body up to 12 inches

An earsplitting crack of thunder announced the storm. Then the heavens split open, releasing pounding rain. Marooned on the bird feeder outside my window, a gray squirrel flattened itself against the floor of the feeder, as far under the roof as possible. Still, the pelting, blowing rain occasionally reached it.

Using its God-given instinct, it stretched its tail along its back until its tail almost reached the tip of its nose. Then it puffed its tail up to cover as much of itself as possible. Crouching beneath its own umbrella, it stayed quite dry!

Animals must adapt quickly to changing surroundings. They use their God-given instinct to protect themselves. But in our machine and electronic age, we humans have learned that if we wait long enough, our problems might be solved for us. So our ability to instinctively react has become dulled from lack of use. Sometimes that spells trouble for us.

"Wisdom rests in the heart of one who has understanding" *(NASB)*. Understanding comes by study, thought, and practical work. Today take the opportunity to learn and do all you can. Then ask God for guidance so you'll be ready for whatever may come.

TALK BACK: Describe a time you needed to use your instinctive abilities to solve a problem. What happened? What did you learn?

74

The Common Raven

Home: Remote areas in the Northern Hemisphere
Size: To 27 inches, 3.5 pounds

The common raven is the biggest bird in the crow family. It's also the largest songbird. It has a thick neck, a wedge-shaped tail, and black fingerlike feathers that spread wide at the ends of its wings.

Ravens generally live in flocks. Riding on rising air currents, they call out with a loud *cwonk, cwonk*. They build nests of sticks lined with mud, grass, and animal hair. And they eat dead animals and garbage.

They usually avoid humans, who have long considered them pests. But my daughter, who lives in Alaska, has befriended ravens. She and her family toss bread out into their yard for the birds.

Suddenly one or two ravens will appear. Soon, high overhead or from over the mountain, more ravens will show up. They circle in the air, then swoop into the yard to eat.

How do they know that food is there? Do they have a keen sense of smell, or long-distance eyesight, or some communication system that lets them tell each other about food?

Won't it be wonderful in heaven to be able to ask Jesus how everything works? I look forward to His showing us all sorts of things. With the psalmist we can say, *"For you are great and do marvelous deeds. . . . I will praise you, O Lord my God, with all my heart."*

TRY IT: Put a bird feeder in your yard. See how long it takes to attract birds.

75

Sand Dollars

Habitat: Sandy shorelines
Size: To 3 inches

With my grandchildren, I stood on the beach in Sitka, Alaska, during the lowest tide of the year. We wanted to search for sand dollars.

As the waves receded, we spotted dozens of them half buried in the sand. Soon we'd gathered a mound of the flat two-inch disks, mottled scarlet and brown.

Unlike white sand dollars that wash up onto beaches, these were alive. We held them carefully, noticing the flower-like looping design on the top and the small mouth hole on the bottom. We also saw the velvety spines that help these creatures move across their sandy home. Then we returned them, right side up, to the ocean.

Fifteen minutes later the area became covered again by waves. Now unseen, the sand dollars would continue their existence, making a difference in the balance of marine life.

Just as we didn't notice the sand dollars during regular tide, you don't always see evidence of the Holy Spirit. But Jesus promised, *"The Counselor, the Holy Spirit, whom the Father will send in my name, will teach you all things and will remind you of everything I have said to you."*

Sometimes you do sense the Holy Spirit's presence. Maybe your conscience pricks you, or you find the strength to do the right thing when it's hard. At such moments you may realize that He's always with you, visible or not.

CONTACT: Thank You, God, for caring so much that You send the Holy Spirit to help me know right from wrong.

Those Weeds!

A weed is a plant that grows where you don't want it to. And if you've ever gotten rid of weeds, you know you can use one of two methods.

With the first method you simply pull off the tops of the weeds so they don't show. This method is quick and easy, and everything looks great—for a day or two. With the other method you gather all the leaves between your fingers, grasp the main stem, and gently tug, removing the leaves *and* the roots. Then the weed will never return.

A beautiful rosebush can actually be a weed. So can pansies and daffodils, if they grow where they don't belong.

It's the same with the activities you get involved with. You study, read, practice your music, walk your dog, groom yourself, and do research on your computer. These are good activities.

The problem comes when you go overboard with any activity. For instance, if you spend hours in the bathroom instead of helping with the dishes, you've got a weed. Reading or studying when your parents have asked you to do chores creates a weed.

There are two ways you can handle habit weeds: (1) on the surface pretend to be doing what you should; or (2) get rid of that habit before it gets a stronger hold on you! The Bible says that there's *"a time to keep and a time to throw away."*

TALK BACK: What habits do you need to "weed" out of your life?

Nipping at Heels

Itsy was a friendly dog with long, golden fur and shining brown eyes. When I visited her owners, she wagged her tail and jumped up to greet me.

The whole time I was at her house, Itsy relaxed on the carpet. Her eyes stayed glued on whoever was speaking. Then as I left, Itsy hurried to the front door, wagging her tail and panting a cheerful goodbye.

But when I stepped out the door, Itsy's personality changed. Once I'd turned my back, she rushed at my heels and nipped at them.

When I turned to face her again, she wagged her tail in a fake welcome. I learned that I had to walk backward out the door and to the street, for Itsy was a backbiter!

Are you a backbiter? Are you really nice to people's faces (as you should be), but then talk badly about them behind their backs (as you shouldn't)? Do you pretend to be happy when someone achieves a special honor, but then grumble when they aren't around? It's wrong to be friendly to others just to cut them down later.

The Bible says, *"An unfriendly person cares only about himself. He makes fun of all wisdom"* (ICB). Ask God to keep jealous, two-faced behavior out of your heart, for there's nothing nice about a backbiter.

MISSION: Next time you're tempted to say something unkind behind someone's back, ask yourself if you're just jealous.

Sandhill Crane

Home: Siberia, North America, Cuba, Mexico
Size: Wingspan to 6.5 feet

During migration season I enjoy watching thousands of sandhill cranes. They stop to eat and rest in the cornfields at the edge of the Tennessee River.

These large, cautious birds thrust their long bills deep into the earth to find roots, tubers, and corn. They eat hungrily, for it takes a lot of fuel to fly from Florida to Canada and beyond. After eating, the birds sometimes toss cornstalks high into the air. Then they jump up and down in a beautiful courtship dance.

Without any noticeable signal, groups of cranes will take off and head northward. With their necks stretched forward and their feet out behind them, they form large energy-saving V's as they fly. Their noisy chatter keeps them in touch with one another.

The Bible says, *"Even the birds in the sky know the right times to do things" (ICB)*. But how do they know when to migrate? And who tells them where to fly?

I believe that God gave them the instinct to know these things. Birds that "listen to" their instincts generally live longer, more comfortable lives.

Someday we will also migrate. And God has given us the Bible and the Holy Spirit to provide us with the guidance we need. If we're "listening" to God's communications, we can rely on Him to safely lead us to heaven, our final destination.

CONTACT: Lord, help me to accept Your guidance in all my decisions. Thank You for leading me. Amen.

Coatimundi

Home: Southern U.S., Mexico, South America
Size: Body length up to 26 inches

The coatimundi is a masked, ring-tailed cousin of the raccoon. With short front legs and long back legs, it scrambles through the woods and fields. Overturning rocks, it pokes its long nose into every crevice it can find, looking for insects or other small creatures to eat.

I once owned a coati, but he almost destroyed the house. He turned over pillows, pushed books off shelves, nosed open cupboards, and checked every corner for spiders. Finally I took him to exercise and hunt in the flower garden.

During his exercise time I turned over rocks for him so he wouldn't crush the plants. Noisily he'd gobble up every insect and crunch each snail he found, his eyes moist with pleasure as he ate.

Persistence is very important. It involves sticking to your task, not giving up, and finishing what needs to be done. It means leaving no stone unturned in order to accomplish what you should.

Moses said, "If . . . you seek the Lord your God, you will find him if you look for him with all your heart and with all your soul." Speaking of persistence, staying true to Jesus is the most important thing of all. Be like the coati. Don't give up!

MISSION: Think of something that's difficult to do. For the next two weeks work extra hard on that thing. Then ask yourself if it's still as difficult. What made the difference?

Swallow-winged Puffbird

Home: Central and South America
Size: 5-12 inches

The swallow-winged puffbird hardly ever descends to the forest floor. It comes down only to build its nest.

In its mind the colorful puffbird seems to have a picture of the ideal nest, and it really works at it! With its long, stout beak it tunnels as far as seven feet into a termites' nest. Then it hollows out a cozy chamber and lines it with leaves. To keep predators from finding its nest, the puffbird carries the removed dirt away from the entrance.

Both parents incubate the eggs. But when the chicks hatch, the father sits on them while the mother goes to find food.

Maybe you know somebody who, like the puffbird, seems to do everything right. They're friendly, make good choices, and cheerfully serve God. Their ideals are so high that watching them helps you understand how God wants you to be. They inspire you to set high ideals for yourself.

The apostle Paul told his friends, *"Follow my example, as I follow the example of Christ."* Actually, Christ had the highest ideals of anyone, for He wanted to be like His Father. Nothing was too much for Him to give to reach that goal.

As we learn more about Jesus, we'll also continually set our ideals higher, becoming more like Him.

MISSION: Observe two outstanding Christians. Choose a characteristic from each that you'd like to develop in your life.

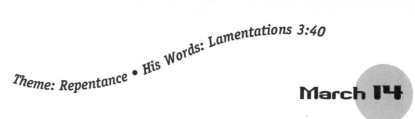

Black Widow!

Home: Tropics, North America
Size: To 1 inch, including legs

Black widow spiders aren't as deadly as their reputation suggests. Still, they can inflict a painful, sometimes deadly bite.

They prefer warm, sheltered places, so they build their webs beneath houses or in garages or trash heaps. The female is larger than the male. She has a red hourglass-shaped mark beneath her abdomen. The male has a narrower abdomen with red dots along his sides.

Black widows wait in their webs until an insect flies into it. When the victim becomes entangled, the spider wraps more webbing around it. Then it stabs the insect, injecting it with venom and digestive fluid. The venom paralyzes the insect, while the digestive fluid liquefies its insides so the spider can just suck it out.

Males and females come together only to mate. Afterward the female sometimes will heartlessly kill her mate. Then she makes a cocoon and lays her eggs inside, and carefully protects them until the babies hatch.

When you get entangled in sin you may feel uneasy and want to repent. But you may worry that God won't forgive you. When the prophet Jeremiah saw the people around him sinning, he said, *"Let us examine our ways and test them, and let us return to the Lord."*

God has promised to forgive you if you're truly sorry. He'll also help you do better. So go to Him today!

TALK BACK: What's the first sin you remember committing? How old were you? Why do you think you remember it?

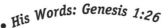
Oh, That Litter!

You've probably seen places where people threw trash. Fast-food containers, pop cans, bottles, old batteries, fishing lines, and discarded objects left a messy appearance.

Each American discards about a ton of trash a year. Unfortunately, it doesn't vanish on its own. Though paper disintegrates within a few years, plastic takes decades to break down. Aluminum cans and bottles don't decompose at all. Trash not only ruins our soil but can affect the quality of our underground water supply.

Litter also creates a hazard to wildlife. Animals can get their necks or feet trapped in six-pack rings and tin cans with lids partially attached. Small creatures crawl into bottles, then can't escape. Water birds become entangled in fishing lines. Discarded fishhooks may become embedded in birds or small animals, leading to infection and a painful death.

What's our responsibility to the earth and its creatures? When God created humans, He said, *"Let them rule . . . over all the earth."* This includes properly caring for the world we've been given. It means carefully disposing of our trash and not buying things we know we'll just throw away.

MISSION: Help keep your habitat clean! Start a recycling club in your school and neighborhood. Find ways to reuse things. Clean up a park. Flatten cans, cut up six-pack rings, and dispose of your trash properly.

83

The Worst Kind of Litter

Yesterday we discussed environmental litter. But there's another kind of litter that's even more hazardous. It's called "mental litter."

The adult human brain weighs about three pounds and contains 100 billion nerve cells. It's our control center. Without our brain we couldn't think, move, feel, or speak. It also provides us with short-term and long-term memory.

Short-term memory stores temporary facts, such as the prices of items in a store. But input that affects our emotions is often stored as long-term memories. That's where mental litter can collect.

Suppose you watch an unclean video. Even after you've confessed, the scenes may occasionally pop back into your mind. Satan loves to make you remember this mental garbage, because he wants you to concentrate on it instead of on God's better way of life. He hopes to discourage you enough about your failures that you'll quit trying to do right.

Of course, the best way to keep from creating mental litter is to avoid doing wrong in the first place. But everyone makes mistakes. So what's the solution? When unwanted memories return, ask Jesus for help right away. *"The peace of God, which transcends all understanding, will guard your hearts and your minds in Christ Jesus."*

Remember, once Jesus forgives you, you're *completely forgiven,* and He'll help you think of better things.

TALK BACK: What's your earliest memory? Why do you think you remember it?

Chinese Water Deer

Home: China and Korea
Size: To 2 feet high and 30 pounds

Chinese water deer look reddish-brown in color. They're shy, and live in small groups near water.

This is the only species of deer in which the male has no antlers. Instead, his teeth form two long, sharp tusks. He uses these to defend himself or to compete with other bucks for a mate.

Females also are unusual. Instead of having two teats like other deer, they have four. They need them all, though. Producing up to seven fawns at a time, they must nurse them in rotation.

The fawns can walk almost immediately, but at first they stay hidden in the tall grasses. Their mother carefully guards them, and they remain with the family group for several years.

When frightened by a predator, these deer immediately run. Then, if they can't hide, they flatten themselves on the ground and lie quietly to avoid being seen.

You probably think of deer as tenderhearted and gentle. If you have these qualities, you'll want to do what's right. So if a godly parent, teacher, or friend points out behaviors you should change, you'll listen carefully. With David you'll say, *"I hurried and did not wait to obey your commands. . . . Lord, your love fills the earth. Teach me your demands"* (ICB).

Why not be like a deer today?

TALK BACK: Why is it hard to accept correction? How can you decide if another person's opinion is valid?

Hairy Trickster

Home: North, Central America
Size: Similar to a house cat

Get a box!" my husband, Bob, called as he returned from his morning walk.

Unzipping his jacket, he pulled out three baby Virginia opossums. They had little white faces and pointy pink noses. But their sharp teeth warned our hands away.

Their mother had been hit by a car, so we adopted them. We named them Eeney, Meany, and No-mo.

Away from their natural habitat, opossums often become roadkill, because they seem to get confused by cars. But in their natural habitat, they're clever.

They carry leaves for their nests by pressing them against their tummies with their tails. When born, the bee-sized babies find their way into their mother's pouch and attach to one of her 11 to 13 nipples for about 10 weeks. Then they ride on her back as she travels, holding on with their naked tails.

Hunting mostly at night, opossums eat anything they can find. In the daytime they stay in their nest or climb a tree, using their thumbed paws to grasp branches. Some hang from their tails. When frightened they "play 'possum," pretending to be dead until danger has passed.

When you get out of your natural "habitat," you may end up in situations that are beyond your ability to handle. But if you trust in God, He'll guide you through. The Bible even promises, *"He will command his angels concerning you to guard you in all your ways."*

TALK BACK: Though God watches over me, what responsibility do I have to stay safe?

86

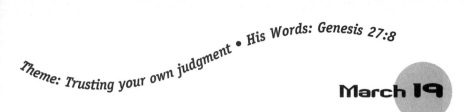

The Green Bathtub

Home: United States
Size: To 11.5 inches

Blue jays are bold, noisy birds that scavenge picnic areas. Once while camping I watched a mother blue jay with her chicks. First she taught them to preen themselves. Next she tried to teach them obedience.

I'd left a green melon rind on the picnic table. When one of the babies flew to investigate it, the mother scolded the chick and chased it away. But back on the "family branch," the chick kept eyeing the tempting pink juice in the rind.

Finally curiosity conquered! The baby returned to the picnic table, tasted the melon, and then hopped into the juice. What a wonderful time it had splashing in that green bathtub!

But when it returned to the branch, something was wrong. The sugary juice had made its freshly preened feathers poke every which way. When it tried to fly again, it plummeted to the ground!

Jacob trusted his own judgment (and his mother's). So he tricked his father into believing he was his brother, Esau. His mother had said, *"Now, my son, listen carefully and do what I tell you."*

Unfortunately, what seemed like a clever idea wasn't. Years of trouble followed Jacob.

His story shows that it's important to weigh your own and other people's opinions. Ask yourself if the idea goes against God's instructions in the Bible. Then request His help in making your decisions. After all, who needs a green bathtub?

TALK BACK: How do you logically decide if an activity is right to do?

The Fastest Sprinter

Home: Mainly Africa
Size: To 130 pounds

Maybe you've watched sprinters in the Olympics. They must take off quickly if they want to lead the pack. Their shoes, made with sharp spikes on the soles, give them traction.

I wonder if the athletic shoe companies got inspiration from the cheetah. Over short distances this catlike animal is the fastest runner in the animal kingdom.

When it spots prey, it secretly stalks it. Then it shows itself, sending the herd running in a fearful frenzy. The cheetah has strong claws that stay exposed like a dog's. So it can grip the loose ground and reach a speed of about 68 miles per hour.

But it can hold this speed for only about a minute. If it can't catch its prey within that time, it gives up the chase and saves its energy for next time.

Being quick is important. Sometimes you'll have to make rapid decisions. Friends might ask you to join them in smoking a cigarette or take a dare to shoplift or do other unwise activities. Deciding right now that you won't do these activities is your best defense.

Being quick to say yes to Jesus is also important. He sends the Holy Spirit to speak to your heart. When you sense Him calling, don't hesitate! As the child Samuel did, say, *"Speak, for your servant is listening."* You'll be glad you did.

MISSION: Practice immediate obedience to those in charge.

That Porous Cuttlebone

Home: Shallow, sandy-bottomed sea waters
Size: To 2.5 feet, including tentacles

Maybe you've seen a cuttlebone. Cage birds like to nibble on this white, porous object, which gives them calcium.

Cuttlebones come from cuttlefish, which are related to the octopus but are smaller. Cuttlefish have four pairs of short tentacles around their mouths and two longer tentacles. They use these for catching food.

Narrow, rippling fins rim their bodies and propel them. Cuttlefish hide during the day by changing their color to match their surroundings. Then at night they hunt for sea creatures.

Cuttlefish can float at any depth or just lie on the sea floor. They achieve this versatility by filling their porous cuttlebone with varying combinations of water and gases. Controlling what they put into the cuttlebone determines where they can stay.

Have you ever blurted out something unwise, unkind, or unclean? Then you told yourself, "I've got to watch what I say!"

Your mind is like cuttlebone. What you put into it determines where you'll hang out and what you'll say. So be careful what you let in.

The Bible says, *"He who guards his mouth and his tongue keeps himself from calamity."* The beginning of that "keeping" starts with what you let into your brain.

MISSION: The moment something bad pops into your head, ask God to help you get rid of it!

89

The Moth That Saves the Cypress

Home: Okefenokee Swamp, Georgia

The beautiful orange zale moth lives in the Okefenokee Swamp in Georgia. It lays its eggs on the heath vine that climbs the swamp cypress tree.

When the larvae hatch from the eggs, they feed on the heath vine. It's the only food they can eat, and their feeding eventually kills the vine. But this is good. If left unchecked, the parasitic heath vine would kill the swamp cypress tree.

If the swamp cypress tree died, new heath vines couldn't grow. That's because these are the only trees the vine can live on.

So if the moth larvae didn't kill the vines, all the swamp cypress trees would die. Then there'd be no host trees for new heath vines, and thus no food for the moths.

Even the smallest creatures in nature help keep things in balance for the good of all. Likewise, the little things you do and say are important in God's overall plan. Your efforts to be honest, kind, willing, and caring help keep your world in balance.

King David said to God, *"You are good, and what you do is good; teach me your decrees."* You can ask Him to do the same for you.

TALK BACK: What things feel as if they hurt but actually work for your good? What things in your life do you need to "destroy"?

Alligator!

Home: Southern swamps and wetlands
Size: To 20 feet and 500 pounds

At first glance alligators sunning themselves look like strips of tire tread. They're cold-blooded, so they must regulate their own body temperature by staying underwater much of the time and sunning themselves when they can. They sometimes lie on a muddy swamp or river bottom or float beneath the water's surface, with only their eyes and nostrils showing.

In dry weather alligators dig large hollows that fill with water. The water provides them with protection and also draws other animals. When an animal comes to drink, it might become a quick dinner for an alligator.

The female alligator scrapes together a great pile of vegetation on which to lay her eggs. After depositing up to 60 eggs on the pile, she covers them with more vegetation. She then guards the nest, allowing the heat from the rotting leaves to warm the eggs.

Two to three months later the babies hatch. They begin to chirp, which signals the mother to uncover them. About eight inches long at birth, the babies head for the water, where they feed and take care of themselves. But they stay near their mother for about a year.

Just as an alligator must regulate its temperature, you're responsible for regulating your spiritual temperature. That means you should take every opportunity to learn more about God and *"watch and pray so that you will not fall into temptation."*

TALK BACK: Name some things that help "regulate" your spiritual temperature. How do you know if you're keeping on track?

91

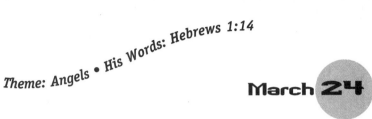

Close Encounter

One day I went exploring Georgia's Okefenokee Swamp with my husband. From our small motorboat I watched for alligators. I'd seen them there before, basking in the sun. But now it was winter, and I didn't spot any.

As we followed the shallow waterways, I did spot many waterbirds flying, eating, and preening. Then we nosed the boat into a shallow cove so we could watch three huge sandhill cranes.

When we started the motor to back out, we realized that we'd run aground. We'd have to either get out and push the boat into deeper water or pole out with the oars. Though we'd seen no alligators, we still didn't like the idea of getting out of the boat. So we decided to use the oars.

As I jabbed my oar against the canal bottom, it moved! Then a big lumpy back reared out of the water and a huge tail whacked the side of our boat!

Obviously, I'd poked an alligator. It had been there the whole time.

Things aren't always as they look. For instance, just as we didn't see or hear the alligator, we don't see or hear angels. Yet they're carefully watching over us, as God has asked them to do.

Speaking of angels, the Bible says, *"Are not all angels ministering spirits sent to serve those who will inherit salvation?"*

MISSION: Tonight make a list of where your angel accompanied you today. What words and actions did your angel witness?

African Gray Parrot

Home: Africa
Size: Wingspan to 28 inches

I heard a little bell tinkle and the pet shop door creak open. But when I turned to look, I discovered that no one had come in. When the sounds repeated themselves, I looked around for the source. The noises were coming from an African gray parrot!

These people-loving birds easily learn to "talk" and mimic household sounds. In the wild they build their nests high in tree trunks. They spend their lives within a small area, eating fruit and other vegetation.

When climbing trees these gray, red-tailed birds grasp the branches with both their bill and feet. Their two outer toes point backward, while their inner two point forward. This gives them a handlike grip and the ability to manipulate their food. Going about their business, these noisy birds constantly talk and call to each other.

Has anyone ever said that you talk too much? Certainly there are times to be quiet, but there's Someone to whom you can never talk too much. The Bible says, *"Pray continually."*

You don't always have to kneel and pray formally. God is interested in everything about you—your needs, fears, and dreams. So while you work, study, or play, you can keep in constant contact with Him through silent prayer. It's even better than talking to your dearest earthly friend, because He always understands what you mean.

GOAL: Besides asking for help when I pray, I'll remember to tell God how much I love Him.

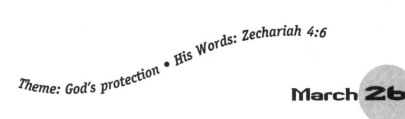

Purple Shore Crab

Home: Intertidal areas
Size: To 1.5 inches

I squatted on the beach, watching tiny purple shore crabs. They're the ocean's cleanup crew. Scampering across pebbles and shells, they pick up bits of decayed matter and put them into their mouths with their pincers.

My grandson, Kevin, brought one over to me. We looked at its inch-wide purplish shell and little protruding eyes. It waved its largest pincer at us. A moment later it pinched Kevin's thumb hard enough to leave little white spots.

Kevin returned the crab to the beach. Though he wasn't hurt, he knew that he and the crab weren't matched in size. He'd win any battle between them!

Sometimes the odds just aren't even. Take David and Goliath. According to common sense, David should have lost the battle between them. Even the Israelites thought so.

But they didn't count on God helping David. That Philistine giant taunted David—and it was the last thing he ever did.

When you're confronted with problems that look impossible to conquer, remember that you don't have to face your troubles alone. Once an angel said to Zechariah, *"'Not by might nor by power, but by my Spirit,' says the Lord Almighty."*

That means that God's on your side. You can count on His strength and wisdom to help you get through life's tough times.

TALK BACK: How can you show strength when facing a bully, even for someone else's benefit?

Greater Bilby

Home: Australia
Size: 3-5 pounds

The greater bilby is a marsupial (a mammal such as a kangaroo, with the female having a pouch for carrying the young). It has rabbit-like ears, silky gray fur, and a narrow, pointy nose that's pink at the end. Like a rabbit, it moves each pair of legs together, though it doesn't really hop.

Bilbies live in shrubs and grasslands, digging spiral tunnels that lead to deep burrows. This is where they spend the hot day. Their sharp sense of smell helps them find insects, other small creatures, and vegetation to eat. They clean themselves by using their long hind claws as a comb.

The female's pouch is upside down. That way it doesn't fill with dirt when she digs. Inside the pouch each of her babies attaches to a nipple until it can manage on its own.

Few bilbies are around today, because cattle and sheep raised for meat and wool claim their habitat. They trample the ground and eat the plants.

Our habitats will change, too. Jesus said, *"But mark this: There will be terrible times in the last days."* Someday we may no longer have the opportunity to study God's Word and worship freely. Then the Bible texts we've memorized will become priceless, for they can't be taken away from us. And God has promised to guide us through those difficult times and take us home to heaven.

TALK BACK: What texts have you memorized that might encourage you in hard times?

95

Hooded Seal

Home: North Atlantic and Arctic oceans
Size: To 900 pounds

Maybe you've seen a picture of a baby seal. This adorable animal has a furry little face and big sad eyes.

Born in late March or early April on an ice floe, the baby hooded seal (called a calf) weighs about 50 pounds at birth. It's known as a blueback because of the color of its fur. It nurses from its mother (called a cow) for only a few days. But it remains on the ice for a couple more weeks before joining the others to hunt.

The bull seal has a large hood of nasal tissue that extends from beneath his eyes to the front of his mouth. When he gets excited, he closes his nostrils and blows air into the hood to enlarge it. To threaten other bulls that get near his cows, he can also close one nostril and inflate nasal tissue from the other. It looks like a big red balloon.

When people get angry they show it in different ways. Some slam doors and say mean things, which isn't good. When you lose your temper you can't think clearly. And losing your cool doesn't accomplish anything, except make you feel foolish later.

The Bible points out, *"A person who controls his temper stops a quarrel" (ICB).* You can choose not to become angry. Try it!

MISSION: Next time you're angry, ask God for help. Decide exactly what's upsetting you. When you've calmed down, talk it out with someone you trust.

The Lookout

Home: Africa, Australia
Size: To 350 pounds

The ostrich is the world's largest bird. Interestingly, it can't fly because its wings are too small. But it has strong two-toed feet. A large nail on the longest toe of each foot gives the ostrich traction and a weapon. So it can run 20 miles per hour and sprint 45 miles per hour.

At nesting time the male scrapes a large hollow in the ground. Then his primary mate lays her three-pound eggs (which contain three pints of liquid). The secondary females surround those eggs with their own until 40 eggs may be in one nest. At night the male incubates as many of them as he can cover. The uncovered ones may not hatch.

Because of their height and keen vision ostriches can see danger approaching from a distance. Then they sound a warning.

Once Cain asked God, "Am I my brother's keeper?" The answer is yes. *"Reprimand the unruly . . . help the weak"* (Phillips), Paul said.

Though you needn't be a busybody, it's your responsibility to protect your family and friends by warning them when you know they're doing something wrong. Though it takes courage to speak up, your influence could save their lives—now and for eternity. God can help you offer your reminders gently and humbly.

TALK BACK: How could you help a friend you knew was shoplifting or thinking of trying drugs? What part does your setting a good example play?

Making Grapevines Strong

Home: Warm climates
Size: Many sizes

In Bible times people cultivated large grape vineyards. Through trial and error the growers learned how to keep a vine healthy and how to make it become strong enough to yield many bunches of grapes.

Explaining discipline, Jesus said to His disciples, *"I am the true vine, and my Father is the gardener. He cuts off every branch in me that bears no fruit, while every branch that does bear fruit he prunes so that it will be even more fruitful."*

I had a hard time understanding this text until I planted a grapevine. It leafed out beautifully, but no grapes developed. So the next spring I did something drastic. I cut off all the branches, keeping only a piece of one to become the vine's trunk. On it I left three tiny buds.

These buds grew into branches, which clung to the fence with their spiral tendrils. And bunches of grapes grew! What I did seemed harsh, but that's what the vine needed in order to grow strong.

Jesus is the vine, and we are the branches. Through the Bible, our consciences, and life's experiences, God "trims away" those things about us that hinder our spiritual growth. Sometimes that cutting hurts! But at the same time He shows us how to cling to Him so we can grow strong and be fruitful.

TALK BACK: What has God "cut from your life" that made you stronger? What else would you like Him to prune away?

That White Stuff

You probably see this mineral in school. It's white and dusty, and it gets on your hands and clothes. It's chalk!

Chalk is made of tiny shells and plant-life bits that once lived on shallow ocean floors. Gradually the sediment hardened and became soft white rock, a form of limestone.

The White Cliffs of Dover on the English Channel are famous chalk cliffs rising from the sea. Big deposits of chalk also exist in Texas, Iowa, and Arkansas. This is evidence that a flood once occurred.

Have you ever made chalk drawings on the sidewalk and gone outside later to find them washed away? Thousands of years ago Someone wrote something special that couldn't be washed away.

After calling Moses to the top of Mount Sinai, God gave this great leader some important rules for safety and happiness. Then He wrote the Ten Commandments. He didn't use chalk, or a pen, or even a chisel—He used His own finger to engrave them on stone!

The Record says, *"When the Lord finished speaking to Moses on Mount Sinai, he gave him the two tablets of the Testimony, the tablets of stone inscribed by the finger of God."*

I believe God engraved the commandments on rock so they could never be erased. He did it to show that those rules are for all times, even today.

TRY IT: If you let God, He'll engrave His guiding words on your heart. Why not let Him do it for you?

Walkingstick

Home: Tropics, warm and temperate regions
Size: 2-13 inches long

One windless evening I saw a tiny branch change positions. Checking it out, I discovered a six-inch walkingstick. Angular and dry, this creature looked like a broken twig. But it stood on two pairs of legs, holding its third pair straight in front of it like a frayed sword.

Later I watched it munch on a leaf. Occasionally it trembled, as though moved by a passing breeze.

There are many varieties of walkingsticks. Each looks like the bark of the specific tree it inhabits. Walkingsticks in North America are smooth and slender, but some tropical varieties may appear shaggy.

Active mostly at night, these insects feed on foliage. During the day they stay motionless so birds don't notice and catch them. If a predator happens to remove one of their legs, young walkingsticks can grow a new one, though adults can't.

Males are rare, so the eggs the females lay often don't get fertilized. They hatch anyway, but are all females. The female babies copy their mother in coloration, habits, and choice of food.

You're to copy Jesus, resembling Him in your words, actions, and attitudes. Paul said, *"In your lives you must think and act like Christ Jesus" (ICB).* That's not always easy, for many worldly things try to catch your attention. But if you ask God, He'll help you reflect Him to those around you.

TRY IT: Watch an insect that mimics its surroundings. What keeps it safe? What keeps you safe?

The Nose Knows— Or Does It?

My dog, Molly, has a wonderful sense of smell. Her nose helps her locate a single raisin hidden in a large room!

On our walks I sometimes see rabbits dashing across the street far ahead. But because Molly is busy sniffing everything, she doesn't notice. Then when we get near the place where I saw the rabbit Molly catches the scent. Her ears perk up, and she tugs at her leash. Though the rabbit is gone, if I let her go, she'll zigzag across yards and around trees and bushes, following the scent along the exact pathway it took. If the rabbit went into the woods, Molly will too.

When I give Molly a new food, she sniffs at it, then turns away. If it doesn't smell like a food she recognizes, her nose says, "Forget it!" But to please me she'll eventually take a reluctant taste. Then she'll gobble it right up. She has to learn that she can't always rely on what her nose tells her but should trust me.

Sometimes what you think is good really isn't, and what you consider horrible really isn't. King Solomon said, *"My children, listen to your father's teaching. Pay attention so you will understand" (ICB)*. It takes time and experience to develop judging skills. So trust the wisdom of your parents when making decisions. They'll do their best to guide you.

TALK BACK: Ask your parents to tell you about a time they needed to trust a grown-up's wisdom. What was the result?

Boa Constrictor

Home: Mainly rain forests, Mexico, South America
Size: To 14 feet

Constrictors are snakes that can squeeze objects. Pythons, anacondas, America's rubber boa, and the boa constrictor belong to this family of snakes.

Boas are good swimmers, but they don't move very fast on land. Still, they have their way of getting food. Looking like dead leaves on the ground, they lurk patiently near water sources. When a small mammal or bird comes to drink, the boa doesn't chase it. Instead, it strikes out, bites onto the victim, and then quickly coils around it.

Boas aren't poisonous. They kill by squeezing so tightly that their prey can't breathe. Once the victim dies, the boa swallows it whole. The boa's patience pays off. It won't need food again for several weeks.

Maybe you have a hard time waiting patiently. Do you wonder, for instance, if Jesus will ever come? When you grow impatient, that's when you need to hold on to your faith and beliefs even more. The Bible says, *"You need to persevere so that when you have done the will of God, you will receive what he has promised. For in just a very little while, 'He who is coming will come.'"*

When people try to discourage you about Jesus' coming, cling to God's promises, just as the boa holds on to its prey.

CONTACT: God, help me to be patient until Jesus comes and not quit watching for Him.

What Bark Does

In the forest you see all kinds of trees. Some look tall and straight; others appear gnarled and weathered. Some trunks feel smooth; others feel scaly or ridged. Some trees have branches that grow near the ground; others have high branches. Some trees prefer damp soil; others thrive in rocky, dry places.

Yet all trees need the same basic things, especially healthy bark. Bark is a tree's skin, protecting it from weather and disease. The bark covers small tubes that run from the tree's roots to its top, carrying sap upward to nourish the leaves and branches.

Fire can destroy the bark, and so can some animals or insects. But as long as a tree has some good bark protecting enough tubes, it will probably live.

If a tree becomes girdled, or completely stripped of bark around its trunk, though, it will die. Without the life-giving sap circulating through the tubes, the tree can't survive. The connection between its roots, leaves, and branches keeps it alive.

You're like a tree, with Jesus as your root. Through the tubes—your mind—Jesus nourishes you. But like bark, your "tubes" must be protected. That means reading, watching, and thinking about good things. The Bible says of God, *"Your commands make me wiser than my enemies, for they are ever with me."*

Following His commands protects you. How's *your* bark today?

MISSION: Start a notebook of texts or ideas that will help you grow healthy bark.

Little Hammocks

It's early morning. You're hiking across a field and notice pieces of cloth draped between stalks of grass.

Curious about these hammock-like strips, you kneel beside one. The webbing reaches as far as 18 inches, then comes nearly together at the center, creating a funnel shape. Down in the funnel hole you see something move. It's a spider! You realize that you're actually looking at spiderwebs, their strands spun so closely together that they look like sheer, silky fabric.

You blow gently, and the spider backs into the hole. You wait. It returns. Then a fly alights on the "hammock" and rubs its feet together on the slippery web.

The funnel-web spider rushes out and grabs the fly. With its spinnerets located at the tip of its abdomen, the spider spins more silk. Then it uses its hind legs to wrap the silk around the fly. The spider's careful work pays off—it has a meal to drag into its hole.

What use can funnel webs be to you? In a pinch you can use them for bandages, as people did several hundred years ago. And what can you learn from the funnel-web spider? To do your work carefully.

The Bible says, *"A person who doesn't work hard is just like a person who destroys things"* (ICB). Why not plan to always do your best?

TRY IT: Find an abandoned spiderweb. Take a strand and wrap it around several blades of grass. Does it hold?

Orb Webs

Home: Gardens, bushy meadows
Size: To 1 inch

I almost ran into a two-foot web suspended between two bushes. At the center of the glistening silk rested a black-and-yellow spider. How did this creature make this marvelous structure?

The web started with just a piece of silk floating on the wind. It caught on something, and the spider scurried along the silk bridge while spinning a new piece of silk to fasten to the other side. Returning to the center, the spider pulled the longer piece of silk down to form a triangle, then spun more silk to create wagon-wheel-like spokes.

Next, starting at the center, the spider spun a spiral of non-sticky silk (which it would later eat). It fastened this silk to the spokes. Then, working outward, it used the nonsticky silk for scaffolding as it spun a spiral of sticky silk.

Near the center of the web it added two long vertical zigzags to warn birds not to fly into and destroy the web. Finally the spider waited for a careless insect to wander into the sticky trap.

The Bible speaks of evil men who tried to trap David in a web of words. He explained, *"They spread a net for my feet."* But David also said, *"He [God] sends from heaven and saves me, rebuking those who hotly pursue me."* If you're faithful to God, you can trust Him to help you escape webs of trouble.

TRY IT: Blow softly on an orb weaver spider waiting on its web. What does it do?

105

Netcasting Spider

The netcasting spider spins a tight patch of webbing. Then it suspends itself upside down, holding the webbing between its four long front legs.

When an unwary insect approaches, the spider reaches out and stretches the sticky webbing over the insect before it can get away. Finally the spider wraps the insect in its net and enjoys a meal.

Satan casts nets, too. For instance, he uses stories that portray dead people coming back as spirits. This doesn't happen, yet the stories entice people to consider, "What if it were true?" And soon people begin to accept one of Satan's most dangerous nets, the occult (the belief in living spirits of the dead).

Satan knows that what you read and watch gradually becomes more believable to you. And eventually he might get you to accept his deceptions.

At the end of time Satan will even work "miracles" to convince people that he's Jesus. Many will be fooled because they haven't guarded the doorways of their minds. Satan will then slip his net around them.

Jesus said, *"Watch out that you are not deceived. For many will come in my name, claiming, 'I am he.'"* There's just one way to avoid becoming trapped, and that's to be careful what you let into your mind today.

TALK BACK: What activities may lead to belief in the occult? How can you tell when you get on dangerous ground? Is "just checking it out" ever safe?

Web-spitting Spider

The web-spitting spider moves slowly and doesn't have sharp eyesight. Still, it has an efficient way to catch food.

A nighttime hunter, it creeps quietly until it spots a sleeping insect. Carefully the spider approaches the victim, touching it softly with its front leg to measure its distance away. Then the spider spits two zigzag threads of glue over the insect. This pins the victim to the surface. Because it expected no danger, it wasn't watching for an enemy.

Some people say that music is the universal language. It can encourage godly choices or sinful ones. Some lyrics encourage disbelief in God, violence, selfishness, or inviting evil beings to help you get what you want.

You'd think people would recognize this danger. But thousands get "caught" in the web of music before they realize what's happening.

Words set to music stay in our minds, and Satan knows it. Some music can even put people into a trance, leaving them helpless against Satan's deceptions.

How can you keep this from happening to you? Listen only to music that portrays things that *"are true and honorable and right and pure and beautiful and respected" (ICB)*. Whatever takes your thoughts away from Jesus isn't safe to listen to.

MISSION: Memorize Philippians 4: 8. Use it for your guide in choosing music.

Angler Spider

Home: Many areas

The fat, bumpy angler spider becomes active at night. It spins a single strand of webbing, attaches it horizontally to a twig, and hangs from this strand by two of its legs. Then it spins another strand about two inches long and deposits a sticky glob of glue on the end. Waiting quietly, it dangles this web from its front feet.

The angler probably produces a special scent to attract moths. When one approaches, the spider swings its line, bumping the sticky glue against the moth. The spider quickly reels in its stuck victim, then paralyzes it with a bite before eating it. If the spider fails to catch its dinner for so long that the glue ball dries, it simply eats it and prepares a fresh one.

Satan is also an angler, trying to trap you with occultish beliefs. Sometimes he uses fantasy video games as his sticky glob.

Maybe you've seen on-screen monsters or characters die before your eyes, then come to life for another round. Unseen, Satan smiles to himself. He wants you to think that dying is no big deal. If on-screen villains can instantly come back to life, maybe real people can, too. He hopes you'll forget that the Bible says, *"The living know that they will die, but the dead know nothing."*

God's people who have died *will* come back to life someday, but only when Jesus raises them at His return.

TALK BACK: Are there things in your home that Satan could use to trap you?

108

Spider Defense

Spiders don't want to become some animal's meal, so they have ways of defending themselves. Some can jump or run swiftly, some inject a poisonous bite, and some escape into a burrow. Others drop to the ground and, because of their coloration, seem to disappear.

The huge nephila spider from the tropics has one of the most unusual ways of all. It sits at the center of its giant-sized orb web. There it waits for insects to fly by and provide it with dinner.

But birds fly by, too—hungry birds. Spotting the nephila sitting in the open, a bird might approach and hover in the air. Sensing danger, the nephila goes into action. It starts shaking its web, just as though it were jumping on a sideways trampoline.

The rapid movement makes the spider look larger than it is. Also, this moving target is nearly impossible for the bird to grab with its beak. Thus, the nephila defeats the bird's intentions.

How do you protect yourself against Satan's temptations and lies? The Bible says, *"Don't follow the ways of the wicked. Don't do what evil people do. Avoid their ways. Don't go near what they do. Stay away from them and keep on going"* (ICB).

The minute you recognize something that goes against God's will, get away from there. Then command Satan, in Jesus' name, to leave you alone.

MISSION: As a protection for yourself against Satan's deceptions, memorize Luke 4: 8. Use it in Jesus' name when tempted to do wrong.

Chisel Teeth

Home: North America and Eurasia
Size: To 30 inches long and 35 pounds

If an animal doesn't possess the tools it needs, it must find them. For instance, some birds use twigs to stir up ants, and sea otters use stones to break open clams. But beavers carry their tools with them—sharp incisor teeth.

Large rodents, beavers need their teeth to gnaw down trees for food and for building dams. First they anchor a tree trunk with their upper incisors. Next they use their lower ones to strip away large chips of wood. Circling the tree, they eventually chew off enough wood that the tree falls. This leaves a sharp point on each end of the break.

Long ago humans noticed how efficiently a beaver's teeth could shape wood. So they learned to break rocks to create a sharp edge. Metal chisels came later.

Chisels need to be sharpened, but a beaver's teeth sharpen themselves. The back of the lower incisors is softer than the front, so as the beaver's teeth wear away the front remains sharp. A beaver's teeth continue to grow, and it must regularly use them to keep them short.

God has given you certain "tools," or talents. The Bible says, *"Everyone who uses what he has will get more. . . . But the one who does not use what he has will have everything taken away from him"* (ICB). As you use your talents, they'll not only bless others—they'll bless you.

MISSION: With a trusted adult's help, discover what talents you have. Start using them.

Photosynthesis

I picked up a board someone had tossed onto the park lawn. I could tell it had been there for several days, because the grass beneath it looked yellow and limp. Why? Because the board had blocked the sunlight. If I hadn't removed it, the grass would soon have died.

You see, most plants make their own food by using chemicals from their environment. This process is called photosynthesis. In order to convert chemicals into the glucose (sugar) they live on, plants must have sunlight. During a good sunny day, plants can make enough glucose to last them for several days. Then they need sunlight again.

You need sunlight, too. When it shines on your skin, some of your body oils become converted into vitamin D, needed for healthy bones. Sunlight also kills germs. Just don't forget to wear sunscreen when you're outside!

There's another kind of light you need. Jesus said, *"I am the light of the world. Whoever follows me will never walk in darkness, but will have the light of life."*

By placing yourself in His light, you'll grow, too.

TRY IT: Get two small plants. Put one where it gets plenty of sunshine and the other in a closet. Water them both. After a week, check them. How do they look? Now switch the plants for a week. What lessons can you learn about your own body and spiritual life from how your two plants react?

The Fancy Fan

Home: Originally India and Sri Lanka
Size: Tail length 4-5 feet

The peacock, a male peafowl, has iridescent blue-and-green feathers. But what really sets him off is his long train of green covert feathers. Dotted with big eyelike spots, they trail wherever he goes.

When he wants to attract a female, he can raise his tail feathers to look like a fancy fan over his back. Then he struts, rattling them in a proud display. Back and forth he swaggers, keeping the glistening front side of his feathers toward her.

But my mom used to say, "The peacock wouldn't be so proud if he could see the under part of his feathers!" The back of the feathers looks like a bunch of dull, pale sticks!

My mom would make this remark when one of us kids began boasting. It made us think twice about showing off and trying to appear better than someone else.

Obadiah made this remark to some people: *"Your pride has fooled you. . . . And you say to yourself, "No one can bring me down to the ground." . . . But I will bring you down from there,' says the Lord"* (ICB).

Watch out that you don't think too highly of yourself. You may be forced to see what's really under your bright colors!

TRY IT: In your next conversation, how long can you avoid using the words "I" or "me"?

112

Mr. Clean Pockets

Home: North and Central America
Size: To 1 foot

Pocket gophers dig elaborate tunnels underground. As they do they use their chisel-shaped teeth to eat roots from trees and plants, which destroys them. These brown rodents particularly like juicy flower bulbs.

Fast diggers, they create a maze of tunnels, including bedrooms, storehouses, and even a toilet room. Naturally tidy, they push their diggings above ground, leaving mounds of soil at various tunnel entryways. Then they seal the entryways for safety.

Pocket gophers can run backward quickly, their almost naked tail helping them feel their way. They generally stay beneath ground. Occasionally, though, they'll surface to feast on tender stems and tubers.

Then they stuff vegetation into their fur-lined cheek pockets, which extend to their shoulders. After carrying the food to their storehouses, they turn their pockets inside out to clean them.

Someone said, "Cleanliness is next to godliness." God did advise, *"Everything should be done in a fitting and orderly way."*

If small creatures keep their areas neat, shouldn't you? As you learn to be orderly with your belongings, you'll become more orderly with your thoughts, too. And when your thoughts are orderly, it helps you concentrate better and understand God's instructions. That's worth the effort!

TALK BACK: In what way was God orderly in His work of creation?

113

Blue-eyed Scallops

Home: Oceans
Size: About 2 inches long

Fan-shaped and ridged, scallop shells often wash up on beaches. They look like the shell on Shell service station signs.

Related to the oyster and the clam, scallops have two wavy-edged valves with one hinge. They swim by opening and closing these valves. The resulting jet of water pushes them along. Usually, though, scallops rest on the ocean floor with their valves slightly open. For food they filter particles from the water.

Their main enemy is the starfish, which uses suction cups on its feet to pull the scallop shells apart and get to the soft inside. But scallops have about 100 blue eyes around the edge of their mantle (the flesh just inside the shell). These eyes help them know when to close their shell for safety.

Speaking of eyes, do you ever feel as if someone's watching you? Do you ever worry that there's a "big eye in the sky" just waiting to catch you doing something wrong?

The Bible says, *"The wicked flee when no one pursues"* (NKJV). Wrongdoers often run, even if no one's chasing them. So if you worry about unseen eyes watching you, it may be that you're doing something you shouldn't. God could be trying to warn you through your conscience. But remember, His eyes watch you in love, not to catch you doing wrong.

CONTACT: Father, please help me to listen to my conscience, through which You speak.

High Climber

Home: North America
Size: To 500 pounds

Walking through the woods, I heard something crash high in an oak tree. As I watched, I saw a huge paw reach out and grab a branch. Then a gigantic black bear appeared. Ambling along the limb, it paused to break off a branch and bite off the acorns.

Soon two fuzzy black spots appeared—the bear's cubs doing aerial acrobatics! One of them descended to a safe fork in the tree for a snooze. But junior stayed up high with his mother.

Then he crept out onto his own branch, 60 feet above the ground. He walked along it like you'd walk on railroad tracks. As he neared the end of the branch, it began to sag. He stumbled, caught himself, turned around, and then sat down. Amazingly, he didn't fall!

Why? Because his mother had done a good job teaching him where to safely walk. And obviously, he'd been a good student.

In the Bible God provides detailed training for Christian living. He also sends the Holy Spirit to impress your mind and angels to protect you. And Jesus? He not only died to save you, He understands just how you feel!

So if you're wise, you'll carefully observe His life and follow His example. Then when He comes you'll be able to say, *"Lord God, you are my hope. I have trusted you since I was young"* (ICB).

MISSION: Check an encyclopedia to learn how long cubs stay with their mothers. Why?

The Colorful Mandrill

Home: Western Africa
Size: To 120 pounds

The mandrill is a ferocious-looking baboon. Its long red nose has wide ridges of bright blue on each side.

The male is easy to spot. He has a long yellow beard and narrow, staring eyes. When he bares his huge canine teeth, he looks downright mean. But his looks are deceiving. Baring teeth is actually considered a submissive behavior among mandrills.

Mandrills sleep in trees, but they hunt for food on the jungle floor. They live in groups, and as they hunt they grunt to each other, keeping in contact. When predators threaten the pack, the less colorful females and the young mandrills escape into the trees. Protective, the males stay behind until danger has passed.

Grooming each other is an important activity among mandrills. Animals who live together and depend on each other can't afford to fight and hold grudges. So when two mandrills disagree, one will eventually start grooming the other, ending the disagreement.

How about you? If someone does something you don't like, is it hard for you to forgive that person? Do you sometimes feel ferocious inside and hold a grudge? That's a human reaction. But Jesus said, *"Forgive, and you will be forgiven."*

Just as we need God's forgiveness, others need ours.

MISSION: Do you need to ask someone's forgiveness? Should you forgive someone? Let God help you do it this week.

116

Beast or Beauty?

Home: Southern United States, tropics
Size: To .38 inch

The ant lion is a ferocious insect. It builds a cone-shaped trap by backing into dry, sandy ground in a circular motion. While doing this it flips sand out of the pit with its head. Once the pit is a couple inches deep and wide, the ant lion submerges itself in sand at the bottom, leaving its long jaws exposed.

When an ant or other insect wanders over the steep edge, it causes the sand to begin sliding into the pit. The ant lion rapidly flings more sand away, speeding up the avalanche. Finally the helpless insect lands at the bottom of the pit in the ant lion's jaws. Then the ant lion waits patiently for the next insect to tumble in.

Once it's gotten enough to eat, the ant lion spins a cocoon around itself. A few weeks later it emerges as a beautiful imago, a lacy-winged fly. This delicate, gentle creature bears little resemblance to the predator at the bottom of the pit.

Have you known people who acted like ant lions—eager to draw others into a pit of trouble? And then they caught sight of Jesus and began to change. Little by little their harsh personalities disappeared as the Master shaped them into kind, loving people.

It can happen to others. It can happen to you. Remember, *"With God all things are possible."*

TALK BACK: You're supposed to pray for those who hurt you (Matthew 5: 44). What else can you do if someone constantly tries to make trouble for you?

117

The Tree-climbing Fox

Home: North and northern South America
Size: 5-15 pounds

The gray fox is a shy woodland creature that hides in the daytime and hunts at night. Its gray, rusty-tinged coat provides good camouflage and keeps it warm. Scared of humans, it's seldom seen. It preys on small mammals, but also eats birds, eggs, and fruit. Not wasteful, the fox stores what it doesn't eat for later.

The gray fox makes its den in places such as hollow logs or rock piles. Because of its short legs it can't always outrun predators such as wolves. So it does the next best thing—it climbs a tree to get away! Grasping the trunk with its forelegs, the fox pushes itself up with its heavy back claws, finally scrambling to a safe branch. Its bushy tail helps it keep its balance.

Wisely, the gray fox knows that it's no match for larger animals. A tree is its highway to escape.

Solomon said, *"The highway of the upright avoids evil; he who guards his way guards his soul."* When you're tempted to watch or read something evil, you have to turn away in order to escape. Put it out of reach! Also, ask God to help you avoid the temptation, and confide in a trustworthy adult. Your eternal life is worth every effort it takes!

CONTACT: Dear God, please give me the strength, courage, and wisdom to turn away from evil and keep my thoughts on You.

The Humble Horned Toad

Home: North America
Size: 2-4 inches

The horned toad really isn't a toad but a wide, flat lizard. Its "horns," actually huge, pointed scales, make this reptile look like a walking cactus. Colored in earth tones, it's well camouflaged. When startled it runs a few feet, then stops abruptly, blending into the background.

Though it looks ferocious, this toad is really quite gentle. It has an unusual method of defense. When frightened by something coming too close, it can squirt blood for several feet from the forward corners of its eyes.

When my mom was little, country kids didn't have many toys. So she and her friends used to catch horned toads and place yarn harnesses around them. Then they'd hitch the toads to matchbox "wagons" that had cardboard wheels. Using twigs to tap the lizards' sides, the kids would steer them, getting them to race each other or pull loads of pebbles. These humble creatures became quite tame and cooperative.

In speaking about God, David said, *"He guides the humble in what is right and teaches them his way."* God wants to lead you to righteousness. Through impressions of the Holy Spirit and through godly advice by your parents and other adults, He "taps" you in the right direction.

TALK BACK: What does "humble" mean? Does a humble person think they're no good and can't do anything well?

The Ovenbird's Oven

Home: South America
Size: Length to 8 inches and weight to 2 ounces

Imagine carrying 1,500 to 2,000 chunks of wet clay in your mouth. That's what ovenbirds do in order to build their home.

Mixing clay with plant fibers to strengthen it, they lay the floor first. Then they build a thick dome and place a door in the side of it. After carpeting the seven-pound nest with grass and feathers, the female ovenbird lays her eggs. Because the mud holds the day's heat, the eggs stay warm and hatch in about three weeks.

If the birds don't carefully complete their project, their nests will cave in on their babies. But most of the nests are so sturdy that they can withstand two to three years of rainy weather. Still, ovenbirds build a new nest each year, leaving the old nest for other birds.

You know how good it feels to start an exciting project. But it takes lots of work to stick with a task until it's finished. It's easier to give up halfway through and go on to something else. A good motto is "Decide. Start. Stay. Finish."

This principle applies to your spiritual life, too. Speaking of following Him, Jesus said, *"No one who puts his hand to the plow and looks back is fit for service in the kingdom of God."* In other words, if you decide to follow Jesus and then give up, you just might lose out on eternal life. That's too big a price to pay for a little laziness!

FOCUS: I'll develop self-control and finish what I start.

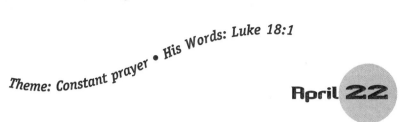

The Tiny Paddler

The European water shrew is about the size of a mouse and has a very long, pointed nose. It alternates sleeping and hunting both day and night. Though it occasionally eats worms or insects on land, it prefers catching a frog, fish, snail, or mollusk in the water.

Because it bobs on top of the water, it has to expend lots of energy in order to dive beneath the surface. Also, once underwater it must paddle constantly in order to stay below. Buoyant air bubbles become trapped in its water-repellent fur and push it toward the surface. After diving, it can remain submerged for only about 20 seconds.

Fringed hind feet propel the shrew, and a row of stiff hairs along its tail form a keel that helps it steer. Since it must consume its own weight in food each day, it sometimes catches frogs or fish larger than itself. It immobilizes them with venomous saliva.

Even the water shrew needs to dry off sometimes. It does this by squeezing through a narrow underground tunnel. The tight fit presses the water from its coat.

The shrew's need to paddle constantly while underwater reminds me of our need to pray constantly in order to stay connected to God. Jesus talked about how we *"should always pray and not give up."*

MISSION: When you wake up, before you even open your eyes, talk to God. Ask Him to guide your day. Remember to "check in" with Him often throughout the day.

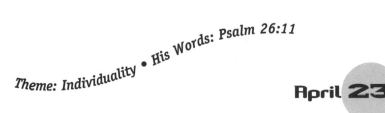

Grevy's Zebra

Home: Eastern Africa
Size: Shoulder 4-5 feet high

There are three living varieties of zebras, all related to horses and donkeys. Each has a unique pattern to its stripes.

The largest, called Grevy's zebra, has narrow stripes that appear vertical on the animal's body and horizontal on its haunches and legs, extending to its hooves. With a narrow head and round, white-tipped ears, it closely resembles a mule. It even brays like a mule!

Grevy's zebra also stands out from other zebras in the way it behaves. It roams arid areas, lowlands, and sparsely wooded plains. Less social than the other two varieties, it forms temporary groups.

The male establishes and patrols a territory for himself and his harem of females, marking the boundaries with piles of dung. He allows other stallions into this territory only if they don't try to mate with his females. If they do, he fights them off, using his sharp canine teeth as weapons.

If your friends make a bad choice when you're with them, do you maintain your individuality and determine to do what's right? Can you say no to wrong activities, even if it makes you different? If so, you, like David, can say, *"As for me, I shall walk in my integrity"* (NASB).

TALK BACK: Why is it hard to be different from other people? Discuss some ways you can guard your integrity and still be friendly with classmates who make bad choices.

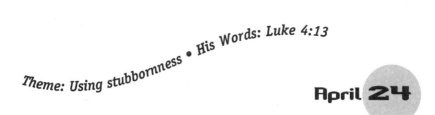
Snuggle Goat

Home: Domesticated in many countries
Size: Adults 125-300 pounds

Yesterday I noticed a full-grown goat in the back of the car ahead of me. It seemed to be enjoying its ride!

Later I discovered a newspaper article about raising goats for pack animals. Although I knew goats are raised as pets or for their hair, meat, or milk, this was a new idea.

I found out that goats are good pack animals for backpacking trips because they can get through smaller places than horses can. Also, they follow their owners like dogs do, so they don't need a leash. And they can eat whatever's available.

Stubborn, goats don't give up easily. People who raise pack goats work with them from birth, bottle-feeding them, bonding with them, and training them to use their stubbornness correctly.

Year-old goats can carry 10 to 15 pounds. Adults 2 years and older can pack 35 to 100 pounds, or one-third their weight. At the campsite they don't need to be tied up at night, but maybe they should be, for they persistently try to get into your tent to snuggle up with you!

Stubbornness is usually considered a bad trait. But it can also be good if it helps you resist Satan's temptations. Jesus turned Satan away by His steadfast refusal to obey him. *"When the devil had finished all this tempting, he left him [Jesus] until an opportune time."*

CONTACT: Heavenly Father, help me to have the right kind of stubbornness, and, as Jesus did, turn Satan away.

123

Zooplankton

Home: Oceans
Size: Microscopic to 3 inches

Zooplankton live in the ocean, particularly near the coasts. These infant animals, including fish and eggs, barnacles, sea anemones, krill (shrimplike crustaceans), and even jellyfish, may spend their entire lives on the ocean's surface. But some, such as sea anemones and octopuses, eventually settle to the bottom to spend their adult life in one place.

Some zooplankton are vegetarian, eating only phytoplankton (small plant life). Some zooplankton feed on each other. But all have one thing in common. Ocean currents gather them into large swarms and carry them long distances.

They serve as the main food for many larger creatures. In fact, whales can eat more than 4,000 pounds of plankton in one feeding. If the currents didn't spread this important food source around, many sea creatures would die.

The story of Jesus is supposed to go to all the world. You have an important part in spreading it. Maybe you're sharing it with friends and classmates through Christlike words and actions. As you grow you may take the good news door to door. Eventually you may even become a missionary. But it's important to start now.

Paul said, *"God, with his mercy, gave us this work to do. So we don't give up"* (ICB). Ask God to give you opportunities to spread the message of His love.

MISSION: With friends visit a senior citizens home. Sing, listen, and share Jesus' love with the residents.

124

Brandy's Wisdom

Brandy, a cocker spaniel, belongs to my friend Dennis. With big, expressive eyes and a tail that does double time, Brandy's a great companion. But good dogs don't get that way all by themselves. They need training and discipline.

Though almost perfect, Brandy has an annoying habit. She loves to pull things off tables, bookcases, or any place she can reach them. When she does that, Dennis punishes her by putting her into her indoor crate for a time-out.

The other day Dennis came home and found sad-eyed Brandy sitting in her crate. She'd given herself a time out! So Dennis checked the house. Sure enough, a crystal candlestick lay shattered on the floor. But Dennis was glad that Brandy had taken control and was disciplining herself!

Self-control and self-discipline go together. As you get older, you need to take over the job of making yourself do what you should instead of leaving that to others. It's within your power to give yourself a talking to and to set limits for yourself. You don't have to let yourself get away with whatever you feel like doing. You can stop yourself before you "pull stuff off the table."

The Bible says, *"If you hide your sins, you will not succeed. If you confess and reject them, you will receive mercy" (ICB).* Why not let Jesus help you in training yourself to do what's right?

TALK BACK: What are appropriate methods of disciplining yourself?

125

That Old Trash Heap

A while back our neighbors cleared a space to build their house. They bulldozed over the lovely meadow that had been sprinkled with rare pink lady's slippers and delicate ferns. When they had finished, they left a terrible-looking pile of bushes, rocks, trash, and dirt.

I was sure it could never be pretty again. But I recently passed the place and noticed a small hill covered with tall grasses, lush vines, spring flowers, and bushes. Butterflies flitted around, hunting nectar. A robin, with a bug in its beak, disappeared into the greenery. God's nature had clothed the ugly waste and made it beautiful again.

When you sin it leaves you in a mess, turning your life upside down. You may wonder if things will ever be OK again. You may even think, *I'm no good. Why keep trying?*

But the Holy Spirit urges you to look to Jesus, asking Him to forgive your sins and help you live right. Then Jesus does something wonderful. He cleans up those sins and gives you the credit for when *He* did right! He counts *you* as perfect!

So when you mess up, don't try to make yourself perfect. Turn to Jesus and let Him bring beauty out of the trash heaps of your failures. Then, as you cooperate with Him, you can say, *"I delight greatly in the Lord. . . . He has clothed me with garments of salvation."*

TALK BACK: Can I earn the "garment of salvation"? Why?

Common Housefly

Home: Universal
Size: To .33 inch

Maybe your mom has reminded you not to leave food lying around. And maybe she's told you to rinse your dishes immediately after a meal and to clean up the yard where your dog stays.

There's a good reason for this. You don't want to attract houseflies. One of the world's worst pests, these insects probably spread more disease than any other creature.

Using their mouths, flies suck up moisture as they crawl on rotting food, decaying animals, or animal droppings. They can even taste with their feet. Because they can't chew food, they must release saliva to liquefy any solid food.

When dining, flies generally release some of their previous meal on whatever they're eating. This is how they pass on diseases. You may have seen flies "washing" their hands. Though they continually groom themselves, they may carry up to a million bacteria, some of which they leave on anything they touch.

You know you should wash your hands and keep flies off your food. But when Isaiah said, *"Wash and make yourselves clean,"* he was talking about cleaning your heart. He understood that sin spreads like a disease and must be controlled. So ask God to help you say no to Satan's temptations and stay clean!

TRY IT: Your feet, like a fly's, are versatile. Blindfold yourself and see how many things you can identify by feeling them with your bare feet.

The Master Hider

Home: North America
Size: To 9 inches, plus tail

The pack rat is a busy grayish-brown rodent with a long bushy tail. A vegetarian, it hunts at night. When disturbed or frightened, it may nervously thump the ground with the end of its tail or by bringing both hind feet down together.

This animal builds a large, untidy nest against a tree, in a rock crevice, by a cactus thicket, in an old building, or on the ground. Made from a variety of sticks and debris, the nest can reach four feet high.

Pack rats (also known as wood rats) have the curious habit of hiding unusual objects in their nests. Abandoned nests have contained treasures such as "lost" watches, eyeglasses, jewelry, tin-can lids, and spoons. Anything that catches the pack rat's fancy might be whisked away and concealed in its home.

Like pack rats that hide their treasures, you might sometimes try to hide your sins. You may think that if no one sees you doing wrong, you can keep it a secret. But your loving God, who sees even sparrows fall, knows what's happening.

The Bible says, *"There is nothing concealed that will not be disclosed, or hidden that will not be made known."* So whether or not any humans are watching, you should act in such a way that it won't matter!

MISSION: Ask God to help you avoid any activities that might make you feel ashamed.

Ant-watching

While hiking I sat down to rest. I noticed a line of black ants struggling to follow each other around pebbles and branches. Each carried an ant egg or a bit of food. These insects were apparently changing homes, and each ant took the exact same path to reach their new hole.

When the line of ants had finally disappeared, I noticed one more ant coming along. It carried a fly wing. As it balanced the wing, it lost the pathway around the pebbles and branches. So it tried to climb the pebble hill. But it was too steep, and the ant dropped the wing.

Repeatedly the ant tried to find its way, but it couldn't. I held my breath, for *I* could see the pathway the other ants had taken. How could I show the lost ant? I couldn't, because there was no way to communicate with it.

Watching that ant helped me understand how God must feel when He sees us struggle. He can easily see the way we should go, and if we'll listen, He'll show us what to do. He promised, *"I will instruct you and teach you in the way you should go; I will counsel you and watch over you."*

God guides you through the words in the Bible and through the instruction He often sends through other people. So keep your ears open!

TRY IT: Find an ant and try to direct it. What happens? Why? What happens when your parent or teacher directs you?

Giant Otter

Home: South America
Size: To 8 feet long

Giant otters live in tropical rain forests. They prefer slow-moving rivers, where they can hunt for fish along the bottom and edges. To capture small bottom fish, otters sometimes swim in tight circles. This creates a "water tornado," which lifts the fish to the surface.

Otters have five toes on each paw connected by a membrane. The webbing helps them swim and also catch and hold fish as they eat them.

Giant otters live, sleep, and hunt together. These sleek brown animals prefer to stay near dense vegetation, where they can quickly hide from their enemies—the puma, the jaguar, and humans.

Just as the otter's "water tornado" brings fish to the surface, people sometimes bring up mistakes others have made. For instance, after someone has wronged you and apologized, you might promise to forgive them. But sometimes it's hard to forget the incident.

Jesus said, *"If you forgive others for the things that they do wrong, then your Father in heaven will also forgive you for the things you do wrong" (ICB)*. God casts your sins to the bottom of the sea and leaves them there forever. And you should forgive others in the same way. Even if you can't totally forget a bad experience, you should live as though it never happened.

MISSION: Memorize Matthew 6: 14. When you remember something bad someone did to you, claim the promise and ask God to help you put the experience out of your mind.

Crabeater Seal

Home: Antarctic waters
Size: To 660 pounds

Crabeater seals live in Antarctic waters. Occasionally, though, they stray north to the southern tip of Africa, New Zealand, and Australia.

Despite their name, these seals eat more krill than crabs. (Krill is a shrimplike crustacean that swarms in antarctic waters.) To catch krill, crabeaters swim rapidly with their mouths open. Once they get a mouthful of water and krill, they close their mouth and strain out the water through the spaces in their five-pronged teeth. They retain only what will serve them as food and discard the rest.

Sometimes people need a "strainer," too. Has someone ever said something hurtful about you? Maybe they accused you of acting in a stupid or harmful way. That's when you need to put your brain's "strainer" to use.

Decide if you can learn something worthwhile from what the other person said. If so, then accept that information. If some of what they said was incorrect, then use your "strainer" to discard the untruth. Determine to grow from what you can, and let the rest go.

As the Bible suggests, you must be willing to *"examine yourselves. . . ; test yourselves."* If you ask Him, God will help you do so.

TALK BACK: How should I respond to a person who says something untrue about me? What are two or three things I can do to improve the situation?

Butterfly or Moth?

Have you ever watched butterflies flit around as though they are hunting for something? They are! These colorful insects can sip nectar only from certain plants, which they locate by scent. If they can't find the right plants on which to feed and lay their eggs, they'll die.

Moths also need specific host plants on which to feed and lay their eggs. Although some brightly colored moths fly during the day, most moths fly at night. You may see them fluttering around bright lights.

Can you tell the difference between a moth and a butterfly? Most moths look fatter than butterflies, and they generally leave their wings open when at rest. Butterflies usually rest their wings straight up and tentlike over their backs.

But there's an even more accurate way to tell the difference between a moth and a butterfly. Look at the antennae. If they look like little feathers, they belong to a moth. If they're slender with little knobs on the end, they're a butterfly's. These little differences reveal the truth.

Some people may claim to love Jesus and appear to be good Christians. But after gaining your confidence, they encourage you to do wrong. So how do you know whom to trust? In a parable Jesus said, *"By their fruit you will recognize them."*

Fruit refers to someone's actions. So prayerfully examine what they do against Bible truth.

CONTACT: Dear God, please open my eyes and give me the wisdom to know what's correct.

Luna Moth

Home: North America
Size: 5-6 inches

While walking I noticed some grass fluttering. Taking a closer look, I spied a huge luna moth emerging from its cocoon. Pale green and velvety, it fluttered its wings, trying to free them.

I wanted to help, but another time I'd watched a moth hatch. It had struggled so much to free itself from its fuzzy cocoon. So after about an hour, I decided to help it by carefully snipping the cocoon threads.

To my horror, the moth drooped and died! Later I told a naturalist friend about it. I then learned that the "struggle" a moth or butterfly goes through emerging from its cocoon serves a necessary purpose. It pumps body fluids into the creature's wings, strengthening them for flight. So my help, though given lovingly, prevented this process and caused harm.

You probably struggle in life, too. God aches to make things easier for you, but in His wisdom He allows you to experience difficulties so you can gain strength for bigger challenges ahead. Under His watchful care you learn to deal with problems. This exercises your faith.

Paul said, *"We also have joy with our troubles because we know that these troubles produce patience" (ICB)*. Don't give up the struggle!

TRY IT: Find a cocoon outside. Without touching it, check its development each day. Make notes about what you learn.

Tiger Swallowtail

Home: North America
Size: Wingspan to 5.5 inches

The tiger swallowtail begins as an egg laid on a willow or other host tree. Then it develops into a brown-and-white caterpillar that looks like a bird dropping.

It feeds constantly, soon outgrowing its skin. So it molts, or sheds the skin. Since its new skin is larger, the caterpillar eats to fill that up. It repeats this process several times, until it becomes a mature two-inch caterpillar.

This caterpillar looks green with big fake black and orange eyespots that scare away predators. Then at its last molt the caterpillar becomes a chrysalis, which resembles a short stick.

Inside this protective chrysalis, the caterpillar spends the winter developing into a butterfly. In the spring the chrysalis splits open, and the butterfly emerges. It plumps its wings and begins searching for a mate. After mating, the black-and-yellow female hunts for the right host tree so she can sip nectar and lay her eggs.

The adult butterfly lives from one week to eight months. So capturing a butterfly even for a little while can be a long time in its life span.

God made many creatures for you to enjoy. Each one needs time to develop its beauty. Like the Bible says, *"He has made everything beautiful in its time."* You can trust God to make your character beautiful, too!

TRY IT: The average butterfly lives for two weeks, while the average person lives about 80 years. If you keep a butterfly for 24 hours, how many people years would that represent?

134

Those Tempting Traps

Trapping used to be a way of life. People would set traps in the forest and near water sources, baiting them with chunks of meat. When an animal smelled the meat and stepped up to take it, the trap would spring closed on its leg.

Even an animal that had escaped a trap might be caught again. The lure of food would override its fear. To stay safe the animal had to turn and run away from the area!

When getting food puts them in danger, some animals will leave immediately, in spite of their hunger pangs. Others will crouch in the bushes, salivating while eyeing the food and working up the courage to go get it.

People can get caught in "traps" too. King David said, *"If I had cherished sin in my heart, the Lord would not have listened."*

How do you cherish sin in your heart? If you watch sinful actions on television and put yourself in the character's place. If you imagine just how you *could* do something wrong and get away with it. If you let yourself long for something you know you can't or shouldn't have.

See, ponder, do happens step by step. But you don't have to follow those steps, if you let Jesus be your guide.

MISSION: When you start thinking of sinful things, ask God to help you put the thoughts out of your mind.

135

Lucy, the Ball Python

Home: Grassy and forested areas of Africa
Size: To 4 feet long

I met Lucy, a ball python, when her owner brought her to visit me. She slowly stretched across the space between us, flicking her tongue to discover what I was. Then she inched along my arm until I was holding her.

Her skin, patterned with yellow "eights" on a black background, felt cool, dry, and smooth. As she moved I felt her strong muscles just beneath the surface.

Ball pythons are constrictors that wrap around their prey to suffocate it. But they're quite shy. When they become alarmed they coil their long body around their head, making a ball (that's how they get their name). This protects their head, their most vulnerable part.

Why did God make one kind of animal bold and another shy? Why did He make grass short and trees tall, water wet and sand grainy and dry? Why did He make some people extroverts and others introverts? And why did He make you like you are?

The Bible says, *"The secret things belong to the Lord our God, but the things revealed belong to us and to our children forever."* You may not understand why things are as they are, but in heaven Jesus will explain everything. Then it will all make sense. Don't you want to be there?

CONTACT: Jesus, help me to be patient and trust You in everything, even though I don't understand why things happen the way they do.

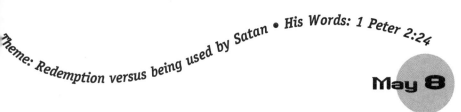

The "Deadly" Tomato

Tomatoes are one of the best foods you can eat, because they're high in vitamins A and C. But they belong to the nightshade family, a group of plants with poisonous leaves and stems. So years ago people thought tomatoes were poisonous. They used them only as decorative plants.

Those decorations did sometimes get used, though. Troublemakers would throw tomatoes at people whose ideas they didn't like! With a *splat* the fruit would hit its mark and leave a messy red stain. Those rascals used tomatoes as weapons!

How would you like to be used as a weapon? That's what Satan wants to do with you. He tempts you, then throws you and your actions at Jesus, saying, "Look at this sinner!" After he's used you, he leaves you lying in the dirt, not caring what becomes of you.

In contrast, Jesus tries to bless you. He wants to help you be truly happy and useful. If you let Him, He'll foil Satan's evil plan, for *"Christ carried our sins in his body on the cross. He did this so that we would stop living for sin and start living for what is right. And we are healed because of his wounds"* (ICB).

CONTACT: Jesus, please help me to cooperate so You can keep me from becoming Satan's weapon.

Dr. Dog

Did you know that dogs can be trained to recognize when a person is about to have an epileptic seizure? Epilepsy happens when information doesn't get transferred between a person's nerve cells. This condition can cause petit mal seizures, which result in rapid eye blinking and loss of awareness. And it can cause grand mal seizures, which result in violent muscle contractions and loss of consciousness.

Many times people don't know when they're about to have a seizure. So they might helplessly fall and flail about, injuring themselves or others.

Joel has epilepsy, but Alex, his little dachshund, can recognize the approach of a seizure. So Alex alerts Joel that an attack is about to come on. That gives Joel time to get into a safe place, away from furniture or high areas.

While the seizure lasts, Alex stays nearby to watch over his beloved master until he regains consciousness. It's obvious that Alex loves to take care of his master.

How do you react around people who have illnesses or must move in a wheelchair? Does the sickness or injury cause you to keep your distance? Someday, when Jesus returns, He'll destroy those problems. Then those who suffer will *"praise the Lord, . . . and forget not all his benefits—who . . . heals all your diseases."*

CONTACT: God, please make me sensitive to others' needs and feelings so I can encourage them.

Grass Rippers

Home: Nearly all countries
Size: To 440 pounds

One day I watched flocks of sheep roaming the hillsides with their shepherds. Unlike cows, sheep rip out grass by the roots, so they must be moved to fresh pastures often. The shepherd carefully checks each field for poisonous plants or predators before letting the sheep graze there.

I noticed how most of the sheep stayed close to their shepherd. If one did stray, the shepherd sent his dog to the sheep's far side to nudge its heels and head it back to the flock. The dog had to work gently, for sheep startle easily and can break their legs when running.

Raised for wool and mutton, sheep aren't real intelligent animals. They can get into trouble if left to themselves. That's why the shepherd lives right in the fields with his flock, watching carefully to protect and provide for them.

Have you ever had to decide what to do in a challenging situation? Next time you face one, remember that you're not dealing with it alone. David said, *"The Lord is my shepherd, I shall not be in want."*

Lovingly your Shepherd "checks the field" for dangers. He sends His Holy Spirit to nudge your conscience when you're tempted to go astray and move you back to the protection of your Shepherd. God's great love for you keeps Him faithful to His promise to always watch over you.

CONTACT: Father, please help me recognize the Holy Spirit's nudgings and be willing to follow His leading.

Nature's Armored Car

Home: South America
Size: To 130 pounds

The giant armadillo is nature's armored car. Covered with a carapace—thick, horny plates that lap over each other—it looks impenetrable. But actually, only its head, back, and sides are covered.

Since it can't roll into a ball to protect its stomach, this shy mammal runs away when danger approaches. It can run faster than most humans can.

A nighttime hunter, the armadillo digs burrows to sleep in during the day. It has five claws on its front feet. The middle claw, which is long, thick, and shaped like a sickle, helps the animal dig into hard termite nests. It then pokes its long, sticky tongue down the hallways to capture any insects there. After a meal it sometimes stands on its hind legs, propped up by its sturdy tail.

How easy is it for people to get through your armor and dig secrets out of you? Solomon said, *"Gossips can't keep secrets. So avoid people who talk too much"* (ICB).

When someone tells you something in confidence, you should keep your lips closed as tightly as the armor fits the armadillo! (An exception would be if keeping the secret would put your friend in danger. Then you should tell a trusted adult.) Likewise, when someone wants to tell you someone else's secret, you shouldn't listen.

How do you like *your* secrets kept? Keep the confidences of others in just that way.

TRY IT: To avoid hearing gossip, politely say, "I'm sure Joe doesn't want that shared." Then leave the area.

140

Cool Cat

Home: Siberia, Manchuria
Size: 400-650 pounds

Siberian tigers live in the far north, where temperatures fall to minus 50 degrees Fahrenheit. Beneath their golden-and black coats, they have thick layers of fat for insulation.

Though the male tigers are loners, the females live in family units. They nurse their cubs in secluded dens. After two weeks the cubs open their eyes, and their teeth begin growing. Within three months they start exploring outdoors.

While still nursing them, their mothers bring them meat to eat. When they are 5 or 6 months old, the cubs begin to accompany their mothers on hunting trips. Before they are 1 year old they start to hunt for themselves.

Siberian tigers prefer to eat wild pigs and deer, but they catch smaller game, too. They must search for prey persistently, for only a tenth of their hunting trips prove successful. When they capture a large animal they eat what they can, then drag the rest to a hiding place to finish later. When game is scarce they often range hundreds of miles to find food. Their ambition to eat keeps them going.

Are you ambitious enough to work hard for what you want, or do you shrug your shoulders and quit? *"If you give up when trouble comes, it shows that you have very little strength"* (ICB), says Solomon. That means that even when reaching your goal seems impossible, don't give up! Like the Siberian tiger on its hunt, try until you succeed.

CONTACT: Dear Lord, help me set good goals for myself and be willing to work diligently to reach them.

The Inky Octopus

Home: Oceans
Size: 3 inches-33 feet

Mollusks, like clams, are soft-bodied animals that usually have a hard outer shell. But even though the octopus belongs to this family, it has no shell. Its soft body consists of three main parts: (1) a head, which includes a parrotlike beak, a very intelligent brain, and two large lidded eyes; (2) a mantle, which contains its gills and most of its organs; and (3) eight arms, each having a double row of suction cups with touch and taste organs.

An octopus's head looks like an oblong balloon with two big eyes on top. These eyes, like human eyes, can move, focus, and close.

An octopus swims headfirst. If a predator disturbs it, it spews a jet of water through its body. This gives it a thrust of speed to escape.

In more drastic situations, the octopus will squirt "ink" into the water. This dark liquid often stuns or confuses a predator. The first ink used for writing and recording information was made from pigments of octopus ink.

God wants to record things in your life, too. He says, *"Let love and faithfulness never leave you; bind them around your neck, write them on the tablet of your heart."* You "write" ideas on your heart when you accept and follow them.

TRY IT: In what way would you like to be more Christlike? Using ink, write your goal down and keep it in your Bible.

142

Octopus Babies

After mating, the female octopus lays about 150,000 eggs in her underwater lair. There she squirts water over them to keep them clean and aerated. A devoted mother, she doesn't leave the nest for the next four to six weeks, constantly caring for and guarding her eggs.

Going without food for so long greatly weakens her, and often she dies. But once the eggs have hatched, her job is finished.

Tiny replicas of their parents, baby octopuses begin life on the ocean floor. Some species, though, float to the surface and live there for about a month. Often the tides will carry them long distances. Then, when they're large enough to return to the ocean floor, they find themselves hundreds of miles from where they hatched.

So they must hunt for a home. Some use an abandoned clam shell, attaching their suckers to the floor and lid and closing it tightly over them for protection.

Baby octopuses travel far without realizing the distance. In the same way, the thoughts you share with others about Jesus will travel far. Jesus said, *"Go . . . and tell the people the message of this new life."* Passed from mouth to mouth, guided and guarded by the Holy Spirit, your inspiring words just might change someone's life.

MISSION: Ask your pastor to help you find some pamphlets about Jesus' love. Give them to people you meet. Smile, and tell them God loves them. Be willing to share what Jesus means to you.

Alpine Ibex

Home: Alps
Size: To 265 pounds

The ibex belongs to the goat family. It lives in high altitudes in some of the world's steepest terrain.

If a wolf, lynx, or bear threatens it, an ibex scrambles up the rocky mountainside to escape. Ibex hooves are cloven and very flexible. So this animal can travel over uneven, slippery surfaces and withstand long jumps.

When winter ends and alpine grass and flowers grow, males congregate in the rocky high country. In the less hazardous areas below, mothers deliver and care for their newborns. After the kids grow strong enough, their mothers lead them to higher elevations, where they can practice running and jumping.

Even with their specialized hooves and their mothers' instruction, ibex kids sometimes fall. That's because they're adventurous, daring, and strong-willed, plus they lack experience.

Today's world tells you it's good to grow up quickly. You're urged to do adult things before you might be mentally or physically ready to deal with them. It's not childish to be patient with yourself, to slow down and take the time to learn to do things right—and at the right time.

In the parable of the seeds you're told to *"obey God's teaching and patiently produce good fruit" (ICB)*. Take time to allow God to guide you in your growing-up process.

TALK BACK: How can I know when I'm ready for greater privileges? How can I prove this to my parents?

Who's the Enemy?

Again and again, the robin would fling itself against my study window. Then it would return to its perch in the crab apple tree, only to spy its own reflection again. Thinking it saw another robin encroaching on its territory, it would try to fight back. It had to protect its nesting site!

I was beginning to feel concerned about the robin. This was the third day it had been fighting its own reflection—something that wasn't an enemy at all. And I knew it would continue its fight until the sun rose high enough that the window wouldn't act as a mirror.

Not wanting to frighten the bird further, I stayed out of my study. But now I needed something from my files. Without thinking, I switched on the light.

Puzzled at its enemy's quick disappearance, the exhausted robin returned to its tree to rest. And I then realized that the light from *inside* the room erased the reflection.

The Bible says about Jesus, *"In him there was life. That life was light for the people of the world"* *(ICB)*. Do you ever fight things that really aren't enemies? When you invite Jesus into your life, He fills you with His light and helps you see things clearly. So why not invite Him to give you light each day?

TALK BACK: What enemies have you fought that you later realized were not enemies? How do you decide whether or not something or someone is an enemy?

145

Garden Snail

Home: Gardens, woods
Size: To 4 inches

You're weeding the flower bed. You notice a silvery trail drizzled across the dirt and climbing a weed. You trace the trail and discover a snail. Its long neck is clinging to a leaf as it eats it.

Four tentacles protrude from the snail's head. The longer ones have eyes at their tips. If you gently touch one, it retracts into the snail's head. The shorter tentacles do the snail's feeling and smelling.

The spiraled, crusty shell on the snail's back is its home. It can quickly withdraw into this shell when insects or birds approach. It can also exude a frothy, unappetizing substance that repels predators.

A snail thrives in dark, damp places, such as gardens or the woods. When the weather gets hot, it must keep itself from drying out. So it retreats into its shell, sealing the opening with several layers of mucus. The mucus hardens and keeps moisture inside. If the snail emerged, it would dry out and die.

By getting baptized you may think that your struggle with temptation will end. But it won't. Just as the snail protects itself, you need to shield yourself with God's armor to keep yourself from "drying out."

You can do this through *"truthful speech and in the power of God; with weapons of righteousness."* God gives you these when you go to Him in prayer and read your Bible.

CONTACT: Kind Father, please help me to seek Your saving power continually.

146

The Best Group

Collective nouns" is a term for creatures or objects that belong together. You've probably heard the term "a swarm of bees." But what about a paddling of ducks, a mob of kangaroos, a spring of seals, a sneak of weasels, or a sloth of bears?

You can almost picture an army of ants marching along, head to tail, carrying food to their nest. But have you seen a dray of squirrels, a parliament of owls, or a down of hares? What about a bed of snakes, a band of jays, and a congregation of crocodiles? Then there's a muster of peafowl and a prickle of hedgehogs!

Every creature is related to others in a specific way. What group names do you have? People? Humans? Kids? Juniors? Teens? Siblings?

Another set of names is given to those who love and honor God. They're called believers, conquerors, brothers and sisters in Christ, the redeemed, and the saved. But the best is the name Paul used when teaching the Galatians. He said, *"For ye are all the children of God by faith in Christ Jesus" (KJV).*

Imagine being one of God's children—loved, protected, and provided for! This is *your* group if you give God your heart.

TALK BACK: What can you and your family do to be called children of God?

147

How Crystals Grow

One afternoon while chasing our horse over a freshly plowed field, I stumbled over something very hard. Turning to see what had tripped me, I discovered a beautiful hexagonal quartz crystal. It had formed on an ugly rock. Clear and colorless, the crystal was about five inches long and two inches in diameter. Its glassy sides sparkled in the sunlight.

A crystal forms when minerals from a liquid or gas solidify. It begins with a microscopic bit of mineral, then grows larger as more liquid gets added. It grows in a very organized way. For instance, a crystal might branch out from one spot, creating a flower effect. The atoms inside the crystal are held together by electrical attraction.

Crystals develop into many sizes. One in Siberia is reported to be as tall as a two-story building!

When crystals are tiny they form perfectly. But as they grow larger, they can lose their perfection, becoming scratched and less transparent.

It's the same with you. When you're tiny you don't have many bad habits. But the longer you live, the more chance you have to develop annoying character traits.

The Bible says, *"Grow in the grace and knowledge of our Lord and Savior Jesus Christ."* In order to do this you must dedicate your heart to Jesus each day. He'll help you stay pure and grow into something beautiful.

TALK BACK: What can you do to help those around you grow in grace?

148

Lobster Moth

Home: Europe, Asia, Japan
Size: Wingspan to 2.25 inches

Have you ever seen anything so ugly that you wanted to stay away from it? The lobster moth might fit into that category.

Yellowish-green or brown, it has sharp ridges on most of its segments. When frightened by a predator, it raises its tail and head. Two long, heavy hairs stick out from the end of its tail.

It poses like a scorpion ready to attack. And it looks as if it might bite at any second. But it's actually defenseless and turns into a pretty moth eventually.

While growing up, you'll meet people who aren't careful about their language. They seem to find a way to make every conversation suggestive or shocking.

Some of your friends might try to imitate people who use bad language. As they do this they may even start acting bad, doing things that will embarrass and hurt them.

The Bible says, *"A wholesome tongue is a tree of life"* (KJV). Guarding what you say helps keep you strong for right.

But what if you've already started down the other pathway? Remember that once it undergoes a change, the ugly lobster moth becomes beautiful. Turning your heart over to Jesus can change you for the better, too.

CONTACT: Father, help me when others are impure in their language and actions. Keep my thoughts clean.

Chicken-Herder Lady

Labrador retrievers are often used on search-and-rescue missions or as guides for people who are blind. These large dogs make loving pets, because they love to be with and please their owners.

My grandchildren have a black Labrador named Lady. As a puppy she wanted to share in everything the family had. When baby Sarah's pacifier kept disappearing, the family scratched their heads in puzzlement. Later they watched while Lady, using her teeth, gently removed the pacifier from Sarah's mouth, then used it herself!

Grown now, Lady has become a good companion and helper. Each morning the chickens leave their coop to go into the woods and scratch for insects. But chickens don't usually come when called, so Kim, my granddaughter, will say to Lady, "Get the chickens!"

With her tail wagging, Lady plunges into the underbrush and gently "herds" each chicken into the open, where Kim can catch it. Lady picks up the stragglers in her mouth and carries them to Kim. She doesn't quit until all the birds are safely home.

Sometimes you might get lost in a thicket of sin. Then God, in His love, sends the Holy Spirit to help you escape. Gently, never forcing your will, He urges you away from trouble and back into the safety of God's way. As Jesus explained, *"When the Spirit of truth comes he will lead you into all truth"* (ICB).

TALK BACK: Why is it important to have the Holy Spirit's guidance each day?

150

American Paddlefish

Home: Central United States
Size: To 7 feet

The paddlefish resembles a shark because of its long nose and pointed fins. Actually its nose, which is one third its length, extends far beyond its mouth and is shaped like a wide canoe paddle! Its surface is covered with hundreds of taste buds that help this fish locate food.

The paddlefish can open its mouth very wide. As it swims it takes water into its mouth, then washes it out through its gills. Plankton in the water gets caught in the paddlefish's "gill rakers." Then it closes its mouth and swallows.

Because of water pollution and construction, paddlefish are losing good habitats, or places to live. In order to lay their eggs, they require deep, clean water with a gravel bottom. The eggs attach to whatever they first touch, and they can't attach to mud!

Have you noticed that Christians are also losing good habitats? Maybe places you used to go are now filled with tempting influences. Maybe even friends you used to hang around with are making harmful choices.

If you really want to be a Christian, you can't afford to be around those influences. The Bible says, *"Let us draw near to God with a sincere heart in full assurance of faith."* Ask God to help you keep your habitat safe!

MISSION: Check your family habitat. With your parents, discuss what should be done to improve it.

Red Howler Monkey

Home: South America
Size: To 5 feet, including tail

If you visit a zoo and hear the red howler monkeys calling, you won't forget it! A cross between a large dog's bark and a roar, it's the loudest sound made by land animals. You can easily hear it for up to two miles!

Red howler monkeys live in jungle treetops and have reddish-brown fur. Their strong hands and sturdy tails help them brace themselves. They normally hunt in the daytime, eating vegetation.

Screwing up their naked, squashed-in faces, they howl in the mornings and evenings and sometimes in between. They make sound by forcing air through the resonant hyoid bone in their throat.

Howlers live in troops of up to 40 monkeys. A newborn monkey hangs on to its mother's underside as she climbs about and feeds with the rest of the troop. Then for about a year it rides on its mother's back.

Howlers are loud and boisterous, which seems OK in the trees. But what about you? Do you know when to be noisy and when to be quiet? When you speak, do you have something worthwhile to say, or is it just chatter? Do you interrupt others or shout over them?

"A word fitly spoken is like apples of gold in pictures of silver" (KJV), said Solomon. Knowing how to use your words and when to be quiet will make you better company for everyone around you.

TALK BACK: Is there ever an appropriate time to be noisy? In what places is it wisest not to talk?

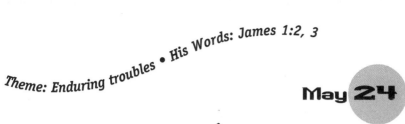

Forest Fire!

In May of 2000 a huge forest fire raced through the mountains near Los Alamos, New Mexico. Flames whipped through the trees and scrub bushes and along desert canyons, gobbling vegetation as it went. The fire left more than 45,000 acres of charred forestland. And it looked useless.

Five months later I traveled through the area. Many hillsides looked black, the trees completely destroyed. But in other areas the fire had moved so quickly that only the grass and lower parts of the trees had been burned. The tops still had green needles!

I also noticed a carpet of flowering weeds, tall waving grasses, and patches of blue, yellow, and white wildflowers. How could they have grown when fire had recently burned all the undergrowth?

Actually, when it's controlled, fire can help nature. It clears out heavy undergrowth that keeps sunlight from nourishing seedling trees. It makes growing room for tender grasses and weeds that provide animal feed. So disaster can turn into an advantage over time.

Trouble in your life can feel like wildfire. And it can destroy you if you let it. But if you learn to cope with each trial by trusting in Jesus, your faith in Him will spring to life. The Bible says, *"Consider it all joy . . . when you fall into various trials, knowing that the testing of your faith produces endurance"* *(NASB).*

TALK BACK: Think of a trial you experienced. How did you overcome it? How did what you learned help you face other trials?

Oh, Those Slivers!

If you've ever had a sliver in your finger, you know that even a tiny one can hurt. No matter how little it looks, all you can think about is getting it out!

God made a wonderful communication system in your fingers. Extra-sensitive nerve endings just under your skin send signals to your brain through nerve fibers. Your brain then translates these signals into sensations of cold, hot, sharp, soft, smooth, and so on.

People who've lost feeling in their fingers become very clumsy, and they often hurt themselves without even knowing it. With a good sense of touch, though, you can notice even the tiniest pinprick.

So-called "little" sins sometimes seem as if they don't matter. After all, how could a tiny fib hurt anything? But when you lie your conscience begins to prick you. Unless you have ignored your conscience for too long, you soon realize that you need to make matters right, just as you need to quickly remove slivers to keep them from festering.

The author of Hebrews said, *"We are sure that we have a clear conscience and desire to live honorably in every way."* God created your conscience to keep you on the right track. So don't limp along with a "sore" conscience—listen to it!

TRY IT: Find the area on your upper leg where you cannot feel a light pinprick. How could this lack of feeling affect you if it covered your whole body?

Clouds

As the sun shines on the earth and sea, it warms the air. The air begins to rise, but the higher it gets the cooler it becomes. Then the moisture it carries begins to condense, forming clouds.

There are more than 100 different kinds of clouds. Meteorologists watch their movements and altitudes to help predict the weather.

High, wispy clouds called cirrus look like angel hair and contain ice crystals. Cirrocumulus clouds, arranged in fluffy rows, look like a tufted bedspread and hold ice. At lower levels fluffy cumulus clouds have flat bottoms caused by warm air pushing upward on them. Nimbostratus, or low rain clouds, look puffy but darken as they become heavier with moisture. Cumulonimbus clouds, which are tall and fluffy, make high towers in the sky, creating thunderstorms and sometimes even hail and tornadoes.

Clouds offer protection from the heat of the sun. They also hold warmth close to earth on winter nights.

In the wilderness a cloud did something even more amazing. It led the children of Israel by day and provided light in the desert at night. What made this cloud so special? The Bible says, *"By day the Lord went ahead of them in a pillar of cloud to guide them on their way."*

It was God's presence that made that cloud so special. His presence will make your life special, too.

CONTACT: Dear God, please give me wisdom to follow as You lead me.

Drifting Down

Have you ever heard the saying "What goes up must come down"? That includes the moisture in clouds, which sometimes comes down as snow.

Here's how it happens. Ice crystals that have formed around dust particles circulate inside very cold clouds. Droplets of water that have changed into vapor collide with these ice crystals, freezing onto them.

Some ice crystals cling together to form snowflakes. Each six-sided shape is unlike any other. As the snowflakes grow larger, they become too heavy to stay aloft. Then they float toward the ground.

Ten to 12 inches of fluffy snow melts down to about one inch of water. At the time of this writing, the largest single-day snowfall recorded in history was 75.8 inches in Silver Lake, Colorado, in 1921. The greatest amount of snow to fall in a single storm, which lasted one week, was 189 inches at Mount Shasta, California, in 1959.

Wind blows snow into great drifts and covers even the dirtiest areas with a blanket of pure white. Then things look fresh and clean.

Every human being has made mistakes that have left the ugly stain of sin on them. But Jesus paid for those sins. So when you ask for forgiveness, He cleans up and covers your mistakes. He promised, *"Though your sins are like scarlet, they shall be as white as snow."*

MISSION: Do you have any unconfessed sins? Ask God to forgive you for them and to give you the courage to make needed apologies.

Rain

When snow or ice crystals fall from clouds, they often change before they reach the earth. For instance, if they pass through warmer air, the ice or snowflakes melt into tiny droplets. These droplets collide with each other and merge, forming raindrops.

Raindrops resemble little cushions with flattened bottoms. The world's highest rainfall is in Mawsynram, India, where an average of 467 inches falls per year. One year at Cherrapunji, India, the rainfall reached 1,042 inches! The lowest known annual rainfall is .02 inch at Arica, Chile. In the United States the lowest yearly rainfall is two inches or less in Death Valley, California.

The Bible says, *"Your Father sends rain to those who do good and to those who do wrong"* (ICB). In this world both good and bad things happen to people who love God and to those who don't. So being good just to have it easy doesn't always work.

But those who turn away from God have to suffer alone through bad times. When trials come to those who love God, He's able to strengthen and encourage them in special ways. Don't you want Him beside you?

TALK BACK: What are some good gifts God gives both Christians and non-Christians? What gifts are reserved for only those who love Him?

Mayapples

Home: Eastern North America
Size: Blossom 1.5 inches, plant to 18 inches high

The mayapple isn't really an apple, and it doesn't grow on trees in the month of May. Instead, this fruit develops in the fall from a flower that blossoms on hillsides or in the woods.

The single stem of the mayapple plant grows from the ground, then branches into two stems, each topped by a 12-inch leaf. These leaves look like nearly opened but tattered umbrellas. Well-hidden beneath the two leaves is one creamy-white flower with a yellow center.

In the fall you can find the "apple," a lemon-yellow fruit where the blossom dropped off. It tastes a little like strawberries and is sometimes made into jellies or pies.

The mayapple doesn't show off its beautiful bloom the way other flowers do. Instead, it hides it beneath greenery. Unless you search for it, you'll never see the blossom.

You probably return to God a tithe (10 percent) of money you receive. Maybe you give other offerings to help with missions or charity work. But how do you give?

Jesus said, *"When you give to the poor, give very secretly. Don't let anyone know what you are doing. Your giving should be done in secret. Your Father can see what is done in secret, and he will reward you"* (ICB).

If you make a big show of giving offerings, it is so others will see how wonderful you are. You become proud and selfish. But when you give secretly, your gift is to God. Only then is it a true gift.

MISSION: Find a way to donate money or clothing to needy people without others (except your parents) knowing.

158

Goby the Mudskipper

Home: Africa to Australia tidal waters
Size: 6-12 inches long

The mudskipper can live both in the water and on land. Like other fish, it breathes through its gills. It keeps them full of water so it can get oxygen from the water.

It also has little blood vessels in its mouth that absorb oxygen. So it can hunt or rest on land as long as it returns often to shallow waters to refill its water chambers.

The mudskipper's eyes perch on top of its head like two huge marbles. They work separately and can retreat inside while the fish digs its burrow. It does this by spitting mouthfuls of mud away from the doorway.

Mudskippers have large, muscular pectoral fins where arms should be. They use these fins to pull themselves out of the water, across muddy places, up the trunks or branches of trees, or through mangrove swamps. Though they go places where you don't expect fish to be, they adapt well in most areas, as long as they can get into water every couple hours.

Jesus wants you to be willing to do difficult things for Him. He said, *"Go and make disciples of all nations, baptizing them in the name of the Father and of the Son and of the Holy Spirit, and teaching them to obey everything I have commanded you."*

You obey Jesus' command by reaching out to those around you. Sometimes doing that isn't easy. But He will help you to be a good example to others as you tell them about Jesus.

TALK BACK: What behavior in others attracts you to Jesus?

A National Symbol

Home: Seacoasts, water areas
Size: Wingspan to 7.5 feet

Because of its proud, independent appearance, the bald eagle has become the national symbol of the United States. Its white-feathered head contrasts with its brown-feathered body, making it look bald.

Eagle parents build huge stick nests in tall trees or on cliffs. There they incubate two or three eggs for 40 days. After the chicks hatch, one parent stays on the nest while the other hunts for prey to carry back in its huge talons. Eagles can spot fish and other small animals at a great distance. They also eat dead carcasses.

With her yellow hooked beak, the mother shreds the meat and feeds it to the babies. What the chicks refuse, the parents eat. Eaglets grow to their parents' size within six weeks.

As time goes by, the parents teach the eaglets independence by soaring over the nest with meat but not giving them any. Hungry, the eaglets spread their wings and follow their parents, clumsily landing nearby. As a reward, the parents drop the meat for them to eat.

It's pretty easy to sit back and let others spiritually feed you. But as you mature you need to develop spiritual independence, studying the Bible for yourself. Paul said, *"Study to shew thyself approved . . . , rightly dividing the word of truth" (KJV).* God will help you understand His Book if you ask Him.

MISSION: Arrange a daily time to spend with God in Bible study and prayer. After one month evaluate your experience. What has He shown you?

What Is a Pond?

How is a pond different from a lake or a marsh?

A lake is deep, allowing water to move about freely. It's so deep that plants grow only along its edges.

A marsh contains quiet water and gets only a few inches deep. Its surface is completely covered by plants with roots.

A pond contains water that doesn't move much. It's shallow enough for rooted plants to cover its muddy bottom.

Some of these plants grow tall enough to extend above the water, while others stay submerged. At the edges, where the pond is shallowest, cattails or other reeds grow. Ponds also nurture floating plants that aren't rooted to the bottom, such as duckweed and pond lilies.

Ponds have several "neighborhoods" that provide shelter, food, and water for the creatures that live there. Each creature has its own specific needs for a home, yet in some way each one relies upon the others.

The psalmist wrote, *"Remember the wonders he has done."* As you consider God's handiwork you can see how He has provided for each creature. You can learn how to protect nature. You can also learn how to work together with others, as pond creatures must do.

TALK BACK: A neighborhood is supposed to provide shelter to those who live in it. In what ways do you help provide "shelter" for the people in your neighborhood?

161

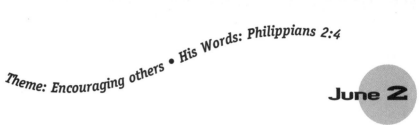

Emergent Plants

Many plants root themselves in the muddy bottom of a pond. But if they also extend above the water's surface, they're called emergent plants.

Emergent plants include sedges, which look like tall grasses, and also pickerelweeds. These have lavender or white flower spikes and large heart-shaped leaves that stand upright or float on deeper water.

The most noticeable emergent plants are cattails. With their swordlike leaves, these edible plants grow in thick patches in shallow pond areas.

Their stems actually hold two flowers—a dark-brown fuzzy female flower that resembles a hot dog, and a thinner yellow fuzzy male flower at the tip of the stem. These flowers spread their seeds just as dandelions do—by floating them on the wind. Cattails also reproduce by sending out underground root stalks that produce more leaves and flowers.

Grouped together, emergent plants provide protection for pond creatures, each other, and the pond itself. Their roots hold the soil, keeping it from washing out during rainy seasons.

In a similar way you and your friends need to shield and support each other. When someone is having a bad day, your kind words or actions can go a long way to prevent "washouts." The Bible says, *"Do not be interested only in your own life, but be interested in the lives of others"* (ICB).

MISSION: Notice how your friends or teachers are feeling. Be ready to offer an encouraging word when one of them seems down.

162

In the Pond's Mud

Have you ever seen bright-blue dragonflies darting about on their see-through wings? It's hard to believe that their lives started in the mud!

The female dragonfly lays her eggs on floating plants or in the sand. When the eggs hatch, the nymphs inside move into the protective mud at the bottom of the pond. There they hunt for insect larvae and worms. But while they hunt, larger creatures hunt for them.

It takes from a month to five years for a nymph to mature. When it's fully developed, it crawls onto a plant that's sticking out of the water. Then it waits for its skin to split. It must also wait for its wings to dry before it can fly. Finally it's ready to hunt for a mate, and a new life cycle can begin.

In order for the dragonfly to develop properly, it requires time at every stage. Nymphs that get impatient often get eaten.

Maybe you get tired of schoolwork and want to hurry on to something more interesting. But don't be hasty! Many things that don't seem important now are very important.

King Solomon pointed out, *"Those who act too quickly become poor"* *(ICB)*. He knew that haste creates big problems. So be like the dragonfly, and try to develop patience. It will improve your life and may even save it!

TALK BACK: Ask your parents to tell you about something they did too quickly. What was the outcome? Why do people sometimes do things too fast?

163

One-Note Specialist

Size: Body to 8 inches, hind legs 10 inches

The bullfrog is a noisy resident of the pond. Green with brown or gray markings, he hides in the water among roots and stems or floats in surface plants. He also dives to the bottom of the pond to feast on any creature that will fit into his mouth.

The bullfrog's "song" sets him apart from other frogs. Echoing across the reeds and water, it sounds like short, deep notes repeatedly played on a tuba.

To produce his call, the bullfrog closes his mouth and nose and squeezes air between his mouth and lungs. The shape of the frog's closed mouth amplifies the sound, which he repeats without change. Then, from somewhere else, his ladylove answers on the same note.

Did you know that your decision to follow Jesus could make someone else unhappy? Seeing you obey God might make them uncomfortable, especially when they want to disobey Him. They might even make fun of you or try to get you to change your mind.

But don't give in! The Bible promises, *"We have come to share in Christ if we hold firmly till the end the confidence we had at first."* So if you stick to your decision—as the bullfrog sticks to his note—you can trust God to bless you.

TALK BACK: Tell about a time you did what was right when others didn't. What helped you stay true to God's will?

164

Coots on the Pond

Size: To 16 inches long

Coots, also called mud hens, live in shallow waters. These dark-colored birds nest in piles of broken reeds at the edge of ponds. Darting among the lily pads and reeds, they hunt for plants to eat. The chicks paddle after their parents, who feed them insects until they can digest fibrous vegetation.

A coot's feet aren't webbed like a duck's feet. Instead, each of its toes has flaps. When the coot pushes its feet backward, the flaps open to create thrust. When the bird draws its feet forward, the flaps close, reducing drag. Unable to take off from land, a coot must run across the water to get enough speed to take off.

Coots seem to enjoy life, and they eagerly "talk" to each other as they paddle about. Though they make various calls, one of their calls sounds like someone repeatedly plucking one tooth of a plastic comb.

The Bible says, *"The blessing of the Lord brings wealth."* The ability to notice and count your blessings is a gift from God. You can learn to be joyful if you choose to concentrate on what Jesus has done for you rather than focusing on problems.

If you watch for blessings, you'll find many to smile about. And have you noticed? Joy is catching!

MISSION: Watch for and list all the blessings you notice today—a rabbit darting across a field, a shy friend's smile, or making an A. Share your list during supper tonight.

Muskrats in the Pond

Home: North America, Europe
Size: To 4 pounds

Muskrats are dark-brown mammals that resemble rats. They live in watery places where there's lots of vegetation. They can swim forward or backward using their flat, scaly black tail to steer.

To create their burrows they make huge piles of reeds in the water, reinforcing them with mud. Then from deep in the water they tunnel into the burrow, chewing out a cozy sleeping place. During the winter when the pond ices over, they eat the dry plants in their thick walls, rebuilding the walls in the spring.

Baby muskrats are born naked and helpless, but within two weeks they can swim, dive, and find some of their own food. After two more weeks, the mother bares her sharp teeth at them and chases them away to establish their own homes. If the pond is too populated, they may travel over land to find another body of water. Abandoned and clumsy on land, they make easy prey for predators.

Have you ever felt abandoned? When Moses was about to die, the children of Israel worried about being without him, especially as they entered the Promised Land. But Moses assured them, *"The Lord himself will go before you. He will be with you. He will not leave you or forget you. Don't be afraid. Don't worry"* (ICB).

Remember, God will always be near you, even when you *feel* alone. It's His promise.

TALK BACK: What should you do if you're accidentally separated from your family? Whom should you trust to help you?

The Pond's "Skin"

Did you know that water is thicker at its surface? Water molecules crowd together, so a molecule under the surface has other water molecules pushing against it. But molecules at the top of the water have nothing to push on them except air, so they expand. This dense water, called surface film, makes a pond neighborhood.

Whirligig and rove beetles live on top of the surface film. They can move across the water without getting wet. They can also feed on pollen and other insects that get trapped there.

Mosquito larvae and water scorpions live on the bottom of the surface film. They breathe oxygen, so their special breathing tubes break the surface to get them the air they need.

Creatures who live on either side of the surface film have one thing in common. They need that surface. If they leave, they can't survive as well.

Jesus is *your* surface film. When you stay close to Him, you're spiritually safe and secure. But if you go away from Him by choosing to break His commandments, you put yourself in danger of being overcome by Satan.

Jesus said, *"Not everyone who says to me, 'Lord, Lord,' will enter the kingdom of heaven, but only he who does the will of my Father who is in heaven."* If heaven is your goal, stick close to Jesus.

CONTACT: Dear God, help me to stay close to Jesus today in all that I do or say.

Walking on Water

Home: Quiet waters
Size: Less than 1 inch

Water striders can "skate" or walk on water. Stretching four of their six legs far apart, they divide their weight among them. Each leg has tiny water-repellent hairs on its end that help these insects walk on the water without getting wet.

Striders like quiet areas, where they hunt for mosquito larvae or flying insects that have fallen into the water. When they spot an insect in the water, they dart across the surface, then stab into the insect's body with their hollow mouth parts. Now they can suck up the insect's juices. While they're doing this, though, they just might get caught by a fish or frog.

Striders have something in common with the disciple Peter. When he saw Jesus walking on water, he wanted to do it, too. So keeping his eyes on Jesus, Peter walked toward Him. But then he grew smug and turned to make sure the other disciples were watching. Immediately he broke through the water's surface and began to sink. Only Jesus was able to save him.

The Bible says, *"He who trusts in himself is a fool, but he who walks in wisdom is kept safe."* When you think you're pretty good or want others to notice the neat stuff you can do, you become proud. Then you run the risk of falling on your face. Remember that it's *God* who makes you able to accomplish anything.

TALK BACK: Oily water makes striders sink and drown. What kind of "oil" might sink you? What precautions can you take?

168

The Redwing Blackbird

Home: Wetlands, pastures, and meadows
Size: About 8 inches

Redwing blackbirds often live near ponds. With their black feathers glistening in the sunlight, they cling to cattails as they call out their musical *oak-ah-reeee*. Flying off, they hunt insects, then return to their perches, showing off their crimson wing-patches and joyfully announcing their return.

Somewhere near the father's perch sits a tidy nest woven from reeds and attached to cattails. There the brown-feathered mother sits on several blue eggs or naked chicks. In the meantime the father enjoys displaying his beautiful colors and singing to anyone who will listen. He doesn't keep his joy a secret.

It was the same way with Peter and John when the authorities wanted them to quit preaching. They "showed their colors," because nothing could keep them from telling about their experiences with Jesus. They said, *"We cannot keep quiet. We must speak about what we have seen and heard" (ICB).*

You can "show your colors" by telling someone how Jesus has helped you. Or by sharing a Bible verse with a friend or speaking up in a gentle way when a classmate says bad things about God. Are you ready to show your colors?

CONTACT: Dear Father, please show me how to be a kind but bold and willing witness for You.

The Growly Pooch

In our neighborhood the dogs used to run around together. They seemed to look forward to meeting every day to follow scent trails or just romp around. When they'd find a cookie someone had dropped, they'd squabble trying to decide who would get it. But basically they got along very well and seemed to enjoy each other's company.

Then a new yellow dog came to the neighborhood. Bold and scrappy, Yellow often jumped the other dogs, trying to become head dog. He dug up people's yards and growled at children.

Before long a few other pooches began acting the same way. They formed a pack and followed Yellow. Soon most of the neighbors chained up their dogs so they wouldn't learn to be annoying, too.

After Yellow bit someone, he mysteriously disappeared. But the dogs that ran with him still run together and act like he did. Their association with Yellow brought out something bad in them that's not easily erased.

The Bible says, *"Do not make friends with a hot-tempered man, do not associate with one easily angered, or you may learn his ways and get yourself ensnared."* It makes a difference whom you choose as close friends. Since you *will* become like them, make sure you know what they're like before you join their "pack."

TALK BACK: How can I choose my friends carefully, while not seeming snobbish?

It Plants Itself

Jesus told a parable about a farmer sowing seed. This farmer walked back and forth across his field spreading seed as evenly as possible. Some of the seed landed on rocky soil, some was eaten by birds, and some dried up before it could sprout. But, as Jesus said, *"Other seed fell on good soil, where it produced a crop."*

Maybe the farmer was sowing oats. Did you know that oats can actually plant themselves? When the oblong seed first drops off the stalk, it's slightly moist. But as the seed dries, bristly fibers along its sides expand, standing it on its "nose."

Then the awn, a long hairlike fiber coming from the back of the seed, begins to coil as it dries. This causes the seed to rotate and drill into the dirt. Long ago Someone noticed the power of the oat drill. People use the same principle in making drills that rotate as they bore into wood or into the earth for oil or water.

Have you wondered how you can help someone come to Jesus? You can tell them the story of Jesus and pray that their minds will be receptive ground for the seed you're sowing. The Holy Spirit will then work on their hearts, bringing them greater understanding of God's truth. You can sow the seed and prayerfully watch over it, but only the Holy Spirit can do the work of the awn.

CONTACT: Father, help me to be a faithful witness to those around me.

171

God's Hands-on Project

The Bible tells us how God created Adam: *"Then the Lord God took dust from the ground and formed man from it"* (ICB). Adam wasn't just "spoken" to life—he was our Creator's hands-on project! And he was made from dust, which is dirt or soil.

God's perfect soil contained all the nutrients needed to grow healthy plants for animals to eat. But once sin occurred, the earth began to die, and the soil's health with it.

So what's dirt or soil, other than what your mom doesn't want you to track in? It starts with rocks broken down by water, temperature changes, or volcanic action. Rocks crumble into sand, clay, or silt.

Soil also includes humus. This is dead plant and animal life broken down by bacteria and fungi. Humus deposits nutrients back into the earth to nourish new plants.

How you treat dirt matters. For instance, if you pour machine oil on the ground, you contaminate it. This affects the food you grow and eat, which in turn affects your health.

Likewise, if you allow garbage into your mind, you contaminate it. Eventually, your whole life will be affected.

God made a way for soil to be regenerated, and He also provides a way for your spiritual life to become new. It's through prayer and accepting His forgiveness for your sins. As you come to Him, He'll reshape you and help you grow more like Him.

TRY IT: What kind of soil is in your yard? Rub some between your fingers. Sand feels gritty, while silt feels like flour. Clay feels gummy when dampened. Why is a mixture good?

Bye-bye, Dirt!

Maybe you've seen news stories about houses built on cliffs. During storms water washes away loose rock and dirt from the cliff, sometimes causing the house to topple.

This washing away of earth, called erosion, affects more than houses. If farmers remove plants from their fields and then plow the fields, they leave no protection from erosion. That's because they've removed the roots that secured the soil.

The same thing happens in the desert. Where plant life is scarce, the soil gets washed or blown away. That leaves only rocks and gullies that fill with silt.

It takes about 500 years for an inch of topsoil to form. But it takes only a few hours for that precious earth to be washed or blown away.

How can you slow down erosion? Leave plants in the ground. Terrace hillsides so that water won't run off it so fast. Plow along the contours of the earth so that little furrows will catch and save the soil. And in windy areas, plant trees to serve as windbreaks.

When tragedy comes your way, it may seem as if all your joy is eroding. But try to remember that God promises not to let circumstances get harder than you can bear. *"He knows how we are formed, he remembers that we are dust."*

He created you. He loves you. He won't let you blow away. He'll be your furrow and your windbreak.

CONTACT: Father, I thank You for helping me through each day.

173

Dive-bombers

Home: Shorelines and sandbars
Size: To 10 inches

When I go to the beach I like to watch least terns. Gray and white, these birds fly along the shoreline just beyond the breakers. With their heads tipped downward, they watch for small fish near the water's surface.

Once they spot one, they hover over it, then fold their wings and dive into the water to catch it. Least terns look a lot like seagulls, but gulls swoop instead of dive.

Least terns live together in colonies. They look for sandy places near rivers or oceans to nest. They also need shallow water to feed.

By building dams across rivers, humans have created deeper bodies of water. This has left fewer places for least terns to live, for, unlike gulls, they haven't adapted well to change. They understand only one way to live and choose only one kind of habitat.

People, too, must sometimes leave their hometowns. Families move or split up, and the members must learn to live without their former relatives and friends. Changing schools and facing a new environment can be scary, but Paul encouraged, *"God did not give us a spirit of timidity, but a spirit of power, of love and of self-discipline."*

With God's help you can learn to adapt courageously to new situations. He's promised to help you cope if you just ask Him to and then, through faith, lean on Him.

TALK BACK: How do you handle change? Whom can you go to for help?

More About Dive-bombers

Home: Shorelines and sandbars
Size: Robin-sized

One evening some least terns flew over my husband and me and landed on a sandy embankment. They noisily scrambled about. When they left, we hurried over and discovered shallow indentations among the shells and pebbles. In each of these bare scrapes lay one to three speckled eggs!

Soon the birds noticed me at their nesting place. Complaining loudly, they dive-bombed my husband's head!

Some of the birds landed near us and dragged their wings as though injured. Small but brave, they tried to lure us away, ready to sacrifice themselves to save their precious eggs.

We didn't want to scare them, so we left. Soon the birds returned to their nests, turned their eggs, and settled over them. During the dark hours they would protect their young from whatever might threaten.

Terns will put themselves in jeopardy to save their babies. Jesus also put Himself in jeopardy to save you. The Bible says, *"The Lord has laid on him [Jesus] the iniquity of us all."*

Jesus paid for your sins by coming to earth and dying on the cross. If He had given in to even one of Satan's temptations, Jesus would have lost His right to return to heaven. But because He didn't fail, you can have a safe eternity with Him.

FOCUS: I plan to invite Jesus into my heart each morning so that He can guide and save me.

June 16

Red Admiral Butterfly

Home: Northern temperate regions
Size: Wingspan 3 inches

How would you like to walk barefoot across a surface and immediately know how it tasted? The red admiral can. God has given this butterfly special taste organs in its feet so it can find nectar and locate a good place to lay its eggs.

Every spring the red admiral migrates northward. Then it lays little green barrel-shaped eggs on nettle leaves or other host plants. When the tiny caterpillars hatch, they pull a leaf around themselves and fasten it with silky threads. This protects them as they feed and grow. Eventually the caterpillars create a chrysalis and fasten themselves near the stem of their food plant.

By the time they hatch into a butterfly, it's almost wintertime. Unfortunately, they don't seem to sense that they should stop traveling northward and go back south. So they try to hibernate beneath leaves or in hollow trees. If it's a cold winter, they don't survive.

It's important to know when enough is enough. Some people tease others, and everyone has fun. Other people take teasing too far, and someone gets hurt.

The Bible says, *"A fool's words start quarrels. They make people want to give him a beating"* (ICB). Just as the butterfly can get trapped in the cold, you can get trapped by your words. So be careful that you don't tease people too much.

TALK BACK: How can you tell when you've teased someone enough?

Ghost Crab

Home: Sandy eastern beaches
Size: To 10-inch leg span

One evening my husband and I sat on the beach alone—or so we thought. Suddenly sand sprayed up from a small hole a few feet away from us. Then two black eyes on long shafts peeped over the edge of the hole. A large crab inched out and scurried sideways to the water's edge, leaving scratchy footprints behind. It was a ghost crab.

If danger appears and this crab isn't near its hole, it will crouch and "freeze." And because it's sand-colored, it becomes almost invisible. That's how it got its name.

The ghost crab digs long burrows in the sand above the high-tide level. There it spends the hot part of the day, becoming active during the cool of the day and at night.

When it emerges it cleans its diggings, finds scraps of food, or dashes to the ocean to fill its gill sacs with water. It must do this periodically to keep from suffocating. But during this dash to the ocean the crab risks being captured by a bird.

In your Christian walk you also become exposed to spiritual dangers. Yet if you ask God to be with you, you won't have to "dash" alone. He'll guide your steps and keep you safe. With love He says, *"Do not fear; I will help you."*

TALK BACK: What are some physical reactions you have when you feel fear? Why is it important to keep a clear mind when afraid? How can you do this?

In the Doldrums

Maybe you've heard the expression "He's down in the doldrums." This usually means that someone's feeling depressed.

This expression comes from an area near the equator. Located on the ocean, this low-pressure place called the doldrums generally has very little wind. So when sailing ships go there they may have to wait days for enough breeze to move them on. They just sit and wait, doing nothing.

Some people get "down in the doldrums" because they have a chemical imbalance in their bodies. Some have suffered tragedy or loss. Others may be just plain bored. And so they sit, long-faced and grouchy.

How do you handle life when you're bored or depressed? Are you hard to live with, making everyone else suffer through your difficulties, too?

I know a way that helps me get out of the doldrums. It works every time. I simply take an "outward look," finding someone else who's having a hard time. As I try to make them happier, I find that life gets better for me, too.

When King David became depressed, he said, *"In you I trust, O my God. Do not let me be put to shame."* Knowing that Jesus will help you makes life better, doesn't it?

TALK BACK: If a friend is depressed and I've done what I could but it didn't seem to help, what should I do?

178

Two-toed Sloth

Home: Northern South America
Size: To 25 pounds

If someone calls you "slothful," it's no compliment! Two-toed sloths take forever to get from one end of a branch to the other. That's why they seem lazy.

These slow-moving jungle animals spend their lives hanging upside down in trees. Their front feet have two long, curved claws, and their back ones have three. These claws give them a sturdy grip.

Moving one leg at a time, these animals inch along the branches. Having feet unsuitable for walking, they seldom leave the trees, but they can swim if necessary. Green algae grows on their grayish-brown fur, providing a good camouflage from jaguars and other predators. Sleeping sloths hang with their feet pressed together and their heads resting on their chests.

Sloths eat leaves and fruit, which can take up to a month to digest! They raise one baby at a time, and it clings to its mother's fur. Weaned after a month, it then eats leaves that have been chewed by its mother. Later on it picks its own leaves to eat while still clinging to her body.

Sloths survive well in their jungle habitat. But slothful *people* don't do very well. Late to appointments and with assignments, they tend to be messy and expect others to do their tasks for them. And that gets old in a hurry! Maybe that's why Paul advised, *"Do not be lazy but work hard"* (ICB). Don't be like the sloth!

MISSION: Think of ways to do your work more efficiently yet well. One idea is to set a timer for just enough time to do your job. Then keep on track so you can beat the timer.

Ball of Pins

Home: Australia
Size: From 5-13 pounds

The spiny anteater looks like a brown ball of pins. It has a tubular, hairless nose and two bright eyes.

Living in the wilderness, it eats ants and termites that it digs up with its spadelike feet. What looks like its nose also contains its mouth, a small hole through which it pokes its long, sticky tongue to slurp up insects.

Only two kinds of mammals hatch from an egg, and the anteater is one of them. The mother lays her egg while lying on her back. Then she pushes the egg into her pouch. After it hatches, the baby remains in her pouch for eight weeks until its spines start growing. Then the mother digs a separate burrow for it and nurses it until it's weaned.

The anteater's feet, with strong, sharp claws, make perfect digging instruments. In order to escape dingoes and humans, the animal lies flat on its tummy and digs with all four feet at the same time, rapidly sinking into the dirt for safety.

God created the anteater with a long, curved claw on each back foot. With it the animal grooms its hair and scratches between its spines.

God has provided for your needs, too. With the psalmist you can say, *"Give thanks to the Lord, for he is good."*

TALK BACK: How has God provided for you? Think of a time you really needed something you couldn't get. How did God help you solve that problem?

180

Tuck Away Those Paws!

When I sit down for worship in the morning, Synjee, my kitty, loves to join me. As I hold my Bible in my lap, she snuggles up beside me in the chair. As long as she's quiet, I let her stay.

The trouble starts when I kneel on the floor to pray. Then Synjee stretches across the warm spot I left on the chair and decides to give herself a bath. The licking begins, starting with her paws. If I let it continue, she'll tidy every inch of her body.

Her licking sounds take away from my quiet prayertime, so I open my eyes and tell her "No." She gazes at me with her big blue eyes. Then she tucks her paws beneath her chest and wraps her tail around her nose. With her paws out of sight, she won't pay any more attention to them until I'm finished talking to my heavenly Father.

Just as Synjee tucks her paws away to keep from being tempted, you can keep temptations out of sight. Say you've decided not to eat junk food. Good, but you won't want to walk through the candy aisle at the store. Being around what you've decided to avoid only makes it harder.

The Bible says that when it comes to wrong you should *"not swerve to the right or the left; keep your foot from evil."* That applies to your eyes, too.

MISSION: Ask God for help, then plan how you'll keep from doing something that tempts you.

God's Tiny Rototillers

Home: Globally underground
Size: 5-10 inches

The Israelites were feeling unimportant—as insignificant as worms in the ground. They were afraid and needed God's help. That's when God said to them, *"Do not be afraid, O worm Jacob, O little Israel, for I myself will help you."* God didn't say this to hurt their feelings but to show them that no one is too small for Him to notice and care for.

Earthworms seem pretty ordinary, but they help keep the soil fertile. These rubbery creatures burrow through the dirt by eating it. As the dirt passes through them, they digest bits of decomposing plant life. Their processed dirt—called castings—softens and enriches the earth.

Also, when earthworms burrow and dig little tunnels, they allow air into the soil. Similar to rototillers, they prepare the earth for healthy new plant life.

Earthworms generally stay underground during the day, unless their burrows get too wet. They do come to the surface to push out their castings, which can be found at the entrance to their holes.

I'm glad that no one is so unimportant that God doesn't see and care for them. You have a special place in His plan. And as you do your best for Him, He'll bless even your small efforts.

TRY IT: On your lawn or in a garden or park, watch robins hunt for worms. They hop, stop, listen, then grab. Mark the spot, then try to find the worm's hole and castings. Remember that God notices even these.

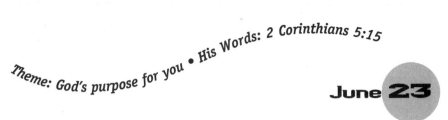

More About Those Rototillers

Earthworms look like a bunch of tiny pink, reddish, or brown rubber rings all glued together. They have long muscles that run the length of their body as well as muscles that circle each ring.

Have you watched an earthworm go somewhere after a hard rain? It stretches forward, becoming long and skinny. Then, holding the surface with tiny bristles that protrude from its body, it contracts its long muscles to pull up its back end. At the same time, it oozes a slippery mucus that helps it slide.

A single earthworm is both male and female! It buries its tiny eggs in the ground in sturdy capsules made of dried secretions. When the worms hatch, they're fully developed and able to care for themselves. Some live 10 years or longer!

Even these plain creatures have a purpose. God created them to enrich the soil. Likewise, no person comes into this world by accident.

God allowed you to be born, to breathe the air you're breathing, and to learn about Him. He has a special purpose for you. Have you wondered what that purpose might be?

The answer is here: *"Christ died for all so that those who live would not continue to live for themselves. He died for them and was raised from death so that they would live for him"* (ICB).

TRY IT: After it rains find a live worm on the sidewalk. Gently touch it. How does it react? Under what circumstances should you react in the same way?

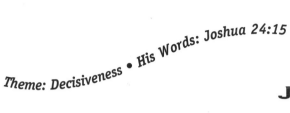

Brazilian Tapir

Home: South America
Size: To 500 pounds

The Brazilian tapir is built like a hippo. It has dark short, bristly hair, rounded ears rimmed with white, and toes ending in hooves. Roaming the forests, it sniffs out vegetation. Its trunklike snout can move about without the animal even turning its head! With this snout the tapir can grasp and break twigs and push food into its mouth.

The tapir lives near water and wallows in the mud to keep cool. Baby tapirs have yellowish stripes and spots, which provide good camouflage. They stay with their mothers for about eight months until they can care for themselves.

A fast swimmer, the tapir escapes predators by plunging into the water. It can stay submerged for several minutes at a time. It can also escape on land, for its weight and tough skin allow it to push through deep undergrowth without getting hurt. When it decides that it's time to move, nothing better get in its way!

Decisiveness can be a good quality. It helps you keep your word and do the right thing, no matter how you're feeling. It keeps you honest. It makes you fair. Joshua said, *"Choose for yourselves this day whom you will serve."*

Deciding to follow Jesus isn't always the easiest way to go. But it's the right way. And in the long run, sticking with that decision will bring you peace and satisfaction.

TALK BACK: When is it easy for you to make a decision? When is it hard? How can you learn to make good decisions?

Zero

Size: Approximately 70 pounds

One evening while feeding my dog, Molly, I spotted a big Siberian husky. He loped along the gully beside my house, sniffing the air and watching me. Later I saw him raiding neighborhood garbage cans, strewing the contents everywhere.

For weeks I'd suspected that a stray dog was around. I'd noticed that when Molly didn't finish her supper, her empty dish would turn up in the woods the next morning.

Zero, as I called him, began coming by my house at feeding time and watching hungrily. I put food out for him hoping to catch him, read his dog tag, and return him to his owner. But because he didn't trust me, he'd sneak up, take the dish, and run.

Then he disappeared. A few weeks later I accidentally left the garage door open overnight. In the morning I found Molly's food supply scattered everywhere. Sadly, the last time I saw Zero he looked very weak. Though I wanted to help, he wouldn't trust me.

Your heavenly Father wants to provide what you need and help you with your problems. King David said, *"Blessed are all they that put their trust in him" (KJV).*

God has given you guidelines, but He doesn't force you to follow them. You can choose to trust Him or keep your distance, grow weaker, and eventually die. In the end you must decide what to do with God's loving offer.

TALK BACK: How do you know when to trust others? How do you know you can trust God?

Moon Jellies

Home: Coastal Atlantic and Pacific oceans
Size: 4-10 inches diameter

The moon jelly is the most common jellyfish. It looks like a clear Jello umbrella with a four-leaf clover shape in its back. To swim, it pulsates just under the surface of the sea.

This jellyfish also has a fringe of short, threadlike tentacles around its outer edge. When a fish touches these stinging tentacles, it gets stunned. The jellyfish then surrounds the fish and pushes it into its mouth.

To reproduce, male and female jellyfish drop eggs and sperm in the water. The fertilized eggs become larvae and attach to a rock or seaweed. The larvae turn into polyps, which look something like half an egg stuck on a stem. The polyps form stacks of tiny pancake-like disks on their tops. Gradually these disks, which are the new jellyfish, separate and float away.

What good are moon jellies? They're part of the food chain for loggerhead turtles and other marine animals that don't react to their stings.

You may wonder why certain creatures were created, but each has its purpose. You may even wonder why you were created. But you can be sure that God has a special purpose for you. Paul said, *"For we are God's workmanship."* As you grow and develop, you'll learn what God has in mind for you.

CONTACT: Lord, sometimes I don't feel as if I have any particular use. Help me understand what You want of me and know that You'll help me achieve it.

Prickly-pear Cactus

Home: Deserts in the Americas

The prickly-pear cactus is made of many large, circular pads. These fleshy pads are covered with needle-sharp spines that are actually leaves. Because cacti live in deserts, they must conserve moisture. That's why their leaves grow hard and sharp.

Prickly pears store water in their pads. Also, their roots grow near the sandy surface in order to collect rainfall. During drought, cacti use the water they've stored, shriveling as they do.

Spines protect the cactus from animals eating it. But prickly-pear spines, when young, are soft and pliable. Only as they age and get exposed to heat and dryness do they stiffen into hard needles.

That's how your habits develop. Let's say you've begun to say mean things or to use bad language. If you don't break those habits soon, they'll grow stronger. Eventually you'll find it almost impossible to make your tongue say only what it should. That's why it's important to set high standards very early in life.

From the time he was little, King David tried to cultivate good habits both in speech and actions. As he grew up he asked God to show him what was right and wrong. He said to God, *"I will watch my ways and keep my tongue from sin."* You can do that too.

TALK BACK: What steps must you take to change a bad habit?

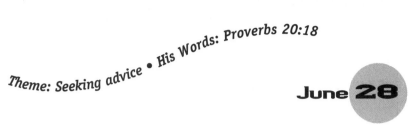

Green Iguana

Home: Tropical Americas
Size: To 6 feet

Iggy, a 16-inch green iguana, lived in an aquarium in my bedroom. A quiet roommate, he'd bask on a branch beneath his sun lamp. But he'd wake up as soon as I put pieces of fruit and vegetables on the sandy floor of his home. Tasting the air with his fleshy pink tongue, Iggy would follow the scents to his meal.

When I'd clean his cage, I'd put him on the bed. Again his tongue would go to work, trying to taste the bright flowers on the bedspread.

In the wild, iguanas climb through trees and bushes searching for food. Their long tails help them balance as they leap from tree to tree. When food is scarce they can survive quite a while by living off the fat stored in their tails.

Though their bright-green color provides good camouflage among the leaves, iguanas often perch on exposed branches above water. When threatened by predators such as large cats or snakes, they raise their dorsal spines and spread out their chin flaps to make themselves look large and dangerous. Or they drop into the water and stay submerged until danger has passed.

What do you do when threatened? The Bible gives good advice about facing an enemy. It says, *"If you go to war, get the advice of others" (ICB)*. In other words, don't fight a battle without first thinking it over and seeking counsel from someone who can see the situation from all sides.

TALK BACK: Name some good ways to fight battles. [Read Proverbs 20:22.]

That Pesky Mosquito!

Home: Worldwide
Size: To .33 inch

You're just settling down to sleep. Then you hear a familiar whiny buzz. You dive under your sheet, but the biting, flying insect gets you anyhow. So you find a flyswatter and bat it around the room. Then you go back to bed, just to have it happen all over again. Mosquitoes don't give up!

Actually, mosquitoes are pretty amazing. The males sip nectar but live only a few days. The females live up to a year feeding on blood, which they need for their eggs.

They lay their eggs in quiet waters. Becoming larvae, the eggs float just beneath the water's surface, using a tube to breathe. When a mosquito hatches, it's soon ready to breed and lay more eggs.

Unfortunately, some mosquitoes carry dangerous diseases. And the female's slender beak is so sharp that she can often insert it into skin without the victim knowing it.

The mosquito's persistence is like that of Satan and his helpers. You tell them to leave you alone, and you think they won't bother you anymore. Then, when you finally relax, there they are, sneaking back to tempt you and make your life miserable.

It's a good thing Jesus can fight off those tempters! Because of Him you can say, *"He has delivered me from all my troubles."*

CONTACT: Father, when Satan and his crew tempt me, help me to always turn to You. Thank You for loving me.

Bald Eagle Experience

Home: Seacoasts, water areas
Size: Body to 31 inches

With a cry the eagle swooped overhead, trying to dodge the crows chasing it. Shaking them off, the eagle landed on a high tree branch. The scolding from the crows grew louder.

Soon the eagle returned to the air, this time carrying something that looked like a nest in one of its talons. Frantically the crows threw themselves against the eagle's foot, forcing it to the ground behind some bushes. But they were no match for the eagle's size and finally flew away.

Despite all the beauty in nature and the enjoyment you can get from animals, you find sadness, too. God created all creatures to live in harmony, and in the Garden of Eden they did. But when Adam and Eve invited sin into their lives, changes took place.

As people shoved God out of their lives, Satan's evil spirit began to take control of everything in nature. Then he did what he enjoys most—ruin things. Plants began to die, and animals started preying on each other instead of eating vegetation. Now you live with what's left.

But God said, *"I am making everything new!"* He'll eventually put things right again. Then all creatures will live in harmony. Aren't you eager for that day to come?

TALK BACK: When you watch the news, what results of sin do you see? What do you look forward to the most when the earth is made new?

The Four-legged Rescue Squad

Size: To 80 pounds

My father-in-law loves to talk about a big brown dog he had when he was a boy. Half Airedale and half mastiff, Bruce considered himself Dad's bodyguard, protecting him from larger boys or other dangers. But sometimes Bruce's protectiveness became annoying.

On hot summer afternoons the neighborhood kids liked to swim in a canal that carried water to the surrounding farms. Dad's shadow, Bruce, would tag along.

One day one of the kids began to splash water. To Bruce, splashing signaled trouble! In a flash he plunged into the water, dragging the "splasher" by his arm up the bank. Proud to have "helped," Bruce carefully watched to make sure no one else was in trouble.

No amount of scolding broke Bruce of his protective habit. Finally, Dad had to tie him to a tree when he and his friends went swimming.

Once God asked Cain where Abel, his brother, was. Cain answered, *"Am I my brother's keeper?"*

The answer is yes. God wants you to help others. When someone is having a hard time, you should do what you can for them. If friends want to get into trouble, it's your responsibility to encourage them to do the right thing. If someone is hurt or sad, you should try to cheer them. Become aware of what's going on around you, and then lend a helping hand.

TALK BACK: If someone doesn't want your help, what should you do?

191

Stick-tight Limpets

Home: Tidal waters
Size: To 3 inches

Limpets live along shorelines where tides rise and fall. They attach themselves to a rock by sucking onto it with their large, soft foot. Then their protective shell completely covers them.

When the tide rises above them, limpets start their search for food. Their foot ripples to move them. With their radula (a saw-like tongue within their foot) they scrape algae from rocks. If you look closely you might see tiny scrape marks on rocks where limpets have grazed.

Limpets secrete a liquid that hardens and increases their shell size as they grow. When hunting, they also secrete a trail of mucus that helps them find their way back to the exact spot they call home. Settling into the very same position each time, they suck onto the rock, wearing grooves in it.

When limpets have attached, they're virtually immovable. In fact, their suction ability influenced the creation of the suction cups used today.

When you learn how Jesus wants you to live, you also should be immovable. Don't let Satan's temptations or peer pressure discourage you from obeying God. When speaking of living for Christ, Paul said, *"Whatever you have learned or received or heard from me, or seen in me—put it into practice. And the God of peace will be with you."* Stick tight to Jesus today!

TRY IT: Press both a dry and a wet suction cup against a window. Which one sticks better?

Elephant Shrew

Home: Africa
Size: 4-12 inches

The elephant shrew is neither an elephant nor a shrew. But it looks a little like a shrew and has a long snout that's flexible like an elephant's trunk. Some varieties of elephant shrews have longer noses than others, and all have mouselike tails. Their fur, which can be yellow, brown, black, or a mixture, provides camouflage.

The elephant shrew lives in dens, rock piles, or leafy nests on the forest floor. Its back legs are much longer than its front legs, so it can leap far. This helps it escape predators.

The elephant shrew uses its long nose to poke into undergrowth or to overturn fallen leaves while hunting insects. With the sensitive end of its nose the shrew finds an insect, then flicks it into its mouth with its long tongue.

Have you ever heard the expression, "He's nosy," or "Her nose is always in other people's business"? Some people search around for juicy morsels of gossip to share. Pretending to be shocked or concerned about what they've learned, they "flick" the information to others. Their wagging tongues often help the stories grow.

King Solomon spoke of this trait when he said, *"He whose tongue is deceitful falls into trouble."* Part of your Christian responsibility is to avoid listening to and passing on gossip about others. God is counting on you to keep your nose—and your tongue—under control!

TALK BACK: How can you politely stop others from sharing gossip with you?

Brave Kitty

One July 4 some children were playing tag in their backyard. They darted through the bushes to escape being "it." Rover, the family cat, sprawled in the sunshine.

Then someone shouted "snake!" The children's mother glanced out the window and saw something slithering toward her family. With a shriek she bounded outside and across the yard toward them.

The commotion awakened the sleeping cat. Spying the danger, shy Rover forgot that he was a cat. Instead he reacted like a dog that feels responsible for its family. He crouched low, dashed through the grass, and with a hiss pounced on the surprised snake.

A frantic tussle followed. Though Rover receiving a lashing from the snake's tail, he didn't give up. Finally the poisonous snake lay lifeless. But Rover had been bitten. Almost instantly the deadly toxins began their work, and he collapsed.

Four days later Rover's story made the news. Though scraggly and weak, he was still alive. His veterinarian said that he was the only cat known to have survived coral snake venom.

Courageous Rover stepped out of character for the good of his family. Someday you may be asked to step out of character either to *give your life* for someone else or to *live your life* for others. The Bible says, *"Greater love has no one than this, that he lay down his life for his friends."*

TALK BACK: Why might some people think that working hard for Christ would be like giving up their lives?

194

Flying Shadow

One evening during worship a shadow flitted between my son, Andy, and me.

"Wow, did you see that?" Andy gasped.

We waited, and after a few minutes the shadow flitted around the living room again, dipping, climbing, then disappearing. It was a bat!

We began to search the room. We looked behind books, under the bookcase, in the artificial greenery, and under the heater. But we couldn't find the bat.

Determined, we continued our search. Finally, when I started to take a picture off the wall, I saw movement. The little brown bat was clinging to the underside of the picture frame. Our persistence was rewarded!

How had the bat gotten indoors? We never found out. But our brief experience made us want to learn more about bats. We discovered many interesting things about them, which we'll talk about during the next few days.

Because we *really believed* that we saw the bat, we refused to give up our search. You must use the same persistence when seeking Jesus. He said, *"When you search for me with all your heart, you will find me"* (ICB).

Do you want Jesus as your Guide and Savior? Do you want Him to be real in your life? Then seek Him diligently, prayerfully, and without giving up.

CONTACT: Father, I know that You are there for me. Help me to keep looking each day until I find You.

195

How Bats Are Alike

There are about 2,000 species of bats, all similar in several ways. For example, bats are the only mammals that fly. Membranes connect their "fingers," producing paper-thin wings. These wings look large compared to their bodies. They also have "thumbs" with hooked claws.

Bats don't build nests. They roost, hanging upside down by their feet. Their babies are born alive and nurse from their mother, just as other mammals do.

All bats have hair and drink water. They're usually social, living in groups for company. Most bats find and eat their food while flying at night. Even though people use the expression "blind as a bat," bats aren't really blind.

There are also many differences among bats. Yet they all belong to the "bat" family, and God provides for each of them.

It's the same with people. God loves every person, whether they're rich or poor, active or lazy. He even sent His Son to die for the human race in order to save it. *"God does not show favoritism but accepts men [and women] from every nation who fear him and do what is right."*

God feels lonely for you if you turn away from Him. Though He has many people to love, there's only *one* of you. *You* make a difference to Him.

TALK BACK: How can you tell that God wants you to be His child? Discuss some ways He's looked after you in the past.

196

Big Brown Bat

Home: North America
Size: Head and body to 2.5 inches, wingspan to 14 inches

Though originally a woodland dweller, the big brown bat has learned to live in populated areas. In daylight it roosts in dry, dark, cool places, such as attics, trees, barns, or under bridges. At night it hunts for flying insects, particularly beetles.

As with other bats, the female is a very good, loving mother. At first the newborn clings to her breast, even as she flies. About two weeks later the baby has grown too big to carry, so the mother hangs it up by its feet in a nursery area used by many bat mothers.

At night she goes out to hunt, and for another two weeks comes back often to nurse her baby. Upon her return she locates her baby by scent, and before feeding it she licks its face.

If danger should threaten before the baby can fly, the mother will call it to cling to her breast as she flies away. Even if the baby has gotten very large, the mother will try to carry it to safety. If the baby doesn't trust or obey her, it might not be saved.

You must trust what Jesus says if you want to be saved. He's provided directions in the Bible to teach you how to live. *"Trust in the Lord with all your heart and lean not on your own understanding; in all your ways acknowledge Him, and He shall direct your paths"* (NKJV).

TALK BACK: How do God's rules help people? How can you learn to trust Him?

197

Mouse-eared Bat

Home: Europe
Size: Wingspan 14-18 inches

Mouse-eared bats grow to about three inches long and weigh one and a half ounces. They have large, lightweight wings. These help them maneuver as they chase flying insects.

Hunting at night, they roost in dark, cool places during the daytime. In order to find their prey they use echolocation. They do this by making sounds too high for humans to hear. The sound waves bounce off the prey and back into the mouselike ears of the bats, helping them locate dinner in the dark.

When mouse-eared bats find an insect they'll fly near it and use their wings like a big hand to scoop it up. Then they grip the insect with their feet to pass it into their mouth. If a bat refuses to catch insects, it will go hungry even with plenty of food around.

Jesus said, *"For God so loved the world that he gave his one and only Son, that whoever believes in him shall not perish but have eternal life."* Because He loves you, Jesus offers you salvation, even though you don't deserve it. You must choose whether to accept His gift or reject it.

To accept salvation, just open your heart to Jesus. You do this by believing that He can save you and by asking Him to be the Lord of your life.

MISSION: Go somewhere private. Ask God to help you accept the gift of salvation that Jesus so eagerly offers you.

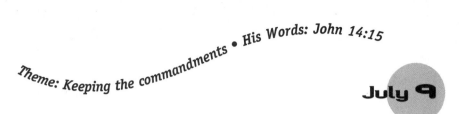

The Yellow-eared Tentmaker

Home: Tropical forests
Size: To 0.8 ounces

The yellow-eared bat lives in tropical forests and eats both fruit and insects. During the day it roosts in banana or palm trees, but it stays alert.

In the tropics it often rains hard or the sun beats down with intense heat. So the yellow-eared bat does something most other bats don't do. When roosting in tree foliage, it builds a little tent by cutting a series of holes in the big leaves so they will fold down all around. This gives shelter from the pounding rain and hot sun. The tent also hides the bat from flesh-eating predators! While wrapped in leaves, the bat stays safe and comfortable.

Some people say it's too hard to keep God's commandments. Others say you don't really need to, because Jesus already died to save you. Yes, He did, and you can trust Him to keep His word and save you if you're willing. But He also said, *"If you love Me, keep My commandments" (NKJV).*

When you understand the Bible's instructions and follow them out of love for Jesus, it's like wrapping yourself in a protective tent. There you're shielded from the rains of temptation and the enemy who tries to make you sin. Make your tent today!

MISSION: Call a local park service to see if there are bats in your area. Make arrangements to observe them.

The Freeloader

Home: Almost universal
Size: To .25 inch

Have you ever tramped through the woods and then found a strange new "mole" on your body? Upon closer inspection, you discovered that it had tiny legs beneath it. It was a tick!

Ticks wait on plants until a creature passes by. Then they jump onto it, finding a sheltered spot to attach to. Slicing into the flesh with their mandibles, they sink their heads into the creature. Then they begin sucking its blood until they're bloated. Finally they drop off the host.

Ticks are parasites because they grow or feed on another organism but offer no benefit to it. They may even cause serious illnesses such as Lyme disease. If you try to remove a tick, often its head or mouth parts remain under your skin.

The problem with ticks is like the problem of using drugs. At first people may not notice bad results, but as the habit sinks itself deeper into their life, it begins to affect them in serious ways. Finally it breaks their health.

It's best to avoid "walking through the woods" of drug use. Don't try it—even once!

Can God help a person who's gotten involved with drugs but now wants to do right? *"'I will restore you to health and heal your wounds,' declares the Lord."* But why not just avoid drugs in the first place?

TALK BACK: Sometimes people are given drugs without knowing it. How can you make sure this doesn't happen to you?

Mistletoe

Home: Trees such as apple, fir, pine, juniper

Parasites occur in the plant world as well as in the animal world. In fact, a common parasite is mistletoe, those green sprigs you see at Christmastime.

Mistletoe seeds get carried from tree to tree by birds, usually in their droppings. The seeds don't grow in dirt and don't develop roots of their own. Instead they attach to a branch and use its water and nutrients.

Once they've done that, the seeds grow into plants, which get larger and larger. Hanging from a tree, mistletoe plants use the tree's shade and its strength. They take from it but never give. In fact, trees that have been invaded by mistletoe often die.

Some people also display parasitic behavior. They take advantage of others' generosity. For instance, someone might borrow pencils but refuse to lend them. Or they might want one of your cookies but hoard theirs. Or they might invite you out to eat but always forget to bring their own money, so you have to pay.

Consistently taking advantage of others is neither nice nor Christian. The Bible says, *"Do for other people the same things you want them to do for you"* (ICB).

TRY IT: Buy a sprig of mistletoe. Plant one of its berries to see if you can make it grow. But don't eat it, because it's poisonous!

Eastern Hognose Snake

Home: Eastern United States
Size: To 3 feet

One afternoon my husband and I discovered a black snake. Belly-up and twisted, it lay on the path with its gravel-flecked mouth hanging open.

"It's a hognose," Bob said, poking it with his toe. "It's dead."

But when we turned around to look again, the snake had disappeared! It had only played dead.

Not poisonous, eastern hognose snakes have wide bodies. They move slowly but have their own defenses.

When something threatens them, they hiss loudly and strike out, but with a closed mouth. If that doesn't scare the intruder, they flatten the front part of their body so it looks more threatening. Then they strike again.

If that fails, they writhe as though dying an awful death. Then they roll over onto their back and lie perfectly still with their mouth hanging open. If picked up, they remain limp and "lifeless." But if they're put back on the ground, they'll roll onto their back again and continue to play dead.

Satan is a predator, and he'll do everything he can to bother you. But you can frighten him away by talking about Jesus or praying to Him. When being tempted in the wilderness, Jesus said, *"Away from me, Satan!"* and Satan had to leave Him alone. With God's help, you can do the same thing.

CONTACT: Heavenly Father, please give me the courage to command Satan to leave me alone and to allow only You to influence me.

The King of Snarl

Home: Tasmania
Size: To 26 pounds

The Tasmanian devil is a black marsupial with pink hairless ears. It looks something like a small bear. In the daytime it holes up in a tree, cave, or digs a burrow. During the night it ambles about and hunts.

Though it prefers to eat abandoned carcasses, it hunts live animals, too. Its strong jaws and large teeth help it crunch down feathers, fur, and bones, wasting nothing.

The mother Tasmanian devil has a backward pouch that holds four babies. She carries them for about nine months. Then she hides them in a cozy nest and goes to hunt. When she brings back meat for the babies to share, they constantly snarl and snap at each other.

Tasmanian devils earned their name because of their growly, unpleasant behavior. They love to fight, never watching out for the other guy.

No one likes to be around growly people, either. When they bicker and find fault with others, it affects everyone. King Solomon was right when he said, *"The north wind brings forth rain, and a backbiting tongue an angry countenance"* (NKJV).

Do you ever act this way? Does it make you happier? It's not easy to change, but with Jesus' help and firm determination, you can. It will make things nicer for others, and you'll feel better, too.

MISSION: Next time you feel like picking a fight, ask Jesus to help you say nothing. Watch what happens.

203

Australian Frilled Lizard

Home: Australia, Papua New Guinea
Size: To 1 pound and 3 feet

The Australian frilled lizard lives in trees. Its long legs stretch so it can reach or jump between branches. And its spiny scales help it blend in.

This reptile has strong hind legs that allow it to run in an upright position across the ground. Basking in the sun keeps it warm enough to move quickly and catch insects and small mammals.

The frilled lizard gets its name from the scaled ruff around its neck. It can spread this 10-inch ruff, which looks like a pleated collar, to absorb warmth from the sun or to frighten off predators. When frightened the lizard also stands on its hind legs, hisses, and thrashes its tail. If that doesn't work, it runs away as fast as it can.

How do you react when someone wants you to do something bad, such as fool around with guns or knives or look at pornography? Do you go along because you don't want to look "chicken"? Or do you resist the pressure and get out of there as fast as you can?

The Bible says, *"Fools mock at sin, but among the upright there is favor" (NKJV)*. It actually takes more courage to resist doing wrong than to go along with it. If that makes you look chicken, then looking chicken is wise!

TRY IT: In front of a mirror practice saying "No, I don't want to do that" in a firm but kind way. Then imagine situations in which you might need to use this sentence.

204

Sun Bear

Home: Southeast Asian forests
Size: 60-150 pounds

The sun bear differs from many other bears, because it spends much of its time in trees. Breaking branches, it creates a sturdy platform 10-20 feet above the ground. This gives it a good view.

It hunts for bees' nests in tree trunks, tearing the nests open with it long, sharp claws. Its slender, probing tongue allows it to slurp out both honey and grubs. It also eats fruit from treetops. While ground-dwelling bears have paws with hairy soles, the sun bear has hairless foot pads, helping it grip better as it climbs.

The smallest of the bear family, the sun bear tends to be shy. Even in the wild it's generally not aggressive. Because of its reputation, it has earned the trust of many Malaysian families and has become a popular pet, for it's gentle and easy to tame.

God has asked you to help spread the gospel to others. He instructs, *"Be sure that you live in a way that brings honor to the Good News of Christ" (ICB)*. To help others want to learn more about Jesus, you must be sure they see something Christlike in your behavior, something that earns their trust and respect. You can show yourself trustworthy by keeping your word, obeying your parents, using good language, and being polite and kind. It's a big job, but if you're willing, God can help you accomplish it.

TALK BACK: Think of a Bible character who was especially trustworthy. How does someone become trustworthy?

The Spotted Sailor

One day a family in India rescued an orphaned leopard cub. Carefully they nurtured her until they thought she could return to normal life. Then they released her into the jungle across the river. She adjusted and eventually had cubs of her own.

Torrential rains came, and the river began to rise. The mother had placed her den on low ground, and the water threatened her babies. So, carrying them in her mouth one at a time, she swam across the river. Then she took them back to the only safe place she knew—her old home with the kind family that had rescued her.

Eventually the floodwaters went down. The mother swam back across the river and returned one baby to the den. But apparently deciding that swimming was too dangerous, she dropped the second cub into her previous owner's canoe. Then she waited for him to ferry them across.*

Just as the leopard remembered the owner who helped her, you should remember that Jesus is happy to help you. He said, *"Call upon me in the day of trouble; I will deliver you, and you will honor me."* Jesus loves you so much that He was willing to die to rescue you.

TALK BACK: Name some ways you can help a friend in trouble. How can prayer help?

---

*Eugene Linden, "Can Animals Think?" *Time,* Sept. 6, 1999, p. 59.

Nests

Birds can build a cozy nest using just about any material—grass, twigs, string, animal hair, spiderwebs, moss, mud, feathers, even saliva. Most birds also seem to know how to attach their nest to a surface so it will stay stable and secure.

In windy areas a wise bird places its nest in the crook of a tree or someplace else that is sheltered. After all, heavy winds can cause such a shaking of the branches that the eggs or chicks might be knocked out of the most secure-looking nest. This means disaster for the bird family.

Near the end of time this earth will experience a shaking. God said, *"Once more I will shake not only the earth but also the heavens."* This shaking will test your loyalty to Jesus and the Bible. During this time people who profess to follow Jesus but haven't kept a secure relationship with Him will fall away. Even some spiritual leaders may become disinterested, be fooled by Satan, or frightened of persecution.

No one else can keep you in a saving relationship with God. It has to be your choice to let Him hold you tight. Determine today to ground yourself in the truth and to not let yourself be shaken away, no matter what happens.

TALK BACK: What are some things that might "shake" people out of the church. How?

Common Wombat

Home: Australia, Tasmania
Size: To 90 pounds

The common wombat has a heavy body and short legs. It looks a little like a cross between a bear and a badger. Strictly vegetarian, this marsupial has chisel-like teeth that continually grow. At night each wombat heads for its own feeding grounds to rip up vegetation with its strong forefeet.

The wombat uses its long claws to dig a burrow. This burrow may extend from 15 to 100 feet in length and have several entrances. The animal lines its sleeping room with bark, and makes tunnels just wide enough to pass through.

If chased by an enemy, it hurries into its burrow, blocking the passageway with its hind quarters. If the enemy doesn't go away, the wombat kicks it with its powerful hind legs.

Wombats have only one baby a year. After birth, the tiny infant crawls into its mother's backward-facing pouch, where it stays attached to a nipple for six months. Then the mother teaches the baby to forage. It's ready to live on its own at 18 months.

Just as the wombat tries to hide from its enemies, people sometimes try to hide their sins. Have you ever done something wrong and then hoped that you wouldn't be caught? Maybe you didn't want everyone to learn what you did.

While you may fool those around you, though, there's Someone who knows the truth. David said, *"O God, thou knowest my foolishness; and my sins are not hid from thee"* (KJV).

CONTACT: God, help me to do right so I won't need to cover up what I've done.

The Amazing Hoatzin

Home: Amazon basin
Size: Chicken-sized

The hoatzin looks like a pheasant. It has a crest on its head, red eyes with long eyelashes, and a blue face. It lives in a large stick nest in a tree above flooded areas.

The baby hoatzin hatches with its eyes open and with claws on the tips of its wings. After it grows down on its body it starts scrambling through the branches, exploring its leafy world.

If a predator approaches, the baby produces an unpleasant smell to discourage it. If that fails, it jumps from the tree and dives underwater until the predator leaves. Then, using its clawed wings, it climbs back up the tree trunk to its nest. The wing claws disappear as the chick matures.

The parents grind vegetation, insects, and water creatures in their throat. When the babies get hungry, they thrust their beaks deep into their parents' open mouths and help themselves.

Some people, like hoatzin chicks, take an active part in caring for themselves. They willingly help with what needs to be done and are aware of what is going on. They know it's important to make the most of their opportunities.

Solomon said, *"The desires of the diligent are fully satisfied."* This means that if you don't just sit there and wait for things to be done for you, you'll be happier.

TALK BACK: What have you done lately that needed to be done but that no one asked you to do? How did you feel about it?

Training Those Vines

In my yard I have a walk-through trellis. A yellow jasmine vine climbs up it. The vine often hosts butterflies and fat bumble-bees that drink its nectar.

Not long ago I trimmed some unruly branches off the vine, but more have come back. Now they're growing in all directions!

It isn't hard to train the vine to grow where I want it to if I work with it often. If I neglect it, though, those wandering branches grow every which way. Soon I end up with an uncontrollable mess that can block my passageway or even pull down the trellis.

In the Garden of Eden Adam had the job of training the vines. You may have trained a pet to obey. Without training, both vines and animals can become a nuisance. People can, too.

That's why God has given a very special job to your parents. He said, *"Train a child in the way he should go, and when he is old he will not turn from it."* He wants them to raise you to be obedient and loving. That means that sometimes they must correct you. They have to "trim off" habits that would someday hurt you.

What's your responsibility? To accept the training, and to ask God to help you be willing to grow.

MISSION: In a store observe some young children whose mothers ignore them. How do they behave? Without correction, what might be the outcome?

Twinkle, Twinkle, It's No Star

Habitat: Most areas other than polar or arid
Size: To .5 inch

You're taking a night walk along a country road. It's warm and humid. Suddenly you see a star twinkling, but it's not in the sky. Instead, it's bobbing through the trees! Then more little lights flash at you from both high and low.

You've spotted fireflies, sometimes called glowworms or lightning bugs. More than 2,000 species of these beetles have been discovered, and at least 60 species live in North America.

Though most beetles have hard shells, fireflies have soft abdomens with light organs at the end. These organs produce a greenish-yellow light. The light creates no heat and doesn't even seem to use up a firefly's energy!

Fireflies spend about two years as wingless ground dwellers, feeding on other ground dwellers. Once the males develop their wings, they live only about two weeks. During this time they must mate, so they fly around blinking. With their large eyes they watch for the females to blink back at them.

Have you noticed how quickly you spot light when it's dark? Jesus said, *"You are the light of the world."* What a wonderful opportunity you have each day to bring the light of His love to someone else! Your smiles, helpful actions, and encouraging words will do just that.

TRY IT: If you live in firefly country, try to mimic the males' blink and flight pattern with a tiny penlight. See if you can get the females to respond to you.

211

"On the Peck"

If you can, visit a chicken yard. Quietly watch the hens scurry around, picking up grain or chasing insects. Listen to their good-natured chuckling.

Before long, though, you'll probably notice a hen that's not happy. Blustery and cranky, she'll eye the others. Then, seemingly for no reason, she'll squawk, flap her wings, and begin pecking at them.

As a child I sometimes woke up feeling grumpy. Then I'd find myself complaining about my sister or growling at my brother. My mom would pin me with her eyes and say, "Look who's on the peck this morning!" Yes, I was on the peck just like a grumpy old hen!

How do you handle yourself when you wake up feeling grumpy? Do you let your feelings build deep inside, then attack someone? Or do you slip back into your bedroom and ask Jesus to change your heart so you won't hurt anyone?

When James was teaching people how to live a Christian life he said, *"Do not become angry easily. Anger will not help you live a good life as God wants"* (ICB).

Everyone feels grouchy from time to time. The problem comes when you let yourself stay in that mood. Instead, ask God to help you behave in a Christlike way.

MISSION: If someone has done something to upset you, gather up your courage and talk it over with them calmly rather than picking on them.

Brimstone

Lot and his family lived in Sodom. In this city people tried to please only themselves, not caring who they hurt in the process. Then angels came to give Lot a message from God. He was to leave the city, for God was going to destroy it. *"Then the Lord rained upon Sodom and upon Gomorrah brimstone and fire from the Lord out of heaven" (KJV).*

Fire coming from heaven would be scary enough, but brimstone too? What's that?

Some of my friends visiting Bible lands hiked through the wilderness area believed to be the ancient location of Sodom and Gomorrah. They noticed scorched earth and strange dirt balls sunken into holes. When they opened a dirt ball, they discovered a brimstone rock inside. It had obviously burned so hot that it melted a hole into the earth!

Actually sulfur, brimstone burns so hot that it can melt through anything it touches. Though sulfur gets spewed from volcanoes, there are no volcanoes in that immediate area. That's why I think the Bible story is true. How else did that brimstone get there?

So why can't archaeologists find ruins from those old cities? Well, when God destroys something, He destroys it all the way. And someday He'll destroy every bit of sin! It will be gone forever, never to hurt you again.

TRY IT: Check in an encyclopedia to learn the many uses for sulfur. Is everything God created useful in some way?

John Dory

Home: Eastern Atlantic Ocean
Size: To 18 pounds

The John Dory fish looks like an old grump that didn't get its way. Its pouting expression comes from its long, upward-slanting lower jaw that creates a down-turned mouth. But in hunting, that lower jaw comes in handy!

The shape of the Dory's body also helps it hunt efficiently. Like a flattened cookie standing on end, the golden or olive-brown fish is so thin that it's hard to see head-on. Also, protective spines sticking out of its upper and lower fins make it an undesirable meal.

The Dory weaves through grasses looking for smaller fish. When it spies one, it bursts toward it, shooting its protruding lower jaw at the target. As the water rushes into the Dory's mouth, the prey washes in with it.

An old legend claims that it was a John Dory that held a coin in its belly for Peter to pay the tax collector. The large dark spot on either side of the fish is said to be Peter's fingerprints!

While we don't know whether or not this is true, we do know that Jesus performed a miracle that day. He told Peter, *"Take that coin and give it to the tax collectors. That will pay the tax for you and me"* *(ICB)*. With that action Jesus showed that it's our responsibility to pay our fair share to the government.

FOCUS: You probably don't pay taxes yet, but do you return tithe and offerings to the church? Can you find ways to give more to God's causes?

The Praying Mantis

Home: Warm to tropical areas
Size: From .5-12 inches

There are about 2,000 species of the praying mantis. These insects appear green or brown, depending on their habitat. Some have wings, while others don't. They seem to be "praying" because of how they hold their front legs in front of them.

Mantises have large eyes and can turn their heads. They use camouflage for protection and hunting. Instead of moving about seeking food, they simply settle on a twig or leaf and wait. Holding up the insides of their front legs, which are lined with spines, they can spring out and grab an insect that wanders by. Their spines make it hard for insects to escape their viselike grip.

The flower mantis from Africa and the Far East looks like a flower. Nectar-seeking creatures come right to it, and the mantis grabs and eats its prey, then holds still for its next meal. What looked good to the insect was really a trap.

In many cultures it's popular to drink alcoholic drinks. Satan has made it seem harmless and even glamorous. But alcohol slows the brain and clouds reasoning powers. What Satan makes look good is really a trap.

The Bible says, *"Do not drink wine nor strong drink"* (KJV). Why not vow to keep liquor from becoming any part of your life?

MISSION: Watch the newspaper columns for a week. Count how many crimes committed included alcohol consumption.

Big Things Come in Little Packages

Home: Southeast Asia islands
Size: 3-6 ounces

In school I was always the smallest in my class. Because I looked younger than the other students, I had to work harder to prove my abilities.

Zacchaeus had the same problem. The Bible reports that Zacchaeus *"wanted to see who Jesus was, but being a short man he could not, because of the crowd."* But Zacchaeus didn't give up. Instead, he climbed a tree to see over people's heads.

The tarsier is another small creature. Its head and body measure only six inches, though its tail grows almost twice as long. It also has long hind legs that help it spring great distances. This mammal can scamper through the branches at lightning speed or jump from a tree and capture a bird in flight.

The tarsier's huge startled-looking eyes give it excellent night vision. And its cupped ears help it locate prey. With its long fingers and thumbs it can quickly reach out and grasp an insect for dinner.

The tiny tarsier functions as well as a large animal does. You, too, can do what you need to do, no matter what your age or size. You may have to stand on tiptoe or find another way to accomplish a task, but that's OK. With the good brain God gave you and with determination and hard work, you can accomplish whatever you choose.

CONTACT: God, thanks for the abilities You've given me. Please show me how to accomplish the things You want me to.

Growing Rice

Home: Warm, humid countries

Rice, actually a grain, is the main food for about half the world's population. It must be grown at just the right time and under exact conditions.

First, farmers plant rice seeds in prepared beds. Within a month or two the seeds have sprouted. Then, wading through fields flooded with a few inches of water, the farmers press the roots into mud.

The farmers keep the water at the right level, and the sun shines down on the plants. Eventually rice kernels develop along the tall grassy stalks. When they look plump the workers pull up the plants and head for the threshing area.

Many people thresh rice kernels by hand, beating the stalks against something to dislodge the rice. In some places machines do the work. The rice may be left in its natural brown form or milled to remove the outer layers and make it white, which also removes most of its nutrients.

Planting God's seed in people's hearts must be done carefully, too. When you share the truth about Jesus' wonderful gift, it may take a while for people to grasp what salvation really means. They need to be "watered" with loving care and respect while the Son shines on them.

Jesus said, *"The harvest is plentiful, but the workers are few."* Will you work along with the Holy Spirit to plant and tend the seed?

MISSION: Make a list of people you want to pray for. Find ways to reach out and show them Jesus' love.

I'm Outta Here!

Octopuses can grow to be more than 20 feet across. Invertebrates, they have no skeleton either inside or outside their bodies.

While fishing one day, a man snagged an octopus that measured about eight feet across. Its body was the size of a small watermelon. Thinking it would taste good, the man stuffed the octopus into a wooden box on the deck of his boat. Carefully securing the lid so his dinner wouldn't escape, he fished awhile longer and then headed back.

After docking the boat and selling his fish, the man picked up the box to take it home. Puzzled because it wasn't heavy, he carefully opened the lid and peeked inside. The octopus was gone!

Then he noticed a two-inch knothole in the side of the box. Somehow, because of having no skeleton, the octopus had managed to squeeze through that small hole and climb over the side of the boat!

How serious are you about wanting to go home with Jesus? Enough to make sure you let nothing stop you from worshiping Him and doing His will? Do you take every opportunity to grow more like Him?

The Bible says, *"Love the Lord your God with all your heart."* Only those who put Jesus first in their lives will escape this world and live with Him in heaven. Don't let sin box you in. Find the way of escape, and take it!

CONTACT: Father, help me to love You more.

Kingfisher

Home: Areas in Europe and the Far East
Size: Body to 7 inches, beak 1 inch

The common kingfisher has a rosy breast and blue feathers on its back and wings. This bird is blessed with persistence, and it needs it!

When hunting for food the kingfisher perches a few feet above the water until it spies a fish. Then it folds its wings and nose-dives into the water to capture the fish. After popping to the surface, the bird flies back to its perch.

So what's so amazing about that? Well, though many other birds can swim, this one can't!

Kingfishers nest in steep banks of dirt over water. If they don't find a ready-made burrow, they fly at the cliff and run smack into it with their beaks until they've chipped out a small hole. Then they dig an up-sloping tunnel with their feet. After enlarging it at the end, the female lays her eggs.

When the chicks are born, they immediately learn to share. After one chick has eaten a beakful of food from its mother, it moves to the end of the line until each of its siblings has had some. But as the chicks get older they forget this good quality!

After Jesus returned to heaven the disciples shared, too. The Bible says, *"Day after day, in the temple courts and from house to house, they never stopped teaching and proclaiming the good news that Jesus is the Christ."* It's great to share, especially the gospel story and the warmth of Jesus' love!

MISSION: Be kind to salespeople you meet. Give them a pamphlet, and tell them that God loves them.

219

Fun or Cruelty?

The little dachshund barked at a passerby. Then it circled around the tree at the end of its rope.

Suddenly a neighbor dog, running loose, rushed toward the dachshund. Then it veered off at the last second. Again and again the neighbor dog rushed toward the dachshund, turning aside just beyond the end of the little dog's rope. The dachschund went wild trying to defend its territory while the bigger dog panted happily.

Monkey One sat in the treetop with two bananas. Chattering, it held one banana out to Monkey Two. But as Monkey Two eagerly approached, Monkey One stayed ahead and just out of reach.

When Monkey Two paused, Monkey One held out the banana again, just to repeat the whole scene. Monkey Two finally gave up and, with its tail hanging down, went to another tree.

Gentle teasing, when everyone involved enjoys it, can be fun. It can make a person feel noticed and even special. But sometimes animals and humans take teasing too far, and someone gets hurt. It also hurts people when others laugh and poke fun at them when they make a mistake.

Solomon said, *"It is as sport to a fool to do mischief"* (KJV). In other words, foolish people make a game of other people's discomfort. If your goal is to be more like Jesus and to treat others as He treats you, you'll make sure your teasing is always kind.

TALK BACK: What instances of unkind teasing have you witnessed? What were the results?

Seventeen-year Cicada

Home: Eastern United States
Size: .75-1 inch

The cicada (sih-kay'-duh) beetle starts life as an egg. Its mother deposits the egg in a slit she cuts in a branch. A few weeks later the egg becomes a brownish nymph, dropping to the ground.

Using its strong front feet, it burrows into the dirt. There it locates tree roots and drills into them with its beak to drink the sap.

Seventeen years later the cicada, now a big brown beetle, comes out of its tree burrow. It climbs up a tree trunk to shed its old skin, uncovering crumpled wings. During the hours it takes the wings to plump up so the beetle can fly, the insect is totally helpless and may fall prey to hungry birds.

The male cicada makes a lot of noise. Using the sound-producing organs below his abdomen, he "rattles" in rhythm with other cicadas. His harsh call sounds like metal being scraped along the teeth of a stiff comb.

Some cicada species spend 13 years underground, others only two or three. Considered pests, they all eat vegetation. But though they exhibit the same habits, each species matures at its own rate.

People grow at different rates, too, both physically and spiritually. *"There is a time for everything,"* said Solomon. So take the time to grow all you can, and be patient with those who may need more time.

TALK BACK: Is there a church teaching that's been puzzling you? Who could help you figure it out?

221

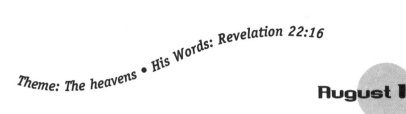

What Is a Star?

Home: Universe
Size: Variable

On a clear, moonless night away from light sources, you can see about 2,000 separate stars. And throughout the year different stars come into view. That's because as our earth revolves around the sun, we face a different direction during dark hours.

The 6,000 stars that we can easily see over a year's time are nearby neighbors. Well, they're nearby in universe terms. These stars, just like our earth, are traveling at rapid rates. But because space is so large, they appear to stay in the same position.

A star is actually a sun. Suns, which are composed mainly of hydrogen gas, produce their own light. Nuclear fusion (like hydrogen bombs blowing off) produces the light. Planets only reflect light that shines on them.

Stars range from one tenth the size of our sun to hundreds of times its size. Some stars always burn brightly, while others vary in brightness. Like our sun, stars produce great heat and light. Their light reaches across billions of miles to us as little beacons of God's love.

Another heavenly body affects our lives. It's spelled S-o-n. God's Son shines His love on us to guide us. In fact, He calls Himself *"the bright Morning Star."* You can always depend on the light He gives you.

MISSION: From the library check out a star book with good illustrations. Refer to it as we talk about constellations.

Milky Way

Home: Outer space
Size: 100,000 light-years across

It was midnight. Most of the airline passengers slept as I pressed my face to the window. Looking into the inky blackness, I searched for familiar constellations. And then I noticed a ragged band of light trailing across the sky. It was the Milky Way, more visible to me than ever before.

Suddenly our heavenly Father's greatness seemed even more real to me. Evolutionists believe that our galaxy "just happened." But I'm a creationist, and I believe that God put it here. With the psalmist I say, *"Praise him, sun and moon, praise him, all you shining stars."*

The Milky Way galaxy to which Earth belongs is about 100,000 light-years across and contains some 200 billion stars or suns. The light these suns produce reaches through the depths of space so that even your eyes can see the glow! If you could view this entire galaxy from its edge, it would look like a huge, bulging disk, with arms of light spiraling out like a pinwheel.

You probably can't begin to comprehend how large the universe is. But God, who created and cares for all this greatness, still has time for *you*. Isn't that amazing?

TRY IT: It's easiest to see the Milky Way during the summer. On a clear night find a dark place away from city lights. First look almost directly overhead, then let your gaze trail southward. Can you find its glow?

What's a Light-year, Anyway?

Long ago astronomers studied the night skies, wondering how they could measure distances from one object to another. You see, beyond our sun the next closest star to us is about 26 million *million* miles away.

Eventually they settled on calculating stellar distances by a measure they called a light-year. That's the distance light travels in one year. Light moves at 186,000 miles every second, or 5.88 trillion miles in a year. That's fast enough for a light beam to circle the earth seven times a second.

Our sun is close at 93 million miles away. Its light arrives in about eight minutes. To help visualize the distance between it and the next-closest star, Alpha Centauri, think of our sun as the tiny dot over an i. Alpha Centauri would be another dot of the same size a mile away!

Considering these distances, it boggles my mind that our prayers reach heaven quickly enough to be answered by God! They travel much faster than the speed of light, for He said, *"Before they call I will answer; while they are still speaking I will hear."* When you need God's help there's no place too far away for Him to hear you!

TRY IT: Calculate this one. Ellen G. White suggests that it will take us seven days to get from earth to heaven when Jesus comes for us.* If we travel only at the speed of light, how many miles away is heaven?

---

* *Early Writings,* p. 16.

August 4

Never the Back Side

Home: Milky Way Galaxy
Size: Diameter 2,160 miles

The moon is the only heavenly body that we can see details of with our naked eye. Whether fully or partially illuminated, the moon's features appear the same all the time.

But I've always had a question. The moon spins on its axis as it circles the earth. The earth also spins on its axis, once for each day/night time period. So if both bodies are spinning, why do we see the same side of the moon all the time?

The answer surprised me. The moon travels around the earth in a counterclockwise direction. It takes 27 days, seven hours, 43 minutes, and 11.5 seconds to do so. For each trip around the earth, the moon rotates on its axis one time. So since the moon spins once every time it orbits the earth, the same side of the moon is always facing earth.

When you don't understand something, don't give up. Ask questions. Check resources. Ask God to guide your thinking. This is even more important when it comes to spiritual subjects. The Bible says, *"Happy is the man who . . . gains understanding" (NKJV).*

TRY IT: Use oranges to represent the sun, moon, and earth. Place the "sun" on a table. Mark an X on the "moon." Move the "earth" around the "sun," rotating it rapidly. Move the "moon" around the "earth" as it travels around the "sun." Keep the X toward the "earth." See how it works?

225

What Is a Constellation?

In Bible times people often slept on their flat rooftops. Gazing at the sky, they did mental dot-to-dots with the bright stars they observed. They made up stories about the "pictures" they saw, and many of those stories became legends.

Stars that people grouped became known as constellations. Astronomers eventually learned that a constellation's stars are just far-flung suns that look like they belong together.

In the Northern Hemisphere people see different constellations from those they see in the Southern Hemisphere. But some constellations, such as Orion, are visible in both areas. At the equator people can see all the stars and constellations during the course of a year.

"God is the one who made the star groups Pleiades and Orion. He changes darkness into the morning light. And he changes the day into the dark night. . . . The Lord is his name" (ICB). God has given you the Bible to light your pathway. When you study only portions of it, you don't get the whole picture. But when you study it all, it's as if you're standing at the equator. Then you can more easily see everything you need in order to live a successful Christian life.

TRY IT: On a star chart find Polaris, the North Star, the Big Dipper, Cassiopeia, and Orion. Then go outside and try to locate them. After a week check them at the same hour. Have they moved to a different position? Why?

Why Earth?

Size: Equatorial circumference, 24,902.4 miles

Why did God create our home on earth? Planets such as Jupiter and Saturn are larger.

But a day on Jupiter lasts only 9.9 hours. Also, Jupiter spins so fast that at its equator it has problems holding on to its matter!

If God had put us on Venus, we'd need big-time air-conditioning. The heat climbs to 890 degrees Fahrenheit! Plus we'd be surrounded with thick smog.

On Mars the temperature varies between minus 225 degrees Fahrenheit to 60 degrees Fahrenheit. That's too cold for many plants to flourish, and there's no water.

God knew what He was doing. He placed us just far enough from the sun to allow good temperatures. He provided days long enough to grow our plants, and a world that doesn't fling us off! He put water here, and oxygen for us to breathe. This place was just right!

The Bible tells us that when He finished creation, *"God saw all that he had made, and it was very good. . . . Thus the heavens and the earth were completed in all their vast array."* I can just imagine God standing there with a great big smile on His face. And as He thought of what was to come, He thought of you. I think His smile got even bigger!

MISSION: What are the hottest and coldest places on earth? What things are necessary for humans to survive there?

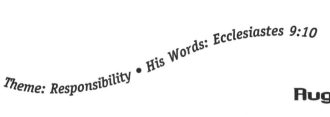

Earth Pig

Home: Ethiopia, Africa
Size: To 180 pounds

The aardvark looks as if it were made from spare parts of other animals. It has donkey ears, a long pig snout, a humped back covered with bristly gray hair, a sturdy tail, and sharp digging claws.

The aardvark digs a large underground sleeping burrow. If a wildcat, human, or other predator enters the burrow, the aardvark rapidly digs and pushes a wall of dirt between itself and the intruder. It can also use its claws and heavy tail in self-defense.

Aardvarks, also known as earth pigs, help control Africa's hordes of termites and ants. Active at night, they tear into the tall, concrete-hard termite nests. Then they poke their sticky foot-long tongues into the exposed passageways and slurp up the insects. Often they open the nests so carefully that they don't totally destroy them and can eat there again.

King Solomon said, *"Whatever your hand finds to do, do it with all your might."* It's important to do your best in all your responsibilities. Being careless in schoolwork or home duties causes problems. But managing your responsibilities carefully and completely, without reminders, leaves you with a feeling of satisfaction. It also causes others to trust you. And that's worth working for!

TALK BACK: In what areas do I want to do better work? What can help me reach these goals?

228

Those Hand-me-downs

Home: Seas of the world
Size: To 5 inches long

Maybe you have an older brother or sister who passes their outgrown clothes to you. Wearing hand-me-downs is a good way to recycle.

The hermit crab also wears "hand-me-downs." Its head and front legs have a tough covering, but its soft hind portions must be protected. So it finds an abandoned shell of another sea creature. Then it backs into the discarded shell and hangs on. When danger comes, the crab retreats completely into the shell, closing off the opening with its hard head.

As it keeps growing, the crab must change clothes again. So it hunts for a vacant shell that's larger and makes a quick switch. When it's out of its protective shell, it's in danger of being eaten by a predator.

Don't you think people spend too much time worrying about getting just the right look from their clothes? Though it's good to be clean and neat, it isn't what you wear that makes you a worthwhile, nice-to-know person. It's what's beneath the fabric. You. That includes your attitude, character, personality, and devotion to doing right.

Jesus said, *"Do not worry, saying, . . . 'What shall we wear?' . . . Your heavenly Father knows that you need them [clothes]. But seek first his kingdom . . . and all these things will be given to you as well."*

CONTACT: God, I know that when I accept Jesus, He covers me with His robe of righteousness. Help me to make wearing that special "hand-me-down" my goal in life.

229

One-Point Landing

Home: North America
Size: Wingspan to 50 inches

Red-tailed hawks are easy to recognize. In flight they spread their rusty-red tails and fingerlike feathers. They soar overhead, looking for mice or small rabbits. Baby hawks depend on their parents long after they've gotten their feathers, for they must be trained to hunt and be expert fliers.

One Sabbath while driving in the country, I surprised a pair of hawks perched on a fence. With them was their baby. Startled by my sudden appearance, the parents spread their wings and flew into the nearby woods, calling to the baby to follow. With a squawk, it wobbled into the air, then pumped furiously, careening toward the woods.

Gaining a little altitude, the baby bird headed toward the tree where its parents waited. Then it attempted a landing. Instead, it ran into the tree trunk with a whack and tumbled to the ground. Stunned, it waited before climbing up the trunk to its parents' side.

How do you feel when you fail at something? Do you give up? Or do you grit your teeth, pray a little prayer, and then try again? Everything you learn to do takes practice. Satan's best tool is discouragement, but you can remember David's words: *"Be strong and take heart, all you who hope in the Lord."*

MISSION: Memorize today's encouraging text for when you experience a temporary failure.

The Warty Old Warthog

Home: Africa, open grasslands
Size: 220 or more pounds

Warthogs are quite a sight. They get their name from two fleshy warts on each side of their face. Then they have nearly hairless skin and four upturned enamel-covered tusks. They use these tusks, which are lethal weapons, to fight off predators.

Warthogs wallow in mud to cool themselves, because they have no sweat glands. Small family groups called sounders consist of a couple females and their young. These groups stay together to protect the young.

They like abandoned aardvark dens for their homes. Adult warthogs enter their dens backward, keeping their heads toward the entrance for protection.

Warthogs have eyes set high on their head. That helps them watch for enemies while they kneel to eat vegetation. Their knees become heavily calloused from being on them so much, but the calluses provide needed protection.

Take a look at your knees. Are they calloused from kneeling? Psalms says, *"Come, let us bow down in worship, let us kneel before the Lord our Maker."*

Does this mean that you shouldn't pray unless you're kneeling? I don't think so. When you're in church or having your devotions, you should kneel in reverence. But there's never a time when you can't send a prayer to God. You can talk to Him while involved in an activity or while falling asleep in your bed. The most important things are to be reverent and to keep in close touch with Him.

CONTACT: Lord, help me to remember to talk to You often throughout the day.

Horsefly!

Home: Universal
Size: To 1 inch

How I love to dive into a river and float with the current to shore. But there's nothing that ruins my fun as much as being discovered by horseflies! Those pesky black buzzers bite both animals and humans, leaving a painful welt.

Horseflies live in moist areas and eat only liquids. Males feed on plant juices, but females must have animal blood before they can lay their eggs. As adults they live only a few weeks, so they must get those blood dinners in order to complete their life cycle. Once they find a victim, they bite into the flesh, then lap up the blood.

The female searches for a damp place, then lays a clump of 100 to 1,000 eggs. Soon after the larvae hatch they crawl into mud or beneath the water to feed. During droughts they wrap themselves in mud to keep from drying out, and can live for several months without eating. It's when they become adults that they get so pesty.

How do you deal with annoying things that spoil your fun? Experiencing problems without getting grouchy is an important skill to learn. The Bible says, *"A prudent man sees danger and takes refuge."* But what about when you can't hide from the trouble? You can learn to make the best of things and choose to be cheerful anyway.

MISSION: Happiness is a choice, so next time something goes wrong, choose to stay cheerful. See how your pleasant attitude helps you cope better.

The Sleepy Mouse

Home: Europe
Size: To 1 ounce before hibernation

The dormouse sleeps nearly half its life. Carefully weaving grass and bark together in the crook of a tree, it makes an enclosed nest that's snug and warm. Here it curls up and snoozes during the day.

At night it uses its padded feet to scamper along even the tiniest branch. With its hairy tail for balance and its mobile wrists and ankle joints, it's very surefooted as it hunts for tree flowers, nuts, and fruit.

When it's time to give birth, the female builds a larger nest. There she guards and suckles her babies for two months until they can care for themselves.

In winter the dormouse hibernates so soundly that it can be moved without waking it. While hibernating it lives off extra fat it put on in the summer. Because of its sound sleep it's vulnerable to attack by predators.

Though you don't hibernate, you need sleep too. Without enough rest your body and your brain don't work well. Isn't it wonderful to know that if you put your trust in God, you can sleep in peace? You can do this because He doesn't need sleep. The Bible says, *"He who watches over you will not slumber."* Aren't you glad that His eyes are always open?

TRY IT: Growing people need about 10 hours of sleep a night. For two weeks chart how much sleep you get. Is it enough?

233

Hoodoos

Banff National Park has an impressive river gorge. It's been formed over hundreds of years by water draining from the steep Rocky Mountains. The water has eroded away soft rocks and clay, leaving a canyon with some very strange sculptures called hoodoos.

These tall, upright sections of clay came about by water rushing around them and by wind and rain erosion. Now they stand looking like cloaked soldiers protecting their river.

Ancient residents believed that an evil spirit hid in each hoodoo. So superstitious people stayed far away from the river at night. Even when going for water during daylight, they moved past the hoodoos with great respect and a watchful eye!

You may smile at these beliefs, but many people know only superstition and fear. They haven't heard of their caring heavenly Father. When they learn the truth, they no longer need to fear the hoodoos in their lives. They find peace as they learn about their loving Maker.

When you sacrifice your money to help people teach those who live in superstition, you're a partner with God. Jesus said, *"Whatever you did for one of the least of these brothers of mine, you did for me."*

MISSION: Find a way to help a missionary on a regular basis. Maybe you can go without something you want and donate that money or find an after-school job. Pray that God will show you what to do, and then do it!

Hammerkop, the "Hammerhead"

Home: South Africa
Size: Wingspan to 3 feet

The hammerkop has reddish-brown feathers and black wading legs. Its long, broad bill points in one direction, and a thick crest of feathers pokes out behind the bird, giving its head the shape of a hammer.

Both mates work together to construct their nest, which takes them about six weeks to complete. They build their six-foot, dome-shaped nest in a tree or on a rocky ledge. One mate brings sticks and passes them into the entryway, while the other works inside. Later they line the nest with mud and grass. In order to protect their chicks, they make a side entry, narrow tunnels, and foot-thick walls. When finished the nest can support the weight of a human!

Besides being an expert builder, the hammerkop is an announcer. When it's about to rain, this bird calls out a warning with its shrill, harsh voice, alerting other birds to take cover.

Noah was also a builder and an announcer. As he constructed the ark, he warned of the coming rains and preached God's plan for saving people from the Flood. But people jeered and mocked him. Still, he stayed true to his purpose. Finally God said, *"Go into the ark, you and your whole family, because I have found you righteous in this generation."*

Wouldn't you like to be as steadfast as Noah?

CONTACT: Father, please give me courage to stand for the right and tell the truth about You, even if others make fun of me.

235

Mountain Viscacha

Home: Andes Mountains
Size: 2-6 pounds

Mountain viscachas look like rabbits wearing squirrels' tails. They live in elevations of up to 20,000 feet.

They spend their mornings sunbathing on rocks. While doing so, they groom themselves by combing their fur with the stiff hairs on the soles of their feet. In the afternoon they graze on lichen, moss, and coarse grass, chewing each tough mouthful carefully.

A guard viscacha watches for predators. This guard sounds an alarm if it spots danger. Then the quick-moving viscachas scramble into their dens in the rocks or burrow into the ground.

Viscachas have luxurious coats. Trapping body heat between their hairs, they stay insulated and warm. If they get too warm, they merely raise their hair to let some of the heat escape.

You can learn something from viscachas. Grooming your mind by memorizing Bible verses can protect you from Satan's lies. Bible promises also provide you with a safety net, insulating you against discouragement. David said, *"I have hidden your word in my heart that I might not sin against you."*

MISSION: Work on your spiritual insulation. Each week learn several verses that will help you be obedient to God, that promise you God's physical protection, and that describe how to receive eternal life.

The Mystery of the Ditch

Bruce, my father-in-law's huge Airedale/mastiff, had a way of annoying cats. If he chased a cat and it swatted at him, Bruce would simply turn around and sit on the creature.

One of Bruce's habits annoyed more than cats. You see, a small ditch ran through town. Several days a week water from a canal flowed through this ditch so people could water their gardens.

But then one day only a trickle of liquid came through the ditch toward the far end of town. Homeowners began to complain about selfish neighbors using it all. And then they found out what was really happening.

Bruce had gotten hot too—until he discovered the miracle of the ditch. He enjoyed lying in it, blocking it with his big body, and letting water flow over his back to keep him cool. Meanwhile, the dammed water flooded into the street.

How do you react when you've innocently done something, then learn that it hurt someone else? Do you shrug your shoulders and forget about it? Or do you apologize and see what you can do to repair the damage?

Jesus said that when *"you offer your gift to God . . . , and you remember that your brother has something against you, leave your gift. . . . Go and make peace with him"* (ICB). In other words, make things right. If your heart is filled with Jesus' love, you'll want to do just that.

MISSION: Is there someone you need to make things right with? Don't delay! Do it today!

Feral Hogs

Home: Cumberland Island National Seashore, Georgia

Cumberland Island, a protected wildlife area, is home to feral hogs. Feral animals are wild descendants of previously domesticated animals. Spanish settlers brought the hogs to the island in the 1560s. When they moved away, they set the hogs free. These roving animals have caused so much destruction that land management personnel have tried to move them off the island.

While visiting the island I enjoyed looking at the unique landscapes, plants, animals, and birds. I hoped to see some of the remaining feral hogs, but they avoid humans. So I never saw them, though I did see evidence of their presence.

Frequently I found the ground torn up where hogs had rooted for tender plant roots. This destroys root systems that hold the earth in place during heavy winds. Feral hogs also roam the beaches and dig up loggerhead turtle nests. Now endangered, loggerheads lay eggs only every three years. So when a nest is ruined, three years' worth of babies are killed.

Humans tend to be destructive to nature, too. Some chase wild animals, pick and discard wildflowers, and carelessly destroy creatures' burrows. By doing these things they make life harder for animals by ruining their habitat or food source.

God made the wild creatures as a blessing. The Bible says, *"Good people take care of their animals, but even the kindest acts of the wicked are cruel"* (NCV).

MISSION: Learn of nature conservation groups in your area and visit one. Make a nature protection plan of your own.

Barred Owl

Home: Woodlands, river and swamp areas
Size: Length to 21 inches

A pair of barred owls live in the woods in our neighborhood. Like other owls, they're secretive and hunt at night. With their eyes toward the front of their heads, owls have binocular vision. Yet when it's too dark to see their prey, their acute hearing picks up even the smallest rustling of a mouse in the foliage.

With specialized feathers that muffle the sound of their movements, they can swoop down on a creature before it even knows they're around. Grasping their meal in their talons, they take it to their roost to devour. Owls help control the rodent population.

On early-morning walks I sometimes hear one of the owls calling in the darkness to its mate. The rhythm of the call is much like a rooster's crow: *Whoo—whoo————who-WHOOOOooooo*. When the owl's in the far woods, I have to make listening for it my whole focus, because its hoot isn't frequent or very loud. But waiting for its call is worth it.

You need to do the same thing when you hear God calling you. The Bible says to *"hear the word of the Lord."* If you stop what you're doing and give Him your full attention, you'll be able to understand what He's trying to tell you.

TRY IT: Go outside at night and make a list of the sounds you hear. What faint sounds do you notice that you might not have if you weren't paying attention?

Gullible Gulper

Size: To 8 feet tall

While visiting a wild-animal park I watched a male ostrich approach my car. He lowered his head and looked at me through the side window. Fluttering his beautiful long eyelashes, he put his broad beak up against the closed window. In greeting, I touched the glass.

Immediately he opened his beak, closed his eyes, and gulped, as though I'd given him something to eat! I put my fingers on the glass again. Repeatedly he opened his beak and gulped down "nothings." I decided he must be gullible.

Ostriches normally eat vegetation and insects. But a single ostrich was known to have eaten a roll of film, three gloves, a comb, a bicycle valve, a handkerchief, a pencil, a piece of rope, part of a gold necklace, several coins, and a clock! What wasn't meant as food he took for food!

Unfortunately, some people are just as gullible. They believe anything they're told, not using their abilities to separate truth from lies. Eventually they may find themselves in trouble and looking very foolish!

Christ said, *"Be careful that no one fools you" (ICB)*. Only you can control what you allow into your mind. While asking God's direction, carefully examine every idea and activity presented as good. Make sure you're not gullible in what you "swallow."

TALK BACK: What guidelines can I set up for myself to make sure I believe only truth?

How the Flounder Changes

Home: Salt and fresh waters
Size: To 7 pounds

The mother flounder lays her eggs underwater. Then the eggs bob to the ocean surface. Once hatched, the babies feed on small surface organisms. While growing they move toward shallow coastal waters.

Then something remarkable happens to each baby flounder! Though the rest of its body remains basically the same, one of its eyes begins to shift until both are on the same side of its head! Finally, the flounder swims on its side, eye-side up.

By vibrating its big, flat body it stirs up sand on the ocean floor, then sinks into it. As the sand settles it partially buries the flounder, hiding it from bottom-dwelling mollusks it plans to hunt. This amazing fish can also change color to match the sand!

When Jesus takes you to heaven, you'll also change. But your change will happen in an instant. The Bible says, *"We will all be changed—in a flash, in the twinkling of an eye, at the last trumpet."*

Your desire to sin will end. Physical or mental challenges will disappear. So will diseases. You won't need braces or hospitals or cemeteries. Won't it be fun to see the joy on Jesus' face when He makes you into a perfect creature?

TALK BACK: When He comes, why won't it take long for Jesus to change your body? In what ways can He help you change right now?

The Dreaded Earwig

Home: Worldwide, excluding polar areas
Size: To .5 inch

Have you ever heard that earwigs like to crawl into human ears to lay their eggs or hide? It's not true! But earwigs do look scary, with their sharp pincers out behind. They use these to hold their prey and also to unfold their delicate wings from beneath their wing covers.

Earwigs have slender antennae that help them search for food and hiding places. Active at night, they live in dark crevices or under dead logs or garden litter, where it's cool and protected.

Unlike many insects, the female earwig is an attentive parent. After laying 20-50 pale eggs, she guards them from predators. She also licks and turns them to remove bacteria and mold.

Once hatched, the nymphs look like a smaller and paler version of their parents. The mother feeds her nymphs for about 10 days, until they can forage for themselves. But family groups often stay together until the end of the summer.

God has provided animal parents with the instinct to care for their young. He's done the same for human parents. Though you may not always appreciate your parents' instructions, that's the job God gave them.

He also said to children, *"Honor your father and your mother, so that you may live long in the land the Lord your God is giving you."* Notice that this commandment comes with a promise!

MISSION: Even when you don't feel like it, resolve to follow God's plan by obeying your parents.

242

Alpine Marmot

Home: Alps
Size: 8-12 pounds

Alpine marmots live in the Alps on steep slopes above the tree line. With their families, these rodents dig spacious burrows that have many entrances, tunnels, rooms, and even bathrooms!

They hibernate during the winter. But as soon as the snow melts, they scurry around outside, collecting and drying grass for their burrows. Clever in building, they also line their tunnels with stones to improve drainage.

These marmots may live in ground so hard that it's difficult to break it with a pick. Yet their sharp digging claws can burrow through it in a hurry. If a rock gets in their way and they can't remove it with their claws, they don't give up. They keep at it until they've loosened the rock with their teeth!

Maybe there are things you wish you could do better, such as hit a ball farther or swim across the pool underwater. Maybe you want to create an impressive project for the science fair or learn to play the violin. Maybe you want to be a doctor and need an A in math.

Paul said, *"In all the work you are doing, work the best you can" (ICB)*. Don't give up! Dig in, and keep working on it! If you have good and reasonable goals, God will help you reach them.

CONTACT: God, help me not to give up when things are hard, but with Your help to do my best.

Growing Down

Home: South America
Size: Adult, to 3 inches

Most frogs start as little tadpoles that hatched from eggs. They quickly develop into tiny frogs that eat voraciously and grow larger. But the paradoxical frog is different.

After hatching, it immediately feeds on plant matter (though its mother eats water creatures). And while still a tadpole the baby grows to approximately 10 inches long! It looks like a huge fish beside its three-inch mother.

Then, after reaching this length, the baby grows legs and loses its tail. When it's finally full-grown it's only one-third the size it was when it was a baby!

Adult paradoxical frogs don't leave the water to hunt food. Instead, they use their long fingers to comb through the mud at the bottom of the pool and grasp insects and other water creatures. At rest, they float among surface water plants, with only their eyes and nostrils above water. Their croak sounds like a pig's grunt!

You can't always judge someone by how they look or behave. Though actions often speak louder than words, there's much more to a person than what shows on the surface. Inside are buried needs, hopes, and feelings. Jesus said, *"Do not judge according to appearance, but judge with righteous judgment" (NASB)*. That means we should use God's love as our guide when drawing conclusions about others.

TALK BACK: What makes it hard to make accurate judgments about why someone acts a certain way?

244

The Granddaddy Pine

A large, healthy-looking pine tree had fallen across the road and been cut away. I tried to count the rings on its trunk. Narrow rings showed dry years, and wide ones revealed years with plenty of rain. Pitch, the tree's blood, had dribbled down the cut and hardened into two-inch strands.

Looking at the fallen tree made me sad, but then I realized that it has new possibilities. As it decays, grubs will burrow into its bark. Birds will feast on those grubs. Small animals will make their homes in the shelter of the log. Needles and wood will decompose to nourish the soil. Thick mosses will grow on the tree's sides, creating plant communities that will supply food for other creatures.

You know, the results of sin are awful. Sin kills plants, animals, and people, leaving a painful emptiness. Yet God has promised, *"You will be sad, but your sadness will become joy"* *(NCV)*. Though sin must run its course now, God is strong enough to take bad circumstances and bring something good out of them.

When things go wrong it hurts. But you can trust God. He loves you and will bring you blessings, even from your hardest experiences.

TRY IT: Help nature. Plant a mature tree seed in a small pot. Water it and cover it with plastic wrap. Then keep it barely moist until it sprouts in a couple months. Remove the plastic wrap and keep it moist. Transplant it outside in the spring.

The Bird That Spits

Home: Cool coastal areas
Size: Gull-sized

Northern fulmars look like gulls, except they have large nostril tubes. Nesting in open areas, the fulmar chicks become easy prey for animals and other seabirds.

Yet these birds have a good defense. When threatened, fulmars make a coughing sound, then lunge toward the intruder, spraying it with a yellowish, oily liquid from their stomachs. Any predator within five feet gets covered with a stinking mess that clings to its feathers or fur and causes matting.

Actually, everything about fulmars smells awful, even their eggs. But maybe that's necessary, because the parents must leave the chicks for long periods of time to hunt for fish. Baby fulmars even spit at their parents until they recognize them, but the liquid doesn't seem to affect fulmar feathers.

Do you know someone who spits out hateful or impure words when they're angry? Maybe they're upset with their parents, or they think the umpire made a wrong call. Or maybe they're just trying to shock others.

Paul said, *"The tongue also is a fire. . . . It corrupts the whole person, sets the whole course of his life on fire."* Once spoken, unkind or impure words can never be unsaid. Even if you apologize, those words could shadow the rest of your life. So pray that God will help you have control over the words you use, for they can destroy more than a few feathers.

TALK BACK: If someone calls you a name or lies about you, what's the best way to respond?

246

Where Did Your Pet Come From?

Some people buy unusual pets, such as primates or exotic birds. Often, though, these animals are captured in a cruel way.

For instance, to catch a baby chimp, the mother—and often the whole family—is killed. And because of stress and poor care, a high percentage of baby chimps die before they reach the pet shop.

Colorful wild birds suffer, too. Trappers coat branches with a sticky substance so the birds can't fly away after landing. Once captured, they often have their beaks taped shut and their wings taped to their bodies. Next they're stuffed into cages for long plane or boat journeys. Many of them die on the way. Others die later because they simply can't adjust to confined surroundings.

Even animals that survive capture and transport have problems later. For instance, when pet alligators grow too big for the bathtub, their owners sometimes release them in places where they can't survive. Or tropical fish get released into lakes and die.

The Bible says, *"Do not muzzle an ox while it is treading out the grain."* That means to treat animals with kindness. Remember, you're a caretaker of God's creatures.

Before buying a pet make sure it was bred and born commercially and wasn't captured in the wild. God made animals for you to enjoy, and they should have enjoyment, too.

MISSION: Check pet shops in your area. If they buy captured animals, tell them what you've learned above.

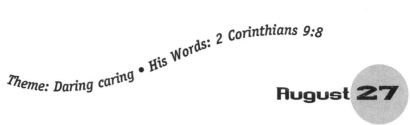
Super Sniffer

Dogs have a keener sense of smell than humans do. In fact, their ability to smell so well has earned some of them special jobs. For instance, basset hounds, bloodhounds, retrievers, and spaniels have been bred as hunting dogs. They might even hunt for money!

Some people, hoping to get rich, travel to foreign countries to buy illegal drugs. They plan to sell them back home for a profit. They usually carry large amounts of cash in their suitcases so their purchases can't be traced.

But Bodie, a springer spaniel, has been trained to recognize the odors of many kinds of currency. At Heathrow airport in Britain, he wanders through the luggage area sniffing the suitcases about to be put on a plane. When he smells a lot of cash, he barks and scratches at the offending bag. Officials can then learn whom the bag belongs to and make an arrest, when appropriate.

You're at an age when you're discovering your talents and abilities. As your capabilities develop, you'll be able to do some things especially well, because God has blessed you. The Bible says, *"God can give you more blessings than you need. . . . You will have enough to give to every good work"* (ICB).

Won't you stop to remember who gave you those talents? Won't you use them wisely and dedicate them to Him?

TALK BACK: How can you discover what your talents and abilities are? Which ones would you like to develop?

The Prophet Worm

Some people think woolly worms are prophets. They insist that these fuzzy little caterpillars predict how hard the coming winter will be.

A woolly worm has 13 bands of hair across its back—one for each week of winter. These bands may be black, brown, or orange.

People believe that if a band is black, it means very cold weather that week. Brown means cold weather. And orange means mild weather. Starting from the front of the worm and working toward its back end, they try to see which weeks will be frigid and which weeks will be mild.

Many people claim to be prophets, too. They foretell fortunes and events. People flock to them to see what tomorrow will bring. But their record of failed prophecies speaks the truth about their genuineness.

In Bible times God sent prophets to warn about future events. How did they know what was about to happen? The Bible says, *"For prophecy never had its origin in the will of man, but men spoke from God as they were carried along by the Holy Spirit."*

God also spoke to Ellen White through visions, giving her messages that help people today. You can know she was a true prophet by the many things she wrote that have been proven to be correct.

MISSION: Look up what Ellen White said about tobacco when popular doctors were prescribing it for health purposes. Then check what medical research has since found to be the truth.

The Tipsy Bird

Home: North America, Europe, Asia
Size: To 8 inches long

The cedar waxwing is a velvety-looking brown bird with yellow-tipped tail feathers and a pale yellow breast. On top of its head sits a feather crest that it can raise or lower. It also looks as if it's wearing a little black mask.

Not as large as robins, waxwings travel in flocks. They nest in trees late in the summer, building nests of grass, leaves, bark, and mud. There they rear three to five chicks. They don't really sing, but whistle softly.

Cedar waxwings are active and have big appetites. Though they eat fruit and insects, their favorite food is berries. Upon discovering a berry bush, it doesn't take a flock long to strip it clean.

Occasionally they find overripe berries that have fermented. They gobble them down anyway, and it makes them tipsy. Then they flop around on the ground until they sober up enough to get into the trees again. During this time predators can easily catch them.

Though the poor birds don't know better, humans have reasoning abilities. You can figure out that drinking alcoholic beverages makes people drunk. It causes many accidents in which people lose their lives. And some people who tried alcohol out of curiosity or to "fit in" became alcoholics. Maybe that's why God impressed Solomon to write, *"Wine is a mocker and beer a brawler; whoever is led astray by them is not wise."*

MISSION: Visit an area where drunk people congregate. Watch for a while. What do you see?

Those Glowing Pulsars

A pulsar is a small star the size of a city. It contains more material than the sun does. Spinning very fast, a pulsar flings out light beams and radio waves that travel thousands of light-years to reach the earth.

Containing lots of energy, a pulsar appears to blink, or pulse. The pulsations, or electromagnetic waves, are so regular that they're used to set atomic clocks, the most accurate timepieces. These waves also carry sounds, which can't be heard unless decoded by a receiver.

Like a pulsar, you transmit your own kind of waves. They affect everyone who comes in contact with you. Do your "transmissions" tell people that you love God? Do they help others see how loving and kind He is? Do they make them want to learn more about Him?

As you demonstrate to those around you what God is like, hopefully they'll say, as the psalmist did, *"O Lord, our Lord, how majestic is your name in all the earth!"* Hopefully they'll accept Him as their God, too.

TRY IT: Take a friend and two small flashlights to a dark street or field. Walk away from each other, then blink—or pulsate—the flashlights. How far apart must you get before you can no longer see each other's light flashing?

251

Two Miracles

Uadim Boutov grew up in Russia. Raised a Communist, he was taught that belief in God is foolishness. In fact, talking, reading, or listening to anything about God was considered a crime to be severely punished. The government even scrambled the signals of Christian radio programs with other radio signals.

Then one day Vadim and a friend found an old radio in the trash. Radios were expensive, so they tried to fix it. Miraculously, it crackled to life. That's when they heard the story of Jesus and His love for them—another miracle. Their hearts filled with joy, for they knew they'd found truth!

Unfortunately, that radio never worked again. Yet Vadim had heard enough to keep him searching for God until he found Him. Today he's a Seventh-day Adventist evangelist.

Radio broadcasters use transmitters to produce electromagnetic waves. Some waves travel only in a straight line. That's why you lose a signal when driving far away. Other waves bounce off the ionosphere, layers in the earth's atmosphere that conduct electricity. They deflect the signal to another spot on earth.

Jesus said, *"This gospel of the kingdom will be preached in the whole world as a testimony to all nations."* When you can't go to faraway lands yourself, radio waves can go for you, spreading God's precious gospel to those who long for truth.

TALK BACK: How can you help spread the gospel right now?

"I Don't Want It; You Can't Have It"

Home: Eastern North America
Size: To 3.5 inches

Ruby-throated hummingbirds are among the smallest birds. Glossy green with whitish undersides, they dart around, chittering at each other as their wings whir. Often they pause in midair to poke their needlelike beaks into flowers for quick sips of nectar. They can hover like an insect and can even fly backward!

The female hummingbird weaves two-inch nests from plant down held together with spider silk. There she incubates two pea-sized white eggs, caring for the chicks until they're grown.

During the spring and fall my hummingbird feeders stay busy, but often no bird gets much to drink. You see, delightful as hummingbirds are, they're selfish!

Even when they're not hungry themselves, the males chase each other away! Flashing their red throat patches, they rise like tiny helicopters, warning each other to stay away. Beak to beak, they battle as if they were enemies.

Selfishness isn't an attractive quality. Some people don't want their outgrown clothes, but they're too possessive to share them with others. Instead they throw them in the trash!

King Solomon talked about sharing when he said, *"If your enemy is hungry, give him food to eat; if he is thirsty, give him water to drink."* Now, that's the spirit of unselfishness, a quality Christians will try to develop as they grow closer to God.

MISSION: Volunteer to help an elderly person who lives nearby.

Amazing Journey

Home: Eastern North America
Size: Without their feathers, bumblebee-sized

Ruby-throated hummingbirds need so many calories to keep warm that they must eat about every 10 minutes! Their wings beat 50 to 80 times a second, which is at least 3,000 beats a minute! They can fly about 27 miles an hour.

During the day they consume three fourths of their body weight in nectar and tiny insects they find in flowers. But when it's cold and flowers don't bloom, how do they find food? Some migrate across the Gulf of Mexico to Central America, traveling over more than 500 miles of open water.

Once they start their flight over the Gulf, there's no place to rest or eat. So they must store up plenty of fat ahead of time to survive such a journey. Their God-given instinct tells them when and where they can supply their physical needs. If they ignore this instinct, they'll never make the journey and will die.

David said of God, *"Your hands made me and formed me; give me understanding to learn your commands."* David knew that God created humans with the ability to choose whether or not to follow His directions. Through the Bible and by the Holy Spirit, God will guide you. Like the little ruby-throated hummingbirds, you can be safe in Him.

TRY IT: Using the information above, figure out how many hours ruby-throated hummingbirds take to cross the Gulf. How many wingbeats must they make during that time?

254

Click Beetle

Home: Eastern North America
Size: To 2 inches

Remember how you needed help when learning to ride a bike? You wobbled, had trouble with turns, and fell off. But did you quit trying? Certainly not! Like a click beetle, you tried until you succeeded.

On its back the click beetle has two huge spots. These spots, which look like eyes staring at you, make predators think the insect is too big to swallow. But if a predator still tries to attack, the salt-and-pepper-colored beetle drops to the ground and plays dead.

If the beetle falls onto its back, it waits until the danger is gone and then does a back bend. With a loud *click* it snaps straight again, and the force pops it into the air! It will continue doing this until it lands on its feet and can safely scurry away.

Often you must learn to do new things. When you have a difficult time and even goof up, you may feel discouraged. But in order to succeed in life you must be willing to try, experience failure, and then try again until you get it right.

Paul said, *"Let us not become weary in doing good, for at the proper time we will reap a harvest."* Ask God to help you keep your eyes on your goal and succeed.

MISSION: Name something that's hard for you to do. Next time it causes you difficulty, tell yourself, "I can do all things through Christ, because he gives me strength" (NCV). Then, with God's help, keep trying.

The Mighty Midget

Home: Northern Hemisphere
Size: 8-11 inches long

The least weasel is small but ferocious. It has a long, low body with reddish brown fur on top and white underneath. Very flexible, it can enter and follow narrow mouse tunnels.

This lightweight animal prefers to hunt mice, but it also eats songbirds and their eggs, rabbits, squirrels, moles, and even chickens. Though it weighs less than a small banana, it will attack animals many times its size—and win the battle.

The least weasel marks its territory with a skunklike scent. Then, if the rodent supply is sufficient, it mates in the springtime. The mother teaches her babies to hunt, and within 12 weeks they're on their own.

Sin has made many animals predators, but weasels do something that bothers me a lot. They don't kill only what they need for food but slaughter entire nests of creatures, continuing until each animal is dead.

It reminds me of people who pick on others, tormenting them until a fight occurs or the victim runs away in tears. These "people predators" make themselves feel powerful by abusing others.

The Bible says, *"Whatever you do, whether in word or deed, do it all in the name of the Lord Jesus."* That means not scorning. Not picking on others. Being kind to those around you. So think twice before you tease. Don't be a weasel!

TALK BACK: What's your responsibility if you see someone picking on someone else? Should you mind your own business, or should you interfere?

The Mighty Zorilla

Home: Africa
Size: 2-3 pounds

The zorilla resembles its relative, the American striped skunk. Bold black and white stripes run the length of its body to warn predators away. But if an enemy pursues it anyway, the zorilla does a handstand and squirts strong-smelling liquid at the enemy's eyes. This temporarily blinds the pursuer, allowing the zorilla to escape.

Zorillas are carnivorous and eat almost any creature they can catch, even following it into its burrow. They sometimes catch chickens, but farmers usually tolerate zorillas because they help control rodent populations.

When zorillas aren't lucky hunting, they eat other animals' kill. One zorilla even kept a group of lions away from the zebra they'd killed! Though it was no match in size to the lions, the zorilla threatened to spray them. So the lions stayed away until it had eaten its fill and left. Using ingenuity, the zorilla accomplished its mission.

Do you sometimes give up if a task you're supposed to complete looks too difficult? Remember the ingenuity Gideon and his few soldiers showed when they had to fight a whole city by themselves. *"For the Lord and for Gideon,"* they shouted as they blew their trumpets and carried candles in pitchers.

They surrounded the enemy, who thought a large army had encircled them. God helped them finish their task. *"For the Lord"* can also become your slogan as, with God's help, you accomplish the seemingly impossible.

CONTACT: God, thank You for helping me to not give up when things look too hard.

Four-legged Baby-sitter

Two-year-old Charlie Grubbs lived with his parents in a cabin in the woods. One winter his mother accidentally locked herself out of the house. As she peered through the window, she became very worried. Charlie, fascinated by the big wood-burning stove, always tried to go near it.

Sure enough, when Charlie saw his mother outside, he headed for the stove. Just then Barney, the family dog, raced across the room. He grabbed Charlie's seat and pulled him backward. Each time Charlie headed for the stove, Barney pulled him away. Frustrated, Charlie began to bawl.

Praying that Barney would keep Charlie safe, Mrs. Grubbs ran to a neighbor's home. She phoned her husband, asking him to bring a house key. Then she returned to her house.

Through the window she saw Barney panting hard as he lay between the hot stove and Charlie. Even though he was exhausted, Barney didn't go "off duty" until Mrs. Grubbs got back inside.

Was Barney a hero? I think so. He did what was necessary to keep Charlie from being burned, even though it wasn't comfortable or convenient.

One time Jesus told a story about some servants who did their best. Their master said, *"You have been faithful with a few things; I will put you in charge of many things."* As you do your best for God's sake, He'll give you chances to do even greater things.

TRY IT: Do something special for someone this week. If they find out you did it, it doesn't count!

258

Electric Eel

Home: Amazon basin
Size: To 100 pounds and 8 feet long

The electric eel is an elongated fish with "shocking" abilities. Its long tail contains electricity-producing organs that help it protect itself and locate and catch food. These electrical plates can produce currents of up to 500 volts, enough to stun a very large animal!

The electric eel has one long fin that runs the length of its underside. It uses this fin to propel itself. On each side of its head sit electric sensors that alert it when fish approach. The eel then sends out intermittent electric shocks that travel through the water and stun the creature.

But if the eel sends too many shocks in a short time, its "battery" wears down. Then it's left defenseless until it recharges.

Electric eels have helped scientists in developing ways to revive and regulate the human heart. For instance, medical personnel sometimes give shocks to a person's chest, which causes their heart to contract and may restart it. Pacemakers are another way to regulate heartbeats.

Your spiritual batteries also go dead if you don't regularly recharge them. You can do this by reading devotional books and Christian stories. But you also need to spend time alone with God, reading His Word and talking to Him. No one else can do that for you.

The Bible explains, *"It is God who arms me with strength and makes my way perfect."* He will give your spiritual batteries a boost each day, if you let Him.

MISSION: Spend private time with God morning and evening.

259

Sensitive Mimosa

Home: Warm climates
Size: Shrub to tree size

The mimosa tree belongs to the legume family. (That means it's related to the peas on your plate.) Its delicate leaves grow in pairs along slender twigs. It also produces pretty yellow or pink flowers and later long pealike pods.

Some mimosa varieties are sensitive to touch. So if a locust or other insect lands on the leaves, they quickly fold together. Then the twig holding the leaves droops, as though it suddenly died. This protects the tree from being eaten by predators.

Soon the leaves reopen, only to close if touched again. But if the same leaves are touched repeatedly, they lose their sensitivity and eventually stay open. Then insects can eat them up.

This is similar to what happens to you when you continue doing something you know you shouldn't. At first your conscience bothers you, but gradually you become less and less sensitive to it. Eventually you no longer realize that you're going against God's will. Without the help of a wide-awake conscience you can get into real trouble.

Through Ezekiel God told His people, *"Change your hearts. Stop all your sinning. Then sin will not bring your ruin" (ICB).* He knew that if people continued tampering with sin, doing God's will would eventually not matter to them and they'd forget Him altogether. Don't let that happen to you!

TRY IT: With one finger lightly touch the top of your hand. Now continue to touch the same place lightly. How long does it take before you hardly feel it?

260

The Mothball Termite

Have you ever had moths or carpet beetles chew fibers in your wool clothes and leave a hole? That's why people use mothballs, which are made of napthalene. This strong-smelling chemical is sugary-white and marble-shaped.

One insect, the Formosan subterranean termite, actually produces its own naphthalene! This destructive termite, which arrived in the United States in a cargo shipment, is native to eastern Asia. But it's spreading northward in North America.

It chews up wood, mixes the wood with soil and napthalene, then plasters the concoction along its tunnels. If the termite takes too long to complete the job, ants or various fungi will enter its home and destroy it. So the termite must do careful work in order to protect its future.

Are you willing to do careful work in order to protect your future? Do you do your homework on time? Do you complete your tasks diligently? And do you remember to ask God's guidance in all your decisions? The Bible says, *"Those who work hard make a profit, but those who only talk will be poor"* (NCV).

The same is true in your spiritual life. You need to establish safeguards to keep you going the way God wants you to.

TRY IT: Find a fallen tree. Look for insect holes and identify what insect made them. What can you learn from how insects protect themselves and their homes from intruders?

261

The Rock That Isn't Really

Home: New Mexico

Long ago two huge volcanoes erupted in New Mexico. Rock and earth blew skyward and burned up, creating volcanic ash. After the ash settled it hardened into tuff, a soft rocklike material.

As creeks and rivers washed over the tuff, it eroded, creating deep canyons and high tuff cliffs. These are now part of Bandelier National Monument, where you can see ancient cliff dwellings built by early Indians.

Living in the desert, these Indians needed shelter from the hot summer sun and the biting winter cold. They also needed a place of refuge from enemies. So they dug into the soft cliffs, scooping out rooms. Inside they built fireplaces for cooking and keeping warm. There they spread their sleeping blankets and stored their food.

They made their homes in south-facing cliffs so the afternoon sun could warm them during cold weather. When wind and rain caused erosion, they repaired the walls with mud. So they stayed safe and dry.

Wisely these ancient people built in the rock. And you can build on an even stronger Rock. Just pray, *"In you, O Lord, I have taken refuge. . . . Since you are my rock and my fortress, for the sake of your name lead and guide me."* Then give your heart to Jesus and determine to do as He wishes. That's building on the Rock!

TRY IT: Trickle water over both a dirt clod and a rock. What happens in each case?

262

Woodpecker Finch

Home: Galápagos Islands
Size: 4-6 inches

The woodpecker finch lives in the Galápagos Islands off the coast of Costa Rica. These volcanic islands get very little rain.

During times of drought finches don't breed, because there wouldn't be enough food to feed their chicks. Still, they like to be prepared, so the male builds several display nests using bark, grass, and twigs. Each nest has a side entry and a roof that provides shade.

Once rain falls, the female chooses a nest, lays her eggs, and stays on them until they hatch. The male brings her food. After the babies hatch, both parents hunt for food.

These busy brown birds eat insects and grubs that live in holes or crevices in branches. If they can't reach the grubs, they don't give up. They get creative, locating a cactus spine or a thin twig. Grasping it with their beaks, they use it to pry the grubs out!

Solomon said, *"Idle people will go hungry"* (ICB). That means you must be willing to work for what you eat. And this principle applies to more than food.

For instance, you may know someone who plays a musical instrument skillfully. Did she just pick up that instrument and automatically know how to play it? More likely it took consistent practice and determination. With anything you want or need to do well, you must work hard. If you don't give up, eventually it will become easier.

TALK BACK: What would you like to do better? How can you accomplish it?

263

The Old Hen

During my teens our neighbors had a small flock of chickens. I enjoyed feeding them over the back fence. As I held up grapes, their favorite food, they'd compete with each other by jumping to pluck them from the bunches.

I knew each of the chickens by name and personality. Grumpy pouted in the corner if she didn't get any grapes. Lady waited patiently, accepting what she got. Feisty chased the others, even when she was full. Fidget nervously picked at herself and wouldn't sit on her eggs. Then there was "Old Mother." She cared for her own eggs and those of other chickens, too.

I heard a story about an old farm hen that had new chicks. At dusk she clucked them into the coop, then tucked them beneath her wings. During the night a weasel squeezed into the henhouse and attacked her. Instead of getting away she sat absolutely still, hiding her babies. She chose to die while protecting them rather than save herself.

Jesus could have come down from the cross, but He loved you too much to let you bear the everlasting punishment for your sins. Even though people mocked Him, saying, *"He saved others, . . . but he can't save himself!"* He held fast, choosing to save you rather than Himself.

Can't you see how important you are to Him?

MISSION: Tonight, while falling asleep, visualize Jesus dying on the cross for you. Ask Him to help you accept His gift of salvation.

Old Foghorn

Home: Most countries
Size: To 440 pounds

One moonless night in Britain my family and I camped on a hillside. After we'd been asleep for about an hour, we heard sheep bleating in the distance. Before long they surrounded our camper.

Though we couldn't see well, we realized that a flock of mothers and babies had joined us. I'd thought that all sheep sound alike, but I discovered that each sheep has a unique voice!

One sheep that I nicknamed "Foghorn" kept getting separated from her lamb. She'd call to it from one side of our camper, her grunting, raspy voice puncturing our sleep. The lamb would answer, bleating pitifully as it tried to find her. Soon we'd hear her on the opposite side of the camper calling again. But by then the lamb had moved, too.

All night the ewes "talked" to their lambs, and it seemed that the babies recognized their mother's voice. In the morning we watched Foghorn nurse her lamb, but when another lamb approached, she butted the intruder away!

Do you recognize your Shepherd's voice? When He calls you through a Bible passage, a Christian song, or during your devotions, you need to be able to distinguish His voice from any other. Jesus said, *"My sheep hear My voice, . . . and they follow Me" (NKJV)*. Listen for His voice today.

TALK BACK: Can you tell by your parents' voices what they're feeling? How do you know? What does your voice tell about you?

That's Not Fair!

Home: Africa, India
Size: To 550 pounds

It's not fair!" Sam growled as Randy again weaseled out of mowing the lawn. They were supposed to take turns, but Randy usually made excuses. Then Dad would tell Sam to do it.

In this world things aren't always fair—for humans and for animals. For instance, female lions work hard to supply their clan with food. Two of them will hide downwind from their prey. Then a third lion will circle around behind the prey, chasing it toward the hiding lionesses. Working together, they make their kill.

But instead of being able to settle down to a nice warm meal, the female lions have to step away. Then the dominant male claims the kill and drags it away. Taking his time, he gorges himself. Only when he's finished eating can the females and cubs dine. It doesn't seem fair, but that's the way it is.

Jesus Himself endured the ultimate unfairness. *"For Christ also died for our sins once and for all. He, the just, suffered for the unjust, to bring us to God"* (NEB).

Yes, He died for your sins and mine. And because of that, we'll soon go home where unfairness will never happen again!

CONTACT: Jesus, keep me strong even when things don't go my way.

Mama Quackers

Ray, a Vancouver police officer, had just gotten out of his car at work. He heard a flurry and felt something tug on his pant leg. Looking down, he found a duck.

Puzzled, he shooed the duck away. But the moment Ray turned his attention to something else, the duck repeated the strange behavior. "What a weird bird," Ray muttered.

The duck became more insistent, quacking loudly as she alternately grabbed his pant leg and then hurried a little away. Finally Ray decided to follow her. She waddled to a storm grate in the street.

Ray bent over and looked inside. There in the drain far below were eight ducklings. Ray found a nearby tow truck and pulled the lid from the ditch. Then, using a vegetable strainer, Ray fished out the fuzzy babies. At last, with a final quack, the mother gathered her youngsters and hurried away.

Contrary to her natural behavior, that mother duck *asked* for help with her problem. And in doing so, she saved her babies.

The Bible says, *"And whatsoever we ask, we receive of him, because we keep his commandments" (KJV)*. When you face problems that you can't solve alone, don't hesitate to ask God to direct you. He may fix your problem Himself, or He may send you to another human who can help. Whatever method He uses, He'll come through for you.

CONTACT: Father, thank You for Your promise for help. Help me to be faithful to You and to believe Your promises.

African Clawed Frog

Home: Native to Africa; brought into California
Size: To 3.75 inches

African clawed frogs have no tongue with which to capture their meals. Instead, they scoop food into their mouths with their front feet. These nocturnal amphibians stay mostly in the water, swimming around muddy pond bottoms or slow-moving rivers.

I've been "frog-sitting" for a friend who's researching these frogs for a class. When he brought them to me they looked like tadpoles. They swam head down, tail up, resembling little whiskered hooks hanging from the water's surface.

But the more they developed, the more horizontal they became. Now two of the four are complete tiny frogs. The other two will soon lose their tails.

One amazing thing about these tadpoles is that you can see into their heads and bodies! You can spot their little organs and watch their legs begin to develop. Nothing is hidden. But once they're fully grown, you can't see inside anymore.

In a prayer David said to God, *"You know when I sit down and when I get up. You know my thoughts before I think them"* (ICB). It's true that your Creator knows everything about you. He understands each of your thoughts, desires, needs, and feelings.

You're so precious to Him that nothing about you is unimportant. Even better than you can see into the tadpoles, God can see into your heart, and He has wonderful plans for you.

CONTACT: Thank You for taking time for me, God. Help me to be aware of Your closeness today.

Bighorn Sheep

Home: Remote western mountains, North America
Size: To 275 pounds

While visiting Banff, Canada, I climbed a narrow trail. It led to a little pocket near a mountaintop. Because of the high altitude, steepness, and cold, I could take only a few steps between rests.

Finally I dropped onto the rocks and peeked into a cupped meadow filled with lush grass and thousands of flowers. There, resting and chewing their cuds, was a flock of bighorn ewes and lambs. I watched as the babies nursed and then scampered about together.

Bighorn sheep, named because of the male's massive, curving horns, belong in such high places unspoiled by the presence of human beings.

The bighorn sheep that lived in the valley below acted different. They begged, licked deadly antifreeze from the roads, and got hit by cars. Outside influences had negatively affected their way of living.

Outside influences can negatively affect you, too. When people around you use suggestive language or tell dirty jokes, God wants you to either stop them or leave their company. He designed you to have a pure mind, and listening to those things can hurt you spiritually and ruin your morals. *"Whatever is pure, . . . think about such things,"* He instructs.

Only God can help you keep your mind clean. Ask Him to help you with that each day.

TRY IT: Taste a little pure sugar. Then sprinkle some salt into it. Does it look different? Taste it again. Is the sugar still pure, or is it polluted? How can this apply to your life?

They Need Help!

Home: Parts of Africa and Asia
Size: To 26 pounds

The ratel resembles a badger. It has a thick body, a large head, and powerful feet. Its coat looks dark underneath and white to gray on the top and sides. These bold, contrasting colors warn other animals to leave it alone.

Known as one of the most ferocious mammals, the ratel fearlessly attacks creatures much larger than itself. Its thick skin is too tough for bee stingers, porcupine quills, or predators' teeth and claws to easily puncture. And if the ratel is grabbed by the nape of the neck, it can turn around inside its loose skin to bite the attacker!

A ratel can bite through tortoise shells, and its powerful claws can dig tunnels up to 40 feet long and five feet deep. It can also spray a skunklike liquid on predators, which sends them running!

The ratel loves honey and teams up with a honeyguide bird to help it find this treat. When the honeyguide, a cheerful bird, spies a beehive, it leads the ratel to it. The ratel rips the hive apart and feasts on honey and grubs. Afterward, the honeyguide cleans up the larvae and beeswax, which it couldn't obtain without the ratel's help. Both creatures go away satisfied.

Even a ratel needs help sometimes, and so do you. The Bible says, *"I guide you in the way of wisdom and lead you along straight paths."*

CONTACT: Lord, help me to accept the guidance of the Holy Spirit as I open my Bible today.

The "Harmless" Sow

When I was little my uncle Emmett raised a few pigs on his farm. Once while visiting him I wandered out to the pigpen. There I watched a mother sleeping while several tiny pink babies pushed against her with their flat noses. How I longed to hold a piglet! But my uncle had said it was too dangerous.

"Too bad Uncle doesn't understand that animals instinctively know I'm their friend," I told myself.

Then one baby came over beside the fence. Seizing my chance, I picked it up. But the piglet began to squirm and squeal in alarm!

The mother moved so fast that I didn't even have time to put the piglet down. With a scream she lunged toward me, eyes blazing. Shrieking in terror, I clutched the piglet and raced toward the farmhouse.

The mother pig crashed through the fence, intent on saving her squealing baby. Luckily someone in the house heard the commotion and opened the front door just in time to let me through. The moment the door swung shut behind me the pig smacked into it!

King Solomon said, *"The fear of the Lord is the beginning of knowledge, but fools despise wisdom and instruction"* (NKJV). My foolish disobedience could have caused more than a broken fence and cracked door. But I learned a very important lesson that day: When instructed by someone older or wiser, I need to listen.

TALK BACK: Think of a time you didn't follow someone's advice. What happened? What did you learn?

271

Giggling Rats

Have you ever seen an animal do something so funny that it made you laugh until your stomach hurt? Most likely it put a spark in your day, leaving you feeling good.

Solomon, a wise king, wrote, *"A cheerful heart is good medicine."* He understood that laughter is healthy. It causes you to relax, and it raises your endorphins (chemicals produced by your body that make you feel happy). It's a fact that sad people become sick more often than happy people do.

Two scientists from Bowling Green State University decided to study the behavior of white rats. Knowing that humans and other primates seem to have a form of laughter, they wondered if white rats do, too.

They found that when they tickled rats, the animals let out ultrasonic whistles that seemed very much like laughter. The rats made the same sounds when playing with each other. It was clear that when they made those sounds they were having fun.

Do you have a sense of humor? Can you see the light side of the mishaps you experience? Yes, you should be serious when it's appropriate, but He doesn't want you to be a sourpuss! It's healthier to have a joyful, sunny outlook on life.

TRY IT: When you're with a group of people, start laughing as though something were funny. Laugh long and hard. How long does it take others to start laughing with you? How do you feel afterward?

272

Snake-necked Turtle

Home: Land and slow-moving water, Australia
Size: Shell to 11 inches, neck and head to 5.5 inches

You've probably touched a turtle's nose and watched it pull its head back into its hard shell. This ability gives it good protection from predators.

But a snake-necked turtle can't do this, because its neck and head are more than half the length of its shell! Instead, this turtle uses an unpleasant odor to discourage predators.

Though more vulnerable to injury, the snake-necked turtle enjoys certain advantages of having a long neck. For instance, when on land it can extend its neck to reach frogs, insects, and small mammals. Underwater, which is this turtle's home, it slowly positions its head beside the creature it wants to eat. Then it suddenly opens its mouth, and the water rushes in, including the intended meal!

At rest this turtle likes to wrap its neck around the side of its shell. And in cold weather it often hibernates underwater or in a burrow on land. It can live up to 50 years.

Each turtle has certain advantages. Isn't it good to know that God has given you advantages and abilities, too? And He helps you make the most of your talents. In fact, the Bible says, *"The Lord will guide you always."*

If you love Him and willingly obey His commandments, He'll gradually show you His special plan for your life. But even today you can start using your talents and abilities for His glory.

TALK BACK: What physical, mental, and spiritual advantages do you have? How can you use them now?

273

Duck-billed Platypus

Home: Australia, Tasmania
Size: To 4 pounds

The duck-billed platypus is unusual for two reasons. First, its mouth looks like a duck's beak. Second, it lays eggs (even though it's a mammal).

The duckbill's beak is pliable and sensitive to touch, like your fingers. Underwater the duckbill closes its eyes, feeling through the mud with its beak. Once it finds a grub or worm to eat, it puts the creature into its cheek pouches. Later on land it discards stones or sand mixed with the food, then eats its meal.

The duckbill's webbed front feet help it swim. And claws on the feet help it dig long tunnels with underwater entrances. These tunnels lead to burrows and can be blocked off with plugs of earth to keep water out.

The mother platypus digs a special nest with a tunnel about 65 feet long. At the end she makes a snug chamber, filling it with soft grasses she carries beneath her tail. Then, holding her marble-sized eggs between her tail and belly, she curls into a ball to incubate them. After hatching, the babies stay in the burrow for about five months.

Just as the platypus needs a sensitive beak, people need sensitive personalities. Recognizing and understanding other people's feelings is an important part of being a Christian. Solomon said, *"An anxious heart weighs a man down, but a kind word cheers him up."* When someone's sad, your kind words and actions can help a lot.

MISSION: Ask God to help you "read faces" today. If you sense that someone needs encouragement, graciously give it.

Who Wants *That* Job?

Home: Worldwide
Size: To 2 inches

The dung beetle eats animal droppings and rotting animal carcasses. You probably think these objects smell bad, but a dung beetle doesn't.

The beetle has an interesting way of gathering its food. First it forms a ball larger than itself from manure it finds. Then, pushing the ball with its back legs, the beetle walks in reverse, moving its treasure to a burying location.

The female dung beetle digs burrows under dung or animal carcasses. Cutting off chunks of dung, she takes them underground to form her ball. Next she lays an egg inside the ball and rolls it into the bedroom chamber.

When the egg hatches, presto! It has breakfast in bed! The larva gorges itself and finally develops into a full-grown beetle.

In burying more dung than they can use, dung beetles rid the pastures and woods of offensive materials. They also fertilize the earth, causing better plant growth. Their seemingly humble job is very important.

People with ordinary jobs are often looked down upon, while those who earn large salaries are admired. But the garbage collector is really as necessary to society as the dentist who fixes your teeth. The Bible says, *"If you treat one person as being more important than another, you are sinning" (NCV)*. You should admire people who faithfully fulfill God's mission for them by carefully doing nonglamorous tasks.

MISSION: Today thank someone who helps make your world better by doing an unglamorous job.

"He's Trained! Don't Worry"

I heard a story about a traveling snake show. As the final act of the show, the owner would allow an enormous boa constrictor to wrap around his body. Then he'd command the snake to unwind again.

But one day things didn't go as planned. While wrapping around the owner, the boa pinned the man's arms against his body. But the owner knew he could trust his boa. When the audience screamed in fright, the man laughed and said, "He's trained! Don't worry!"

Once the boa had completely encircled the owner, the man commanded it to unwind. But the boa didn't obey. The owner began to struggle, but the audience thought it was part of the act.

Each time the man exhaled, the snake tightened its coils. By the time the audience realized what was happening, it was too late to save the owner from suffocation.

Lulled by how things had always been, the owner didn't realize he was in trouble until he was being squeezed so tightly that he couldn't move.

You may think you have a bad habit under control. "It won't hurt me," you say. But as it gradually wraps around you and gets stronger, it can eventually ruin you. A seemingly harmless serpent convinced Eve to distrust God when it said to her, *"You will not surely die."* With God's help you can break those bad habits before they suffocate you!

MISSION: Do you have habits you need to destroy? How can you do it?

276

Saiga

Home: Central Asia
Size: To 155 pounds

Saigas are small antelopes. They live on treeless Asian plains, where they graze on grass and low shrubs, some of which are poisonous to other animals.

The saiga's woolly coat grows thick during cold seasons. And its long, fleshy nose filters out dust and warms cold air as the animal breathes.

A saiga can travel up to 60 miles a day searching for food. When migrating it might cover up to 125 miles per day. When necessary it can run 35 miles per hour.

During mating season bucks fight viciously to win harems of up to 50 females. Many bucks die after the mating season. Fighting and mating take all their energy, leaving them no time to eat.

The females often birth twins. They have them in areas of very short grass so they can spot predators easily. After a few days the young are able to travel with the adults. When fleeing danger, other types of antelopes leap over obstacles, but saigas run around the obstacle.

Everyone encounters obstacles in their lives. Some people "go around them" by pretending they don't exist or by doing something dishonest. But it's much wiser to face obstacles. *"The wise man looks ahead. The fool attempts to fool himself and won't face facts"* (TLB). With wisdom from God and guidance from parents and teachers, you can learn ways to solve problems.

TALK BACK: Suppose a school subject is becoming an obstacle in your life. Discuss some practical ways you can conquer the obstacle.

Rattling Quills, Flying Words

Home: Africa
Size: To 60 pounds

The African porcupine is a vegetarian. Its teeth continually grow, so it wears them down by gnawing on old animal bones. The animal's efficient nose helps it find roots, fruit, and bulbs, which it holds in its front paws while eating.

This rodent's dark brown fur is filled with sharp 12-inch quills that grow along its back from neck to tail. When an enemy approaches, the porcupine tenses the muscles beneath its skin, which raises the quills. Then it loudly rattles them to warn off the predator.

If a foolish animal comes closer, the porcupine will turn and run backward into it, filling it with quills. These quills, which painlessly drop off the porcupine, are barbed so that they work deep into the predator's flesh as it moves. If the wounds become infected, they can kill the predator.

Unkind words can be as damaging as porcupine quills. The Bible says, *"No one can tame the tongue; it is a restless evil and full of deadly poison" (NASB)*. Words said can't be erased, and the wounds they cause can be hard to heal, even after apologies.

Only a close relationship with God can help you control what comes from your mouth. Ask Him today to help you manage your emotions and guard your words.

TALK BACK: When are you most likely to say harsh words? Can you find a better way to express yourself when upset?

278

Copy Ducks

At the county fair I visited a duck exhibit. It had a pool containing an up-ramp, a narrow landing with a grain feeder at the top, and a slippery down-ramp.

To show how new ducklings learn to find food, the exhibitor put 12 yellow babies into the water. Immediately they began swimming around in a tight group.

About five minutes later an adventurous duckling got onto the up-ramp. But seeing its siblings swim away, it left the ramp to follow them. This happened three times.

Only after the exhibitor blocked the swimming passage did the adventurous duckling go all the way to the top. Stretching way out for a nibble of grain, it slipped and slid down the slide, splashing into the water again. Immediately it swam to the up-ramp, climbed it, nibbled again, then slipped and slid. When the others realized what was happening, they all followed!

Have you noticed that it's easier to follow others than to be different? Maybe someone tries to show you a magazine that features impurity or violence. Do you have the courage to turn away? Or, like the duckling, do you silently follow the others?

When facing peer pressure, David said, *"I will set nothing wicked before my eyes; I hate the work of those who fall away"* (NKJV). Ask God to help you deal faithfully with peer pressure.

TALK BACK: Tell about a time you were courageous enough to do the right thing, even though others were doing wrong. How did you feel afterward?

279

Zippy's Game

It was time to clean Marineland's dolphin pool. So the diver put on his flippers, grabbed his gear, and plunged into the water. He always enjoyed swimming with the sleek and gentle mammals.

His job involved removing several items from the bottom of the pool. Swimming methodically, he hunted for them but couldn't locate any of them. Confused, he swam to the surface. Then he learned from onlookers what had happened.

As the diver had made his way along the bottom of the pool, Zippy, a Marineland dolphin, had swum ahead of him. Zippy had picked up each item he neared, and then dropped it behind the swimmer! Zippy had kept doing this, jumping out of the water in delight. The dolphin obviously enjoyed its game of outsmarting the two-legged creature that had come to swim!*

Play, at the right time and in the right amounts, is healthy. It relaxes your heart and brain and helps you feel good. The psalmist said, *"This is the day the Lord has made; let us rejoice and be glad in it."* It's good advice!

MISSION: Take some time each day to go outside and have some active fun away from TV, videos, books, and computer games. You'll be healthier and happier because of it!

---

*Eugene Linden, "Can Animals Think?" *Time,* Sept. 6, 1999, p. 57.

Earthquake!

Beneath the ground are great sections of rock called plates. They slip slowly past each other as they change positions. Sometimes protruding rocks catch on each other, creating stress as the plates move. When these rocks finally break apart you feel an earthquake.

Earthquakes occur more than a million times a year. Some quakes are tiny tremors you can barely feel; others produce terrible destruction to buildings and a tragic loss of lives. The worst earthquakes usually happen near a fault, or crack, in the earth's outer crust.

The San Andreas Fault, running along the West Coast of the United States, has had the most earthquakes in North America. San Francisco suffered two major quakes in the 1900s—one in 1906 and the other in 1989.

A catastrophe such as an earthquake can quickly put an end to people's security. Many lose their homes, and those who survive close calls are glad just to be alive!

In the beginning there were no earthquakes. But after sin took over, God had to wash earth's face. The resulting flood changed how the earth works.

But someday, if we're faithful, we'll go home with Jesus. He promised, *"In my Father's house are many mansions. . . . I go to prepare a place for you"* (KJV). There your mansion will be built on solid ground and will never fall!

CONTACT: Father, when I experience earthquakes in my life, please take care of me and help me trust in You.

Tsunami!

Home: Pacific Ocean Ring of Fire
Size: Generally up to 50 feet high

A tsunami is a wave that's caused by a deep ocean earthquake or volcano. The wave, which may be only three feet high, spreads out in all directions from the point of disturbance. Racing across the water, it can reach speeds of 370 miles per hour.

The problem comes when the wave nears land. As the ocean floor gets shallower, all that water needs a place to go. The only place is up, so the wave grows higher. The slant of the shore automatically pushes some of the water back, and that makes the wave even higher! About 40 tsunamis have hit the Hawaiian Islands since 1819. Others have come ashore in Alaska.

A "tsunami" can also hit someone's life, especially if a person they love dies. Some people suffer depression, losing their desire to eat, be with friends, or do any of their usual activities. Others may deny the death. Some become angry with God or others.

Unless you've experienced the death of a loved one, it may be hard to understand what someone's going through. So what can you do? Be friendly, but don't push. Talk about their loved one with them if they wish. Don't lash back if they get angry.

Pray for them, and be ready to share God's promise: *"Never will I leave you; never will I forsake you."* Then be patient. They'll eventually be able to cope again.

TRY IT: Throw a pebble into quiet water. Time how long it takes for the shock rings to subside.

The Bear Who Disobeyed

Home: North American woodlands

While driving through the woods I spied a black bear nursing two cubs. Other tourists had stopped to watch, so I did too. But all the people taking pictures and coming close made the mother bear worry about her babies' safety. So she began to growl gentle instructions to the cubs.

The smallest one headed for a tree and scurried up to safety. But the larger one looked curious and ambled toward the people. The mother growled again, but junior paid no attention. Then, with a roar, she rushed toward him, flopped him across her lap, and gave him a hard smack across his backside.

Yelping with surprise, the cub rushed toward the tree. Now he was so eager to obey that he climbed right over his little sister, nearly knocking her off the trunk!

You probably don't like to be disciplined. But listen to what Jesus said about it: *"I correct and punish those whom I love. So be eager to do right" (ICB).*

Those in charge of you may discipline you when you get out of line. Generally that's because they care what happens to you and how you grow up. As hard as it may be, it's your responsibility to accept their discipline and learn from it. In the long run, you'll be thankful you did.

MISSION: Discipline should be firm but not cause injury or be cruel. Memorize Proverbs 4: 1. Parents, memorize Ephesians 6: 4.

283

The World's Biggest Flower

Home: Indonesian rain forests
Size: To 36 inches wide

Rafflesia arnoldii is the world's largest flower. Nicknamed the "corpse lily," it smells like rotting flesh. This parasite lives in jungles and attracts flesh-eating insects. As they crawl on the flower, looking for the decaying meat, they pollinate it.

The giant rafflesia has no roots, stems, or leaves. It develops on a woody vine, and its bud grows to about the size of a large cabbage head. After the bud opens, the red or pink flower measures about three feet across, and the petals are about an inch thick. The flower weighs up to 15 pounds!

Some people pretend to be wonderful Christians. Other people may believe their act. But in secret they show their true colors by using bad language and encouraging disobedience. They may even put down people who don't go along with their actions.

How damaging to your eternal life can following these people be? The Bible says, *"Such people are not serving our Lord Christ but are only doing what pleases themselves. They use fancy talk . . . to fool the minds of those who do not know about evil" (NCV).* Those who don't repent and let Jesus change them will be lost.

MISSION: Examine your behavior. Do you try to look good just to get what you want? If so, ask Jesus what you should do about it.

African Wild Dog

Home: African savanna
Size: To 66 pounds

African wild dogs have a shaggy coat that appears to be a mixture of black, white, and tan. Long-legged, these dogs run together in packs. Their large cupped ears give them excellent hearing as they travel the hot savanna, hunting game. Because they're aggressive and work together, they're greatly feared by other animals and humans.

These dogs interrupt their wanderings only while their pups grow strong enough to travel. The newborns stay safe in old aardvark dens. In the meantime their parents go out to hunt, returning to regurgitate fresh meat for the babies to eat.

These dogs are dangerous animals, yet there's something good about them. They value their family. They don't abandon injured or old family members who can't hunt for themselves. Instead, the pack feeds and cares for them.

You also need to look after members of your family and community. You should help and encourage them and let them know that they matter to you. Do you know someone very young, sick, or old? How would you feel in their place? What would you need? Go the extra mile to brighten their lives.

Speaking of believers in his day, Paul said, *"There were no needy persons among them"* because they looked after one another. How are you at watching out for others?

MISSION: Find someone in your church or neighborhood who lives alone. Think up a nice surprise for them, and when you take it to them, spend some time visiting with them.

The Putter-offer

Molly has two favorite times of day—morning walk time and dinnertime. When I begin to mix her supper, her ears perk up, her tail races, and she starts to drool. It takes her no time to finish off her meal and lick her bowl clean.

But because Molly's ears dangle into her food as she eats, I wash them off afterward. When she sees me coming with the little can of warm water, she lowers her head, backs off, and hunches down, begging to be left alone. Now there's no tail wagging or eager drooling.

As she tries to delay me from my job, she only dreads it more each moment. But once the 15-second task is done, she's happy and playful again.

Growing up, I used to have to handwash all the family dishes. I'd clear the table and then try to put off the task, wandering away to do something else. Yet I knew I'd eventually have to face those dishes, and that thought ruined my day. By the time I actually tackled the job the food had become dried and smelly, and it was an even worse job.

Those experiences have taught me an important lesson. As the Bible says: *"Poor is he who works with a negligent hand" (NASB)*. If you have an unpleasant job to do, do it first thing. Then you don't have to dread it all day.

CONTACT: Dear Father, please give me the self-control I need to not put off unpleasant tasks.

Identifying the Real Enemy

Mockingbirds are very territorial. They'll chase off any birds that come near their nests, even other mockingbirds.

Two pairs of mockingbirds live in my yard. In order to get food for their babies, they must pass through each other's territory. Hour after hour I've watched the males chase and scold each other. They became so obsessed that they quit watching for other predators that might do their nests harm.

One day a glossy black American crow entered the yard. Bold and noisy, this bird can grow to be more than 17 inches long. Crows love to tear apart small birds' nests and gobble up their eggs or fly off with their chicks.

When the crow approached one of the mockingbird's nests, the mother called out in alarm. Suddenly the two squabbling males turned their attention to the real enemy. In hot pursuit one dive-bombed the crow from above, while the other attacked from beneath. Working together, they chased off their real enemy.

People waste a lot of time fighting little battles with each other while a more dangerous enemy approaches. That's why the Bible warns, *"Be self-controlled and alert. Your enemy the devil prowls around . . . looking for someone to devour."*

Instead of wasting your time picking on other people, keep an open eye to Satan's temptations. By working together, you and your friends and family can keep him away.

CONTACT: God, help me not to get distracted by disagreements with others so I don't notice the ways Satan is trying to get me.

Good or Bad?

Home: Tropical/subtropical seas
Size: To 5 inches

Cone shells live on the floor of warm seas. Each shell looks like a tight spiral with a narrow-slot opening. At nighttime the snail inside the shell sticks its big slimy foot out of the slot. That helps it slide through the coral reefs to hunt.

As it sucks in water, the snail catches the scent of prey. When it nears its prey, it pokes out its proboscis, a tongue-like tubular organ that contains a poisonous dart. Then it shoots the dart into its prey.

The snail has teeth on its tongue. These teeth constantly grow and contain little tubes filled with venom. When a venomous tooth breaks off into prey, it releases poison, which paralyzes the prey. The snail then swallows the prey whole. Some species have venom that is so potent it can kill an adult human!

God has found a way to bring something good from this poisonous creature. Many people suffer terrible pain from cancer or other diseases or injuries. The drug morphine is often used to lessen their pain, but it becomes less effective over time. Scientists have now found that the poison from certain cone-shell snails can be up to a thousand times more effective than morphine and remain effective!

Isn't it wonderful that something corrupted by Satan can still be useful? The Bible says, *"We know that in all things God works for the good of those who love him."*

TALK BACK: Tell about a difficult experience that ended up bringing good to you.

288

October **7**

The Midnight Washer

Home: United States, Canada
Size: To 46 pounds

Raccoons are busy, intelligent mammals. You can recognize them by their ringed tail and masklike markings across their eyes.

These nocturnal animals hunt for food wherever they are. They eat a wide variety of things, from crayfish and frogs to nuts, fruit, or scraps they find in garbage cans. Though they prefer to live near lakes or streams, they can make their home almost anywhere, even in an attic!

Raccoons have a highly developed sense of touch. They feel around for their food with their nimble "hands," reaching under rocks and into crevices. When they find a piece of food, they sometimes take it to a source of water to wash off sand or unpleasant secretions. Then, holding it with their hands, they put the food into their mouths.

Clean water helps remove impurities. That's why baptism is a symbol of dying to worldly things and having your sins washed away. To help you remember that you continually need God's forgiveness, you'll also want to take part in foot washing during Communion. Accepting the washing symbolizes what Jesus does for you when He cleanses your heart from sin.

During the Last Supper, Jesus said to His disciples, *"Now that I, your Lord and Teacher, have washed your feet, you also should wash one another's feet."*

MISSION: Next time your church celebrates Communion, think about the sacrifice Jesus made for you. Talk about it with your partner as you wash each other's feet.

289

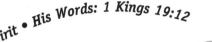

Two Brooks

What an odd brook! I thought as I stopped my bike for a rest.

I'd always thought that brooks gurgled merrily. But this one made no sound. I couldn't understand it.

The water, which came down the hillside, disappeared beneath the wooden bridge where I stood. Brightly colored pebbles covered the bottom of the brook. Along the bank were fresh, green grasses that bent into the water gracefully.

I listened more carefully. Finally I heard a faint splatter. Then, in the stillness, I heard the water swish softly as it disappeared beneath the bridge.

Later I saw another brook that tumbled over rocks and broken branches. It made a lot of noise. And then I understood the difference. Water splashes and makes noise when something gets in its way. But when water moves over uncluttered surfaces, you have to be very quiet to hear it.

That's how it works with the Holy Spirit. He doesn't make lots of noise to get your attention. In fact, Elijah learned that God speaks in *"a still small voice."*

He speaks quietly to your heart through Bible verses you read. He gives impressions and tweaks your conscience. But He never forces Himself on you. Are you listening for Him today?

CONTACT: Dear God, amid everything that happens today help me recognize the Spirit's still small voice and accept Him as my guide.

290

Naked Mole Rat

Home: Africa
Size: 3-4 inches long

Several things make the naked mole rat look strange. First, its hairless wrinkled pink skin looks too big for its body. Second, its ears are just holes in its head. And third, its top front teeth, which appear on the outside of its face, seem to come out of its nose.

Blind, this animal never comes above ground. It lives in a large social group that digs many tunnels and burrows in an area as large as a square mile. Some tunnels are located at food level where roots and tubers, such as the sweet potato, grow. Other tunnels are deeper and wide enough for two animals to pass.

As in bee colonies, only one female and a few males breed. Using their four protruding teeth, the other moles keep the tunnels free from roots and dirt and also hunt for food. All colony members look after the babies, or pups.

Strangely, these moles dig bathroom chambers, but then they eat and roll in their droppings! The scent probably identifies them to one another.

Moles rolling around in their bathrooms remind me of people who use dirty language. They contaminate themselves and all who hear them. Paul said, *"Bad company corrupts good character,"* and it's true. It's easy to begin doing wrong things if you hang around people who do them.

TALK BACK: How can you avoid picking up the habit of using unclean language? What should you do if a friend speaks in this way?

291

Bird-wing Butterfly

Home: Southeast Asia, Australia
Size: Wingspan to 11 inches

The bird-wing butterfly, named for the shape of its wings, is the largest known butterfly. This huge creature flits through the upper stories of the forest, feeding on nectar from tree and vine flowers. Males, with their iridescent emerald or gold-streaked wings, also feed on minerals at muddy riverbanks and sip juices from rotting fruits. The less colorful females generally stay at treetop level.

Butterflies are known for their fragile beauty. Light shining on their wing scales reflects lovely colors as they flit from flower to flower. But they seem unaware of their beauty and go about their business just as plainer creatures do.

Unfortunately, it's different in the human world. Some people who do well at certain things call attention to their talents, craving praise. If a victory goes unnoticed, they're sure to point it out.

But guess what? That kind of pride comes when you forget that all your abilities are gifts from God. He's the one you should be proud of! Of course, you need to do what you can to develop your abilities. But you do that for God's honor and glory, not for your own.

Remembering that humans can do nothing without God's help, Solomon, the wisest man in the world, said, *"Let another praise you, and not your own mouth."* That's pretty good advice.

CONTACT: Dear Lord, help me not to selfishly try to attract attention to myself, but to keep my eyes on You and give You the credit for the abilities I have.

292

Synjee's Long Journey

Moving can be traumatic not only for humans but also for family pets. As our family drove from Tennessee to Washington state, our new home, our kitty, Synjee, showed her discomfort.

She hates riding in the car, so a 2,500-mile trip was pretty stressful for her. Tucking her sweaty paws beneath her, she crouched in the darkness under the seat, occasionally yowling.

For 2,200 miles she rode that way. Then, on the last day of our journey, things changed. Synjee got brave and climbed into my lap. I scratched her ears, and she purred and fell asleep. Upon awakening, she bathed my hand with her tongue. Only as she trusted and allowed me to cuddle and comfort her did she calm down and enjoy the care I wanted to give her all along.

The Bible says, *"The ways of God are without fault. . . . He is a shield to those who trust him" (ICB).* During your lifetime you'll experience times of fear and insecurity, for you don't know what lies ahead. But if you let Him, your heavenly Father will hold you close and help and guide you. It takes trust, but you'll never regret it.

So trust Him today. Trust Him tomorrow. Trust Him always, for He knows what you're going through, and He will work things out for you.

TALK BACK: What's the difference between trust and faith?

Black Spider Monkey

Home: South America
Size: To 21 pounds

An energetic acrobat, the black spider monkey has skinny arms and a long tail that's hairless at the tip. This tail helps it do all kinds of things—balance as it scampers along tree limbs, hang from branches, steady itself, and pick up objects.

With its troop this monkey lives in the forest's upper canopy. There it forages for fruits, nuts, leaves, insects, and birds' eggs. When relaxing, it enjoys grooming its neighbors. Without thumbs on its hands, the monkey can leap between branches better, for thumbs would get in the way.

Black spider monkeys are intelligent. For instance, because they resent intruders from other troops, they break off heavy branches to drop onto trespassers. They also read each other's facial expressions, visual signs that indicate friendliness, playfulness, begging, fear, or warning.

You need to be aware of signs, too. Before Jesus will return to earth you'll witness more wars, diseases, plagues, crime, and natural disasters. And some people who claim to love God will actually honor Satan and insist that you do so, too. The apostle Mark said, *"When you see these things happening, recognize that He is near, right at the door"* (NASB).

Such things are happening now. Don't wait for things to get worse before you give Him your heart. Ask, and He'll help you be ready.

TALK BACK: Are there things you do that hinder your readiness to meet Jesus? How can you get ready?

White-winged Crossbill

Home: Northern North America
Size: To 6.5 inches long

The white-winged crossbill is a busy traveler. It moves from one coniferous forest to another to find spruce cones. God created this bird's bill so it can easily pry seeds from hard, prickly cones.

Most birds' bills come together at the tip, or fit inside each other. But with the crossbill's beak the tips point in two different directions. You can see how a crossbill's beak looks by crossing your fingers. Just as the tips of your fingers go different ways, the crossbill's sharp mandibles do, too, enabling it to pry out tight-fitting seeds from between the scales of cones.

Crossbills are dependent on cone crops. If they don't find a good supply, they won't nest. If they find a good supply, though, they may breed and raise their chicks, even in midwinter. God has given them the instinct to nest only when there's enough food and the ability to adjust to circumstances.

Just as crossbills have been given special tools to do their work, you've been fitted to do what God has in mind for you. Your talents and abilities are your tools. And God has not only supplied you with tools; He'll also help you learn how to use them.

King David praised God for helping him fit into His plan. He said, *"How great is your goodness, which you have stored up for those who fear you."*

MISSION: Determine to trust God to help you in your special lifework.

Sally the Salamander

Home: Wet forests
Size: From 2 inches to 4 feet

I used to have a pet salamander named Sally. I loved stroking her smooth maroon back and watching her roam through the foliage in her terrarium.

Salamanders in the wild make their homes under bark or leaf litter near creeks or ponds. They breathe and absorb water through their skin and secrete a mucus that keeps them moist. Though they're shaped like dry scaly lizards, they always feel smooth and moist.

I would catch slugs for Sally and put them in her terrarium. When she got hungry, she'd capture them by shooting out her long, sticky tongue.

Then one morning I saw that she was dry and quiet. Grief-stricken, I buried her under some pansies. But after school I noticed that she was back in her terrarium!

Surprised but overjoyed, I hurried to greet her, only to find a maroon blob of clay molded to look like Sally. It was a counterfeit salamander made by my brother to comfort me. But it couldn't replace my slippery little friend!

The Bible tells God's truth. But Satan makes counterfeits to deceive people. Those who don't prayerfully accept God's truths end up teaching Satan's lies. Jesus said, *"Their worship of me is worthless. The things they teach are nothing but human rules they have memorized"* (ICB). You must learn to differentiate between the genuine and the counterfeit and then have the courage to say no to anything but God's truth.

TRY IT: Look at expensive and cheap watches. Can you tell the difference between real and counterfeit gold?

296

Finding the Seeker

It's fun to watch wild baby animals. Before long they venture from their nests and start discovering the big world. But sometimes curiosity takes them too far from home.

Baby bear cubs sometimes have that problem. From birth they're carefully nurtured in a protected den. But as they grow older, their mother must leave for short periods of time to hunt for food. That's often when the trouble begins.

Junior ventures to the den doorway. Enticing new scents greet him, and he follows his nose to learn what they are. Eventually he thinks of home again and realizes that he's lost. Lonely and afraid, he cries out for his mother. But she's already searching for him and has spotted him. What joy junior feels when he "finds" her!

The same happens when you begin to look for Jesus. That's when you find that He already knows where you are and is calling softly to you. He says, *"Here I am! I stand at the door and knock. If anyone hears my voice and opens the door, I will go in and eat with him, and he with me."*

No matter where you go, Jesus seeks you, for He loves you and wants to be with you all the time. He'll gladly let you "find" Him today.

TALK BACK: Talk about a time someone in your family was lost. What happened? Who found the lost person?

Small Cat, Big Results

Home: Africa
Size: To 40 pounds

The serval is a small wildcat with a distinctive shape. Thin with an extra-long body and long back legs, it's perfectly built for making powerful attacks. Its small head has long, cupped ears that provide it with excellent hearing as it searches for prey.

Though it sometimes stalks prey, it often hides in tall grass until it hears a small creature approaching. It uses its hearing abilities to pinpoint the creature's exact location, then springs upon it.

An enthusiastic hunter, the serval covers up to three miles a night searching for small animals. Occasionally it hunts during the day and has been observed leaping 10 feet into the air to snag a low-flying bird. There's nothing halfway about how this cat does its job! Though I don't like to think of animals preying upon each other, the serval sure acts enthusiastic.

Part of your task while growing up is to discover what life-work God has planned for you. Whatever it turns out to be, Paul said, *"I beg you to offer your lives as a living sacrifice to him [God]"* (ICB). That means doing the best you can now—with your schoolwork, your chores, and your personal time with God. And it means being ready for greater tasks as God gives them to you.

TALK BACK: Think about the talents and interests you now have or are developing. How can you use them in working for God?

"Make Do" Champions

Home: North America
Size: To 8.2 inches, including tail

In the past people made do. If they didn't have something they needed, they got along without it or improvised with what they had.

Deer mice make do, also. They seem content wherever they are, building snug nests in abandoned animal burrows, walls, or woodpiles. They even use old birds' nests, making roofs of twigs and leaves. In these cozy dens they raise their babies, which are born pink and naked.

Deer mice prefer to eat seeds, but, making do, they also eat greens, berries, nuts, insects, mushrooms, and even gnaw on dead animals.

Our materialistic society encourages you to accumulate money and belongings. It's not popular to make do. But people who focus mainly on getting possessions aren't usually content, for as soon as they get one thing they want another. It's better to focus on what you can become with Jesus' help rather than what you can get.

Paul went through many hard times, often doing without items he really needed. Yet he said, *"I have learned to be content whatever the circumstances."* Instead of his discomforts he chose to focus on his relationship with Jesus and working for Him. You, too, can learn to be content as you live for Jesus.

MISSION: What are some ways you can treat nature with kindness? What specific items can you conserve or recycle in your own home? Make a plan.

Whirligig Beetle

Home: Quiet waters
Size: To .75 inch

As I investigated the stir at the river's edge, I discovered a dozen black beetles. They were swimming in the oddest manner, twirling and spinning. Then they darted a few inches across the surface before spinning again.

It seemed that they didn't know what they were searching for and couldn't decide which way to go. The tiny ripples they created caught the sunlight and sent it in widening circles across the water.

The black whirligig beetle has a third pair of legs that serve as oars to move it through the water. It's at home both on and beneath the surface, for it has two pairs of eyes. One pair looks skyward, the other down. The beetle feeds on insects that live or fall into the water and attaches its eggs to underwater plants. It doesn't bite humans.

Today many people don't know how to live successfully. They rush around trying to make themselves comfortable and seeking ways to look better than others.

But God knew that people would need help knowing how to treat Him and others, and also care for themselves. So with His own hand He wrote down His rules on stone (Exodus 20: 3-17). He said, *"My son [daughter], do not forget my law, but let your heart keep my commands; for length of days and long life and peace they will add to you"* (NKJV).

CONTACT: Dear God, help me not to go in circles but to accept Your rules to guide my life. Thank You for directing me.

300

The Tire Biter

Belle, a neighbor's little black dog, chased our pickup truck whenever we passed her house. Each day she'd wait behind some bushes, then attack us from the side. Barking and biting at our front tires, she'd come as near as she dared.

We'd have to stop until she was out of the way. We told her owners what was happening, but nothing changed.

Then one day Belle wasn't waiting in the bushes. Carefully we eased down the hill, then headed toward home. Suddenly she rushed from a neighbor's garage. Before we could swerve, she'd attacked again! This time the tire hit her.

After leg surgery and a long recuperation, Belle didn't chase our truck anymore. But then gradually she returned to her dangerous habit. Each day she ran a little closer to our truck. Someday her foolishness may be the end of her.

Some people chase after foolishness, too. By messing with drugs or alcohol or shoplifting, they put themselves in jeopardy. Though careful enough to escape the result for a while, their folly will eventually "get them." You just can't flirt with evil and go untouched.

"Folly delights a man who lacks judgment, but a man of under-standing keeps a straight course." In other words, once you know that something's not good, you don't see how close you can get to it. You wisely stay away from it.

TALK BACK: Is any folly occurring in your school or neighborhood? How can you keep from getting caught up in it?

301

Eclipse of the Moon

I stepped outside to check the full moon. I knew that tonight a total lunar eclipse would occur. The moon shone brightly from the cloudless sky, stretching my shadow out behind me.

"The moon doesn't glow on its own," I reminded myself. "It only reflects the sun's light."

I watched carefully. Soon our earth would pass between the moon and the sun. The moon would then be in the earth's shadow, or umbra, creating an eclipse.

First I saw just a hint of a shadow on the moon's left side, as though a cloud had crowded it. Later only half the moon shone. At last, just before midnight, the entire moon's face was eclipsed, or hidden. It looked dark brownish-red, and my shadow no longer stretched behind me.

As I gazed at the moon that had been so bright earlier, I thought about God and you and me. God shines His blessings on us and promises to guide us. When we accept His blessings and follow Him, we feel peaceful and happy.

But sometimes we let other things come between God and us. Then the joy and happiness Jesus provides gets blocked, and we go into a spiritual "eclipse."

When you find yourself in this position, it's important to make things right with God. *"Give all your worries to him, because he cares for you"* *(ICB).*

TALK BACK: When is it easiest for you to go into "eclipse"? What steps can you take to make sure it doesn't happen?

Watch the Eclipse!

Our earth rotates around the sun. At the same time the moon circles the earth. As it does, gravity from the earth, the sun, and the other planets all pull on it. With all that tugging, the moon can't travel in a straight line.

We experience a "new moon" when the moon moves between the earth and the sun at night. Then the side facing earth gets dark.

A week later half the moon is visible. In another week the earth is positioned between the sun and the moon, but not quite lined up. Then we enjoy a full moon.

When the sun, the earth, and the moon are *exactly* lined up during a full moon, the moon goes into total eclipse. It's an awesome sight!

Next Wednesday night, October 27, 2004, most of America will experience a total lunar eclipse. (On the West Coast people will see only the last part.) The midpoint will occur at about 10: 05 p.m. Eastern time. From start to finish, it will take three and a half hours.

David said, *"I see the moon and the stars, which you created. But why are people important to you?" (NCV).*

God keeps billions of heavenly bodies in their places, but He also guides you and me because He loves us so much. Think about that the next time you observe the night sky.

TRY IT: Check a newspaper for the local eclipse time. Use binoculars to view it.

303

The Clown Fish's Secret

Home: Warm oceans, except in the Atlantic
Size: To 5 inches

The giant sea anemone looks like a large sea flower. But it's actually an animal that attaches to the sea floor by a fleshy base. Its stinging tentacles wash about freely in the currents. If a fish brushes against its tentacles, the anemone stings it, then passes the fish to its mouth to eat it.

But the sea anemone and the clown fish have a symbiotic relationship, which means that they help each other. When other fish chase the orange, black, and white clown fish, it takes refuge among the anemone's stinging tentacles. Then the anemone stings the pursuer and makes a meal of it. In the meantime the clown fish eats the anemone's leftovers and even eats the anemone's dead tentacles, thus grooming its host.

Why doesn't the clown fish get stung by the anemone? It does! But only once. That first sting causes it to secrete a slimy mucus that covers its whole body. Then the stings can't affect it again.

You're often bombarded with things you don't want to see or hear. These influences could kill you spiritually. But as you ask for God's presence each day, He gives you the Holy Spirit, your protective shield to guard and direct you. It's only with His help that you can remain spiritually safe.

David said, *"Show me what I should do because my prayers go up to you"* (ICB). Why not make that your request, too?

MISSION: Write down your plan for making sure you create time for God each day.

304

Silky Anteater

Home: Central and South American forests
Size: 12-21 inches long, including tail

The silky anteater is a fluffy little mammal. It spends most of its life in trees hunting for small insects. Spongy pads on all four feet help it cling to branches. It also uses its tail, which is hairless on the bottom, to grasp tree limbs.

Long, curved claws on its front feet allow the silky anteater to tear into ants' nests, and its long, sticky tongue helps it catch insects. Having no teeth, a section of its stomach lined with strong muscles grinds up the insects.

The silky anteater can walk on the ground, but it turns its feet on their sides to do so. If threatened, it holds its sharp claws near its face and lashes out. It tries to hide from its worst enemy, the harpy eagle, among fluffy seedpods in silk cotton trees. Unfortunately, this camouflage doesn't always keep the deadly predator away.

Life isn't easy for jungle animals or for humans. But if you never have trials, you won't gain strength of character. So in His wisdom God occasionally allows troubles to come your way. As you experience His help, your faith and trust in Him grow stronger, and you learn that with Him you can go through anything. *"The Lord helps them and delivers them . . . because they take refuge in him."*

TRY IT: Start a "God's Help Journal." When something bad happens to you, write it down. Ask God to help you learn something positive from it. Later record what you learned.

Burrowing Owl

Home: Open prairies, North and South America
Size: To 10 inches

Owls all have one thing in common: forward-facing eyes that provide binocular vision. This aids them as they hunt. But there are also differences among owls.

The burrowing owl is a ground dweller that lives in abandoned rodent burrows. This owl has longer legs than other small owls, which makes walking along the ground easier. Its mottled brown and white feathers show plainly as it perches beside its burrow or on a low post.

When a skunk, fox, or other predator threatens, the owl bobs up and down or darts into its burrow. If a predator tries to follow, the owl mimics the sound of a large rattlesnake to frighten it away!

Burrowing owls hunt mostly at night and can hover in the air above their prey. They often locate their prey by sound rather than by sight. The South American burrowing owl sometimes shares its burrow with a rodent called a viscacha.

Do you have to share space with a brother or sister? Learning the skill of sharing is a crucial part of living happily in this world.

The Bible says to *"not let selfishness or pride be your guide. Be humble and give more honor to others than to yourselves"* (ICB). In other words, put the other person first. It isn't always easy, but it's the right thing to do.

GOAL: I will learn to be more thoughtful of my family, considering their needs above my own.

306

Jake, the Faithful

Anne was a young schoolteacher in Idaho many years ago. One day she decided to travel home for a surprise visit.

The winter morning looked clear, so she patted her horse, Jake, and set out. Dreams of popcorn and hot cider around the fireplace filled Anne's head as they hurried over the hilly, snowy road. How surprised her parents would be to see her!

Then around 2: 00 p.m. the sky clouded over. Soon strong winds whipped great snowflakes in all directions. Anne tried to spot a farmhouse where she could take shelter. But the blizzard made seeing farther than Jake's ears impossible, and before long, Anne was desperately cold. Though she knew they were near home, she became totally disoriented and then sleepy.

Suddenly Jake stumbled, sending Anne toppling to the frozen ground. Dazed, she lay there, too cold to move. But Jake didn't abandon her, though his instincts could have taken him home to his nice warm barn.

Instead, he whinnied and nudged her with his nose, insisting that she get up. Finally she pulled herself back onto the saddle, then lay across the saddle horn and clung to Jake as he carried her home.

The Bible says, *"The Lord preserves the faithful."* He wants you to be faithful—to your family, your church, and to Him. Sometimes that takes lots of effort, but He'll help you remember what you should do.

CONTACT: Father, I know I can't be faithful without Your help. Please keep me loyal in all ways.

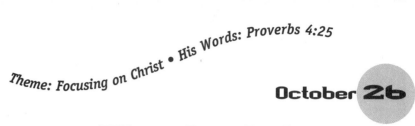

October **26**

The Ocelot

Home: Arizona to Argentina
Size: 25-35 pounds

The ocelot is an illusive wildcat. Most people don't see one unless they visit a zoo.

This cat's golden- or silver-colored coat is blotched with dark brown spots, which helps it blend in with its surroundings. Unlike small cats that curl up when they sleep, ocelots sleep with their heads resting on their front paws. Also, when danger threatens, ocelots usually bound away rather than climb a tree.

Ocelots slink around their hunting grounds at night, then hole up during the day. Their keen sense of hearing and excellent eyesight help them hunt successfully. Long extra-sensitive whiskers allow them to maneuver through narrow spaces in darkness.

Once an ocelot spots a hare, mouse, or other mammal, nothing can distract it. Never taking its eyes off its target, it hunkers down on its stomach and slowly creeps along until it's close enough to rush its prey. Then, with a pounce, it captures its dinner with its sharp claws. Ocelots efficiently help in rodent control.

Part of good Christian character is the determination to keep your eyes and your attention on Jesus as your example. Solomon said, *"Let your eyes look straight ahead, fix your gaze directly before you."*

Keeping your eyes on Jesus is the only safe way to live.

TRY IT: Go outdoors and creep up slowly to observe one of God's creatures. How easy is it to keep it from being aware of your presence?

308

Strangler Fig

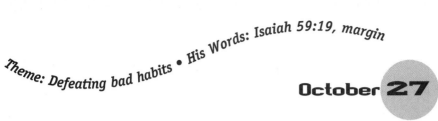

You can find many vines in the Tennessee woods. Some are beneficial, but not the strangler fig.

This vine begins with a seed dropped in a treetop by a bird. The seed sprouts, sending roots into the earth to grow strong. Then the vine encircles its host tree.

When small, the vine seems harmless. But as the tree's trunk widens, the vine doesn't stretch. It cuts off the tree's circulation like a too-tight belt. Then the tree's sap can't rise and nourish the branches and leaves above. The vine must be removed *before* it encircles the tree, or else the tree will die.

It's the same way with bad habits. For instance, some kids argue with their parents. At first they might do it only a little, but before long talking back becomes part of their attitude. Then, like a mighty enemy, the habit wraps around them and holds them prisoner.

But there's hope! When Isaiah talked about Israel's enemies, he said, *"When the enemy comes in like a flood, the Spirit of the Lord will put him to flight."* If you let Him, God will help you defeat and destroy destructive habits while they're little. Then they'll never get a chance to strangle you.

TALK BACK: After listening to a news broadcast, identify some bad habits that were present in the lives of the people featured. How could those habits have started? How can habits be changed?

American Badger

Home: North America
Size: 9-26 pounds

The badger is one of North America's lesser-seen animals. It usually spends daylight hours in its deep underground burrow, then hunts at night.

Built low and wide, this animal has small, rounded ears, a strip of white fur running along its back to its nose, and white stripes on its cheeks. It also has strong legs and sharp claws that allow it to burrow faster than a human can dig with a shovel.

Badgers are loners except during mating and cub-rearing season. Each animal stakes out its own territory and leaves a scent to warn other badgers away. If another animal approaches, the badger growls and snarls and fights it off.

Crafty hunters, badgers chase and catch small mammals, dig them out of their burrows, and sometimes hide in an animal's burrow until it returns. They even eat snakes, because the venom is harmless to a badger unless it's bitten on the nose.

Have you heard the expression "He badgered me"? Badgering means pestering people until you finally wear them down. That's what Satan does. He repeatedly tempts you in the areas of your weaknesses, hoping that you'll give in and do wrong.

But you have a promise: *"Blessed is the man who perseveres under trial, because when he has stood the test, he will receive the crown of life that God has promised to those who love him."* With God's help you don't have to give in!

TALK BACK: What things can you do to make sure Satan doesn't badger you into sinning?

310

Playing Lead Bird

In 1941 the whooping crane nearly became extinct. Only 15 of them were known to be alive. Then conservationists stepped in, carefully breeding and raising them in captivity. In 2000 their population had risen to 375.

Each year some whooping cranes migrate between Canada and Texas. But birds raised in captivity don't always know how to migrate. So in 2000 an exciting project began.

Conservationists tried to teach 13 hand-raised sandhill cranes to migrate. Using a pilot wearing a bird costume and flying a yellow ultralite plane, they hoped to lead the birds from Wisconsin to Florida. Then they would establish the birds in the wild. Next they plan to try this with whooping cranes.

Maybe you know people who have stopped coming to church. Perhaps someone was unkind to them or they got tired of keeping the commandments. Maybe they were just plain lonely. Whatever the reason, you can help them realize that God still loves them.

But sometimes coming back to church is scary. They might feel as if the members are staring at them and whispering.

You can be like the yellow plane leading the flock of birds. Give the former members a warm welcome and treat them with friendly care. Remember, Jesus came *"to seek and to save what was lost."* It's your privilege to help Him lead people back into the safety of a friendship with Him.

CONTACT: Show me the way to help others return to You, Lord.

Okapi

Home: Zaire, Africa
Size: To 550 pounds

The okapi is the giraffe's closest relative. Though its neck is shorter than a giraffe's, it has a similar head shape. Also, the male okapi has the same little nubby horns as a giraffe. And the okapi, like the giraffe, eats tree leaves, using its 14-inch tongue to grasp the branches and strip off the foliage.

Shy and chestnut-colored, the okapi lives in forested areas where it can easily hide. Special horizontal stripes on its hindquarters and front legs mimic light patches falling on foliage. This camouflages the animal's outline, making it hard to spot. To mark its personal territory it gives off a scent from glands situated between the toes of its hooves.

An okapi doesn't like being dirty, so it licks itself with its tongue, which is long enough to clean even its eyelids! When a zoo okapi needs medicine, the keeper pours it on the animal's back. The okapi promptly washes itself clean of the sticky stuff, licking up the medicine.

Because sinning makes people "unclean," God has made a way to get them clean again. Remember when Jesus wanted to wash Peter's feet? When Peter protested, Jesus answered, *"Unless I wash you, you have no part with me."*

Jesus already paid for your sins, so only He can wash you clean. The symbols of baptism and foot washing demonstrate this cleansing. They serve to remind you that you need God to forgive your sins.

TALK BACK: How old were your parents when they got baptized? What difference do they think it's made in their lives?

312

The "Adopted" Butterfly

Home: Europe, northern Asia
Size: Wingspan to 1.5 inches

Large blue butterflies have black spots on their forewings, which are rimmed with grayish brown. These butterflies lay their eggs on thyme plants. Soon tiny yellow caterpillars emerge, then burrow into the flower's head to eat and grow. Later they chew their way out of the flower and crawl to the ground.

A certain kind of red ant loves the fluid these caterpillars secrete from their tenth segment. So a red ant will "adopt" a caterpillar, taking it into its nest. There worker ants feed the caterpillar ant eggs and grubs. The following year the caterpillar goes into its chrysalis stage, emerging after a few weeks as a butterfly.

This process takes three-way cooperation. The butterfly helps pollination as it flits between flowers; the caterpillar gets fed and sheltered, both in the flower head and in the ants' nest; and the ants get to eat the caterpillar's secretions. Each of these functions helps all concerned.

Your relationships with God and your family are like this, too. God puts you where you can be nourished and cared for. You respond to your caregivers with love and obedience, which brings them joy. And God provides for all of you.

The Bible says, *"Good understanding wins favor, but the way of the unfaithful is hard."* As families cooperate with God and each other, they stay happy and secure.

TALK BACK: How do you bring joy to your family? to God? Is there something more you should do?

Falling Stars

You're taking a nighttime walk. Suddenly a brilliant white light streaks across the sky, disappearing into blackness. You've been lucky enough to see a shooting star, or meteorite.

Most of the meteorites we see are actually specks of space dust or small rocks that enter our atmosphere. When they do, they burn with such intense heat that we can see their light for many miles.

When numerous meteorites fall within a short time span, it's called a meteor shower. This occurs when our earth, in its trip around the sun, crosses a field of space debris that's left over after some larger body has broken up into pieces. These pieces also orbit the sun.

During a meteor shower the meteorites seem to come from one point in the sky. That's how it was when I watched the Leonids. Seven of them even left smoke trails that were visible for several seconds after they'd disappeared.

One sign of the end of the world is a great falling of stars. Some people believe that this happened in 1833; others think that this event is still to come. Whoever is right, the result remains the same: *"The sun will be darkened, and the moon will not give its light; the stars will fall from the sky. . . . They will see the Son of Man coming on the clouds of the sky, with power and great glory."*

I want to watch this happen, don't you?

TRY IT: We pass through the Leonids each November. Using a computer, log onto http: //www.earthsky.com to learn when they'll be visible.

Sled Dogs

In the past people in the snowy North owned sled dogs. Bred for strength, intelligence, and thick pads on their feet, these dogs weighed up to 85 pounds and could each pull 50 pounds.

The Denali National Park Service in Alaska still uses sled dogs for winter patrol. When motorized Snow Cats became popular, the park service tried them, but only for a short while. They learned that sled dogs are more reliable than machines! Dogs can figure a way out of tight situations, and they don't break down and leave the musher (sled driver) stranded.

Sled dogs work in teams of 5 to 10 dogs, depending on the load they need to pull. Older dogs get paired with younger, inexperienced dogs to train them.

The lead dog must want to lead, be smart, and be able to stay focused on the job. This animal needs good strong feet, because it must break trail through the snow and find solid footing for the others. On a good day the team can travel 30 miles.

A dog called the "swing dog" works in the middle. When turning, it must run wider than the lead dogs to keep the sled from tipping over. But the most powerful dogs are placed directly in front of the sled to do the strongest pulling.

Working in unity is important in a church, too. Leaders and followers each have special jobs to do. The Bible says, *"Two are better than one, because they have a good return for their work."*

CONTACT: Lord, help me to work well with others.

The Singing Whale

Home: Northern arctic and subarctic coastal waters
Size: To 3,000 pounds

The adult beluga whale is white and has a thicker skin than most whale species. It needs this, because it lives in extremely cold waters and must often hunt for food beneath ice. When it is beneath the ice and needs to breathe, it uses its head and back to break through the thick frozen crust to make a breathing hole.

Belugas are nicknamed singing whales because they continually chirp and make sounds. Sometimes their sounds can be heard above the water! They sing and talk to other whales in their pod or group as they round up schools of fish to eat.

Working together makes them more successful in catching enough prey for the whole group. Though life is harsh in their habitat, they just keep singing.

The apostle Paul believed in singing, too. Picture him sitting in that dark prison cell feeling lonely, hungry, and tired. When things got tough, though, he sang praises to God, reminding himself of the Lord's goodness and care. That helped him get through long days and nights. He even reminded the Ephesians to *"sing and make music in your heart to the Lord."*

When you have problems, try singing praises to God. Sing when you're happy, too. Sing out loud or quietly in your heart. The words you sing and the impressions God sends you will brighten your life.

MISSION: Ask some elderly people what songs encourage them and why. Memorize a song for your times of trouble.

Jumping Spider

Home: Northern Hemisphere
Size: Female .25 inch, male smaller

You're crouching behind a bush while playing hide-and-seek. Out of the corner of your eye you notice movement on a leaf. You watch as a colorful spider leaps and grasps a fly in its front legs, then eats it.

There are at least 300 species of jumping spiders in the United States. They have thick bodies, short hairy legs, and two large eyes at the front of the head. These eyes give them the best eyesight of any creature their size.

Jumping spiders can leap forward, backward, or sideways, and up to 40 times their body length! When hunting they move quietly until they spy a small insect. Then, raising their front legs, they leap at the insect, spinning a safety web just in case they miss their target. That safety web keeps them from falling.

God has given humans a safety web with 10 strands. It outlines what you should do to live in harmony with God and other people. It's the Ten Commandments.

Just as the spider can leap freely when connected to its safety line, you can live freely as long as you follow God's guidelines. Your safety web doesn't limit you but gives you the freedom to grow.

In his song to God, David said, *"Do not let me stray from your commands."* He knew that following God's rules would be a safety net for him.

TALK BACK: Why do some people feel that God's commandments limit them? How do the commandments free you?

317

Those Watching Eyes!

Home: The Americas
Size: 80-230 pounds

You're walking alone through the woods when you sense something watching you. The hair on the back of your neck rises, and your heart races.

For centuries people have feared animals such as the cougar. Also called the mountain lion, the puma, or the panther, this sleek cat used to be plentiful. But now so few cougars remain that they're a protected species.

They became endangered because they hunt deer, domestic animals, and even humans when very hungry. So in order to protect themselves and their livestock, ranchers declared war on them.

Strong and agile, cougars can easily leap forward 23 feet, or spring up in the air 18 feet. They move through tree branches easily and can drop 65 feet from an overhanging limb without injuring themselves. Secretive, cougars prefer being alone except during mating season. Basically nocturnal, they shelter in caves or in rock piles or dense vegetation. Humans and wolves are their only enemies.

Won't it be nice in heaven when people and animals will no longer hurt each other? Speaking of heaven and the new earth, the Bible says, *" 'The wolf and the lamb will feed together, and the lion will eat straw like the ox. . . . They will neither harm nor destroy on all my holy mountain,' says the Lord."*

TALK BACK: How did animals become dangerous if they were created to be gentle?

318

Squirrel Monkey

Home: South America
Size: To 2.5 pounds

My friend's pet squirrel monkey wore a frilly blue dress and bonnet. With her tiny diaper, the animal looked like a funny baby.

She shook my hand politely and accepted the peanut I gave her. But instead of coming to me, she wrapped her gangly arms around her owner's neck. She wanted only her "mama"!

Squirrel monkeys live in troops of as many as 100. Hanging out in trees, they use their tails for balance as they forage for fruit, nuts, birds, and insects. Their paws, made like our hands, allow them to do intricate tasks such as unwrapping leaves to find hidden insects.

The female monkey raises one baby at a time. While tiny, the baby rides on its mother's back, wrapping its tail and hind legs around her. Sometimes females who have no babies carry the young to give the mothers a rest. When the babies get old enough, they scamper around, teasing their playmates and patient mothers.

How much patience do you have? How do you react when your little sister follows or pesters you? If a classmate cuts in front of you in line, do you get angry? The Bible warns, *"Don't become mad quickly, because getting angry is foolish"* (ICB). God also wants you to be patient with people. Developing patience may take a while, but it's worth the effort.

TALK BACK: In what areas does your patience need to grow? How can you begin to improve it?

The Secret of the Cordgrass

Home: Salt marshes
Size: To 8 feet tall

Cordgrass grows in marshy areas along shorelines. It looks tall, tough, and swordlike. During high tides this plant is mostly submerged in sea water. At low tide the water drains off the marsh, leaving the cordgrass mainly exposed.

Strangely, cordgrass needs fresh water to live, yet it grows in salt water. How can this be?

Well, a special membrane in its root pulls fresh water out of sea water. This membrane filters out most of the salt before it can enter the plant's sap. Then special glands along the surface of the plant pluck out any salt that got past the membrane. These glands pass the salt through pores that deposit the salt on the *outside* of the grass blades. At the next high tide, the salt gets washed off the plant. If any of these systems fail to work, the salt will kill the grass.

The theory of evolution teaches that life started from a blob and just kept changing until it worked. But if cordgrass took millions of years to evolve, how did it keep from dying off before it gained the ability to process salt water?

The Bible says, *"In the beginning God created the heavens and the earth."* Things didn't just fall together. A very loving God made them.

TRY IT: Get three plants. For three weeks water one with fresh water and two with salt water. What happens with each plant? How does the soil look?

Sugar Gliders

Home: Australia and vicinity
Size: To 11 inches, including tail

Sugar gliders are tree-dwelling marsupials that look some-
what like flying squirrels. When the trees are too far apart
for them to scramble between the branches, these animals hurl
themselves into the air and spread out their legs.

Do you know how wind lifts your open umbrella and tries to
send it flying? That's what happens with the sugar glider's "wing
flaps." This loose skin between the front and back legs creates a
cupped surface, catch the air, and help the glider sail through the
air. Though the animal can't gain altitude, it can easily glide as
far as 150 feet.

Gliders must move quickly to avoid owls and other predators.
So just before landing they flip the front part of their bodies upward and land on their back feet. This puts them in a position to
scamper quickly up the tree trunk into protective cover.

Obviously, sugar gliders plan ahead. You need to do the same.
*"Counsel and sound judgment are mine; I have understanding and
power,"* God said through Solomon.

God promised to give you the wisdom to know what's wise
and the courage and strength to do it. If you ask Him, He'll help
you look ahead and avoid problems.

**FOCUS: Keep a schedule of homework assignments and
special duties to make sure you've allowed yourself enough
time to complete everything.**

321

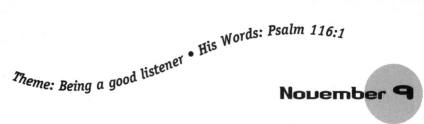

Theme: Being a good listener • His Words: Psalm 116:1

November 9

More About Sugar Gliders

Sugar gliders have soft grayish fur and a white belly. Carrying leaves and twigs with their long bushy tails, they build their nests high in manna gum trees. There they come out at night to dine on fruit, insects, and leaves. But they're called sugar gliders because they love to lick the sweet tree sap.

Up to three babies live in the mother's pouch. As they get bigger, they come out and wrap their tails around their mother's leg or tail. Then they hold on tightly as she scampers around.

Sugar gliders have large eyes that give them good night vision. They also have hairless ears that rotate like a cat's ears so they can easily locate predators. To communicate, they "yap" softly to each other, but only one glider yaps at a time, as though they're in conversation. Their lives depend on their ability to glide, see, and listen carefully.

Do you really listen to what your parents, teachers, or friends say to you? Do you listen to what God tells you through the Bible and His Holy Spirit? Sometimes you might get so busy talking about your own interests that you don't think about what others are saying.

David said, *"I love the Lord, for he heard my voice."* God really hears you, so why not follow His example and become a good listener?

MISSION: When others tell you something, concentrate on what they're saying. If you don't understand, repeat what you think they meant so they can clarify their meaning.

Ring Around Its Neck

Home: Seacoasts, lakes, and rivers worldwide
Size: To 2 feet long, plus tail

Most waterfowl have waterproof feathers, but cormorants don't. Their feathers get waterlogged. That's good, though, because they must be able to sink quickly.

Cormorants ride low in the water. When they spy a fish, they fold their wings against their sides and dive down, paddling with their webbed feet. Chasing the fish deep into the water, they catch it, surface, then swallow it whole.

Asian fishermen use cormorants in their work. They place a loose ring around each bird's neck. They also place a long line, used like a leash, on its legs. Then they wait for the bird to catch fish. Each bird can catch about 100 an hour!

The neck ring keeps the cormorant from swallowing the fish, so the fisherman can collect them. After a fish is taken away, the cormorant simply returns to work, as eager as ever. (Eventually the birds do get fed.)

Do you feel unrewarded for the chores you do? Do you sometimes wonder why you have to perform the same tasks day after day? Isaiah said, *"I have labored to no purpose; I have spent my strength in vain and for nothing."* But then he added, *"Yet what is due me is in the Lord's hand, and my reward is with my God."*

Everyone has to do some boring, repetitive duties. But it's important to develop the self-discipline to complete what's necessary. Though you don't always see the rewards right away, they are there!

TALK BACK: What rewards are there in doing chores? How can you develop the self-discipline to do them?

323

Meerkat

Home: South Africa
Size: To 2 pounds

Meerkats, a type of mongoose, live in the Kalahari Desert. They're very sociable mammals that rely on teamwork to keep their colonies safe. Each animal has a specific job to do.

The hunters sniff out insects and other small creatures to share with the others. The teachers train the young. The baby-sitters supervise groups of young meerkats while their parents hunt.

The sentry watches over the whole colony, standing tall on its hind legs. Tirelessly it peers across the desert scrub in search of predators. When it senses danger, it barks a warning, which sends all the meerkats scurrying into the underground tunnels.

When cornered by enemies, the colony members dig rapidly to create a dust screen. Sometimes they puff themselves up to look larger as they advance on the enemy in a united group. Working together makes the difference between life and death.

When you're given a job you don't like, you might be tempted to complain or try to get out of it. But Paul told the Philippians, *"Do everything without complaining or arguing."*

He understood that in families, churches, schools, and workplaces, many unglamorous tasks must be done. And if everyone cooperates willingly, things will go more smoothly and everyone will be happier. Why not ask God today to help you be a willing team member?

TALK BACK: How does each member of your family help the group? What's one thing you could do to make your family happier?

324

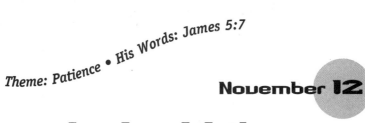

Jackrabbit

Home: United States, Mexico
Size: Around 11 pounds

Did you know that jackrabbits can run up to 50 miles an hour and leap five feet into the air? If you've ever watched them run, you know how quickly they can disappear. Long hind legs give them the ability to move very efficiently and escape predators.

The mother jackrabbit also has a clever way of protecting her babies. After she's given birth, she places each baby rabbit in a separate nest. That way a predator won't find them all.

On hot semideserts and prairies where jackrabbits live there's often little shade. So to escape the scorching heat they dig out forms, which are shaded holes in the sand. There they stretch out on the cooler earth.

God also gave them a special cooling system. Their eight-inch-long ears are thin and filled with blood vessels that get rid of extra body heat. But they patiently wait until the cool of the night before hunting.

Have you ever watched people waiting in line or at a stop-light? Some of them sigh, check their watches, rev their motors, growl and complain, or show their impatience in other ways. But sometimes it's good to have to wait. It can help you learn self-control and give you time to think.

The Bible says, *"Be patient."* It's a good idea to pray for patience, especially as you wait for Jesus' second coming.

TRY IT: Today practice making yourself wait for something you want. Concentrating on something else will help.

Gravity and Air Pressure

Several gases make up the air we breathe. But what keeps air molecules from floating away into space? Gravity—the same force that plunks your baseball down after you throw it—tugs on the molecules, drawing them to earth.

Because molecules all push down on each other, more air molecules stay at low altitudes than at high altitudes. And because higher altitudes have fewer molecules, they have less air pressure and therefore less air to breathe. That's why airplanes must use pressurized air during flight.

The heat of summer and chill of winter also affect air molecules. When molecules in high pressure areas try to flow into low-pressure areas, they create wind.

I've never seen gravity, but when I jump I'm soon back on the ground. I haven't seen an air molecule or the wind, but I've felt their presence on my skin and in my lungs. I've seen branches sway. Therefore, I believe they're there.

I've never seen God, Jesus, or the Holy Spirit. But They've changed some of my bad habits. I hear Them speaking through my conscience. Therefore, I believe They're there.

The Bible says, *"The wind blows wherever it pleases. You hear its sound, but you cannot tell where it comes from or where it is going."* It's the same when you let God work in your heart. You may not know how the changes occur, but they do.

TALK BACK: Gravity keeps the air near earth. But what keeps us near God?

326

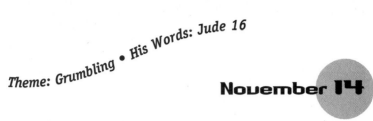

November 14

The Grumbler

Fox terriers are active, smart, and loyal dogs. I used to have a fox terrier named Zannie. White with a rusty splotch across his back and head, he always had a puzzled look on his face.

It seemed as if Zannie could figure out what I wanted him to do almost before I told him. He could leap as high as my head to take sticks from my hand. He could also dig like a gopher. And he loved to go shopping, proudly carrying my package home!

But Zannie had one failing. He was a grumbler! When I asked him to do something he didn't want to do, he'd reluctantly obey. Then, as soon as I turned my back, he'd make grumbling sounds under his breath. If I glanced back at him while he griped, he'd stop—until I quit looking. Somehow, he always had the last word!

Zannie's behavior made me laugh. But in humans grumbling isn't funny! The Bible describes ungodly people as *"grumblers and faultfinders."* They concentrate on every negative thing they can find instead of looking for the positive.

Next time you want to complain, ask yourself why. Is it for a valid reason, or just a selfish one? Is there a better way to respond?

TALK BACK: What kind of people do you enjoy being around? Are you that kind of person?

The Screaming Train!

One dark night I awoke from sleep. I heard the loud rumble of a train approaching. But then I realized something. There's no train track near our house! So what was happening?

Wind began to shake the windows, and my family raced downstairs as the "train" roared closer. Suddenly we heard a screech of tearing metal come from overhead as the chimney cap got twisted. And then everything became silent.

We had experienced the power of a tornado. A few shingles got torn off our house, the front of our house was covered with shredded insulation, our porch chairs got flung into the woods, and our doghouse got moved to a different place, leaving a very confused dog behind! Out back the trees were twisted off like matchsticks.

But the tornado had hopped over our neighborhood! It settled down about two miles away.

There a man was sucked from his bed and put back down on his mattress—outside his house and unharmed! Another man, taking a bath, got deposited—naked but unhurt—in the middle of a parking lot.

Roofs, cars, and furniture were carried for blocks. Clothing waved like flags from the branches of still-standing trees. Entire blocks became nothing but piles of sticks. But fortunately, no one was killed.

What should you do when faced with sudden danger? Aside from having a plan, you can only call on God for protection. *"The Lord will hear when I call to him,"* David said.

MISSION: With your family create a plan outlining where to go in case of a tornado, fire, or other calamity.

Tornado!

As damp air warms, it rises, cooling it off again. That process causes the moisture to condense and form a tall, puffy cumulonimbus cloud.

If the cloud, called a thunderhead, is warmer than the surrounding air, it keeps rising rapidly and can become a thunderstorm. If the direction and speed of the wind change, the thunderstorm may rotate and produce lightning, rain, and hail.

Sometimes a funnel cloud forms. It looks like a tail growing from the cloud bottom. As the wind spins, the funnel may continue to grow, finally reaching the ground with a sucking updraft. Then it's called a tornado.

Like an angry finger spinning at speeds of 300 miles per hour or more, it drags across the earth, turning black from the debris it picks up. When a tornado comes near to or hits a building, it often causes the structure to explode, because the air pressure changes so quickly.

Tornadoes in North America tend to occur on muggy, stormy afternoons. Most often they form in warmer climates, but they've occurred in every state. Some tornadoes give no visible warning before they strike.

Catastrophes may wreck everything around you, but they can't destroy your relationship with Jesus. Your relationship with Him is the most important thing there is. The Bible says, *"You will keep in perfect peace him whose mind is steadfast, because he trusts in you."* Stay close to Him and He will carry you through each circumstance and give you the courage you need to face it.

MISSION: Designate a family meeting spot to use if you become separated during a catastrophe.

The Eye
That Cannot See

Hurricanes and tornadoes are both wind storms. Tornadoes touch down in smaller areas and don't last as long, while hurricane winds cover wide areas and may last several days.

Hurricanes form when high-speed winds rush to a low-pressure area on the ocean and begin circling. The low-pressure center, called the eye of the storm, is very warm and damp. The cooler, denser incoming wind pushes the warm wind upward, gaining speed as it rises.

Fully developed, this storm looks like a huge doughnut. It rotates over the ocean surface, then gradually moves to another area.

When a hurricane hits land it does its greatest damage. As the high winds race around the eye, the storm moves very slowly over an area, giving the winds plenty of time to destroy buildings and crops. First, the wind blows in one direction. When the eye of the storm moves over the area, all is deceptively calm and sunny. Suddenly, though, the other side of the rotating storm hits. There's nothing to do but wait it out.

When a great wind passed over the Sea of Galilee, the disciples panicked, but Jesus remained calm. He prayed to His Father, then raised His arms and commanded, *"Peace, be still" (KJV)*. Instantly, the winds stopped. It was then that the disciples realized that Jesus was the Lord of everything—even the wind.

TALK BACK: What life storms has Jesus calmed for you? for your ancestors?

330

Cockleburs

Home: Wastelands

You've been hiking with your friends. Finally you sit down to eat your sandwiches. That's when you feel a nagging itch on your ankle.

When you scratch you notice that your socks are covered with cockleburs. You try to pick them off, but they cling tightly to the yarn loops of your socks. It takes real work to remove them.

Cockleburs are oblong-shaped fruits of a leafy green plant that grows along roadsides or in fields. The pod of a cocklebur contains two seeds. Covered by prickly, hook-shaped fibers, the pods easily attach to clothing or animal fur. In this way humans and animals help transport the seeds to new areas so more plants can grow.

How can an annoying burr be of any help to humans? After finding burrs on his clothes, George de Mestral became interested in how they held so tightly. He studied them carefully, then invented something you probably use. It's called Velcro, a series of tiny hooks and loops that make closures for all sorts of objects, including shoes.

What can you do with prickly annoyances in your life? If you look at them in a different way, maybe you can learn something from them. The Bible says, *"Diligence is man's precious possession" (NKJV).* There's no telling what your intelligence and ingenuity can accomplish when you have determination and help from your heavenly Father.

TRY IT: What other things could you do with a burr?

331

Crocodile Skink

Home: New Guinea
Size: Approximately 7 inches

True to its name, the crocodile skink resembles a miniature crocodile. While most skinks have smooth, shiny scales, this variety has rough, dry overlapping scales. It also has two horny ridges running down the length of its variegated brown body.

Its triangular head and the yellow ring around its eyes make it easy to identify. Claws on its toes help it dig in leaf litter or hunt through trees to find insects and other arthropods.

The crocodile skink generally moves slowly. If captured by a predator, it simply breaks off its tail. It doesn't even bleed. This sacrifice often saves its life, and it does grow a new tail.

The skink can voice its opinion about things. Its pulsating, chirpy sound resembles one of those yapping mechanical dogs sold in toy stores. Surprisingly, the male skink's voice is a higher pitch than the female's. It seems to communicate for a definite purpose: to let others know that it's around, or to warn intruders away.

How about your communications? When you speak, is what you say for a good purpose and worth listening to? The Bible says, *"But avoid worldly and empty chatter, for it will lead to further ungodliness"* (NASB).

MISSION: Keep track of your conversations today. How much of what you say will uplift God or be encouraging or informative to others? How much is just silly chatter?

Common Blue Butterfly

Home: United States, Great Britain
Size: Wingspan to 1 inch

Common blue butterflies live around plants belonging to the pea family, such as lupine or vetch. These iridescent blue creatures flit from plant to plant, searching for nectar and the right host plants.

Walking through a field, I was surprised to discover fresh cow dung almost covered by a layer of these blue beauties. I wondered how something so pretty could settle on something so ugly!

I learned that "mudpuddling," or grazing on dung, is something the male butterflies do. As they sip juices from the dung, they get minerals they need to produce sex hormones. If they didn't get these minerals, they couldn't fertilize a female's eggs.

The female butterflies are mostly brown with a tinge of blue. And the blue on the males really isn't blue at all—it's just a reflection of light. What appears to be there isn't!

In some ways you're like this butterfly. On the outside you may sometimes appear happy or confident, but inside you know you aren't. Other people judge you by what they see, though.

Only God can see the real you. David said, *"Lord, you have examined me and know all about me" (NCV)*. God understands your feelings, thoughts, and secret wishes. Because of this He can help you solve even your toughest problems. And there's no waiting to get His attention! He's only a prayer away.

CONTACT: Dear Lord, thank You for knowing me so well. Help me to know You, too.

Cliff Swallow

Habitat: Open areas, North America
Size: To 6 inches

The twittering bird zoomed overhead. Soon it folded its slender blue-gray wings and disappeared into a hole in the desert cliff.

A moment later it reappeared, flashing its pale underside as it glided to the marsh. Turning and swooping, it passed low over the water. Darting here and there, it filled its wide beak with mosquitoes and then returned to its nest to feed its babies.

Cliff swallows often hollow out caves in sandy cliffs. Or they build gourd-shaped nests of mud under bridges or eaves. They like areas near ponds or rivers, where insects congregate and mud is easy to find.

God gave these birds the instinct to plan ahead for their safety. They don't nest where animals such as snakes or rodents can catch them. They gather near plentiful insect populations so they can catch their food as they fly. And these family-oriented birds nest close together.

You also need to plan ahead for your safety. Staying in safe areas, choosing friends wisely, and being aware of the ways Satan tries to trap you can help you survive.

Solomon suggested, *"Take heed to the path of your feet, then all your ways will be sure" (RSV).* This means that you need to be aware of what's happening around you and plan accordingly. God will help you if you ask for His guidance.

TRY IT: Observe several kinds of wild birds. How do they ensure their safety? When danger approaches, how do they act?

334

The Great Reunion

Recently I heard about an elephant preserve. This place takes in elephants that the circus doesn't want anymore. Most of the animals are in poor health or injured.

One 50-year-old female elephant had been attacked by a crazed bull elephant. She could barely walk and seemed very depressed.

Then one day the preserve acquired a younger female elephant. Her bones looked like scaffolding beneath her droopy skin. Two thousand pounds underweight, she could barely stand in her holding pen.

Immediately the older elephant perked up and moved as close to the new elephant as she could. Then, crying loudly, she poked her trunk through the bars of her pen and eagerly stroked the newcomer's face. The younger elephant did the same.

Amazed, the keepers opened the gate between the two pens and watched the overjoyed elephants greet each other. The keepers learned that many years earlier the two elephants had belonged to the same owner. In no time both elephants' health had improved, for they were finally happy.

Someday you'll take part in a joyful reunion with absent relatives and friends. The greatest joy, though, will be to meet Jesus face to face! Of that time the Bible says, *"Now God's home is with men. He will live with them, and they will be his people. . . . He will wipe away every tear from their eyes. There will be no more death, sadness, crying, or pain"* (ICB).

TALK BACK: Whom are you eager to be reunited with?

335

Wild Yak

Home: Himalayan mountains
Size: To 2,000 pounds

Wild yaks are on the endangered species list because humans have domesticated so many of them. These animals live in harsh, cold country in altitudes up to 20,000 feet.

Members of the cattle family, yaks have dark-brown hair. This hair hangs in thick pads almost to the ground, allowing the animals to bed down on snow and ice and still stay warm.

In the high mountains yaks must eat hard-to-digest grasses and lichen. After eating for a while they regurgitate and chew their cud (partly digested food) to soften it. Then they swallow it again, continue digesting it, then regurgitate and chew the cud another time. Eventually their well-chewed cud passes through three more stomachs.

While the food digests it ferments, producing a temperature of 104 degrees Fahrenheit in their stomach! That inside furnace helps keep yaks warm.

As Jeremiah learned new things from God, he said, *"When your words came, I ate them; they were my joy and my heart's delight."* In other words, Jeremiah thought about what God had told him and shared it with others.

When you regularly read God's Word, you develop a hunger for it and want to read it more and more. As you "digest" His messages, your understanding becomes clearer, warming your life with His love. It's up to you to "eat."

MISSION: During the next few weeks read the book of John a few verses at a time. Ask God to help you understand what the stories mean.

The Ivory Barnacle

Home: Oceans

If you've spent time at the ocean, you've probably seen barnacles at low tide. Like crowded groups of tightly closed seashells, they cling to rocks, piers, boat bottoms, and even whales.

While exposed to the air, barnacles close their little shell doors to keep from drying out. But once they're submerged, they open their doors and poke out their six pairs of feather-like legs. Swishing these through the water, they capture plankton.

Barnacles begin as tiny, free-swimming creatures that resemble shrimp or crabs. Soon, though, they fasten themselves head-first onto a surface by oozing a brown glue. Soft-bodied, they need protection, so next they secrete a lime substance that forms a hard cone around them. As they grow they secrete larger chambers, dissolving the inner chamber.

Barnacles live in colonies and keep growing, so once they attach themselves to boat hulls they slow the boats down. To get rid of them, captains often dock in freshwater channels, because barnacles can't live in fresh water (except for the ivory barnacle).

If barnacles are discovered early, they're no problem to remove. But once they've protected themselves with a hard shell, they're nearly impossible to get rid of.

When you listen to the Holy Spirit, He will show you what's right and wrong. Then you'll grow strong. Just as the ivory barnacle can withstand all kinds of water, you'll be able to stick tight to God's way no matter what.

FOCUS: David said to his son, "Observe what the Lord your God requires: Walk in his ways." Determine to develop good habits that will help you do that.

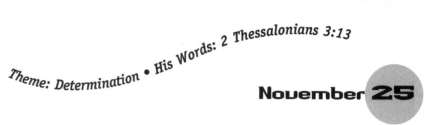

Twig Eaters

Home: Northern North America
Size: To 2,000 pounds

The mother and baby moose peered from the willow thicket as I drove past. The mother stopped chewing, weeds drooping from her mouth. Her tiny calf peeked shyly from between its mother's front legs.

Moose, meaning "twig eaters," are the largest living deer. The males grow heavy antlers up to seven feet across. They use these during the rut, a yearly time when bulls fight to win the right to breed with females. After the rut they shed their antlers, which small rodents gnaw on for minerals.

Moose eat up to 60 pounds of food a day. They have no upper front teeth, so they use their strong horselike lips to strip off juicy willow leaves and twigs. They also wade into lakes to find pond weeds and lilies, sometimes completely submerging themselves. During winter they eat willow twigs, bark, and plants that they can paw out from under the snow.

Because of their fibrous diet they have a four-chambered stomach and do lots of cud chewing. But finding food and digesting it takes almost all their time.

Are you also willing to work hard for what you need? to dig deep to learn important facts? to make yourself do what's necessary to accomplish your goals? The Bible says, *"Never tire of doing what is right."*

If you aren't willing to work physically and mentally, you'll eventually suffer for it. Your choices today affect tomorrow.

MISSION: Today, do your work more carefully than required.

338

Marble or Clay?

You've probably seen pictures of gigantic marble carvings such as Michelangelo's *David* in Italy. The artist had to chip off tiny pieces of stone, carefully working it with a chisel and hammer. Then he had to smooth each little rough edge. Once chiseled, a marble statue stands strong and can't be reshaped.

But have you ever seen a potter make something from clay? Clay can be shaped, reshaped, smashed down, and then worked again, until the creation is just what the potter wants it to be. If there's a flaw in the piece, he can remake it!

As Jesus shapes you, you'll want to stay strong and true to what He asks of you. That's like the stone. But when you make mistakes and get things messed up, it's good to know that your Creator can work with you and remold you, shaping you into someone useful and good.

Isaiah said, *"O Lord, you are our Father. We are the clay, you are the potter; we are all the work of your hand."*

Let God shape your life into what it should be. He'll make it a work of art more awesome than you could ever imagine! Then, with His help, stay as strong and true to Him as marble.

CONTACT: Father, help me not to resist Your work of shaping me. Give me wisdom to know Your will.

Tree Hyrax

Home: Africa's jungles
Size: 5-10 pounds

Though the tree hyrax resembles a grayish-brown guinea pig, it's actually related to elephants and manatees! This nocturnal mammal has unique feet that allow it to climb and live in trees. Its toes end with long hooflike nails for climbing. And the ridged, spongy soles of its feet perspire, helping it grip steep surfaces. A vegetarian, it bites off plant life with its molars rather than with its front teeth.

The hyrax must constantly watch for unseen predators. Cats, snakes, and large birds lurk in the shadows, waiting to catch the small animal. If attacked the hyrax will aggressively fight back by biting. Its warning call, a series of loud screams lasting several minutes, can be heard for two miles through the jungle.

You have unseen enemies, too. They watch for your weakest moments, then whisper lies to you, telling you that Satan's way is better than God's. But as you study about Jesus and His love for you, you'll discover that *"the Lord . . . is our help and our shield. In him our hearts rejoice, for we trust in his holy name."*

While you must be aware and careful, you don't need to fear Satan. Simply give your life and will to God each day.

CONTACT: Dear God, please show Your love to me as I put my hope in You.

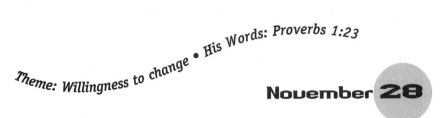

The Quick Changer

Home: African wooded savanna
Size: 100-175 pounds

Impalas belong to the antelope family. Honey-colored, they have a vertical black stripe on their tails and on either side of their rumps. They also have large black-tipped ears. The males sport slender, double-curved horns that grow to 30 inches long.

During the wet season the females and young live in small herds with an adult male. But during the dry season groups of impalas form a large herd, traveling to find vegetation.

Their predators—cheetahs, leopards, and lions—sleep during the hottest part of the day. So that's when impalas go to their water source. That's also when most of their young are born.

When an impala sees a predator approaching, it raises its tail to warn the others. The herd then scatters, racing at 40 miles per hour across the grassland and bounding in great 30-foot leaps. An impala also has the ability to bound 10 feet straight up into the air and turn around before landing. This quick change of direction surprises predators and can save the animal's life.

When you learn that you're doing wrong, you should surprise Satan by quickly changing your ways. God has advised, *"Turn at my rebuke. . . . I will make my words known to you" (NKJV).* Just as the impala would be caught if it hesitated, you can be "caught" by your enemy if you put things off.

TALK BACK: Talk about a time you discovered that you were doing something wrong. How did you react?

341

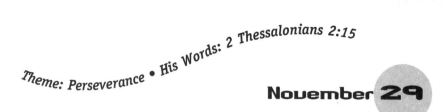

Chuck-will's-widow

Home: Part of United States
Size: To 12 inches

The constant calling from the woods behind our house kept me awake. All night long it went on. I closed the windows and covered my head with pillows, yet I still heard it.

My neighbor told me that the noise came from a Chuck-will's-widow. This bird was calling for a mate!

Chuck-will's-widows were once called goatsuckers, because people believed they sucked milk from goats. These pigeon-sized birds have very wide mouths surrounded by bristles. At dusk they start their hunt for insects—and for a mate, if they don't have one. Through the night they repeatedly call *"Chuck-will's WIDow,"* never giving up.

During the day they sleep. Their mottled brown feathers provide good camouflage when they rest on the ground, where they nest. Strangely, when they perch in a tree they sit parallel to the branch, which is also good camouflage.

When Paul said *"stand fast and hold the traditions which you were taught" (NKJV)*, he was speaking of spiritual matters. But that's good advice for everything you do.

You often face tasks that you don't enjoy. It would be easier just to give up. But like the Chuck-will's-widow, you need to be persistent, asking God to strengthen your self-control.

TALK BACK: What chores do your parents need to remind you to do? Plan a way to remember without being reminded.

Black Smokers

Home: Pacific Ocean floor
Size: To 33 feet high

On the floor of the Pacific Ocean are ridges in the earth's crust. As the earth's plates shift, these ridges separate. Deep molten rock bubbles and boils up through the small spaces between the ridges. When that rock cools, it forms a new crust.

But tiny cracks still remain, so icy ocean water seeps downward. As it filters through the new crust, it collects minerals from the rock. Eventually the water gets so hot again that it bursts back through the ocean floor, like a geyser going off.

The melted minerals blacken the water, making it look like smoke. These minerals settle onto the ground around blowholes, then harden, creating tall chimneys called black smokers.

Just by looking, you wouldn't think so much activity is taking place beneath the earth's surface. Yet the water erupting from black smokers shows only a part of what's happening down deep.

People sometimes start smoking cigarettes because they think it will make them look grown-up. But smoking does more than create puffs of smoke. Beneath the surface, ash settles into the tiny spaces in a person's lungs, filling them so they can't absorb oxygen. Less oxygen creates shortness of breath, and eventually the irritation can cause cancer.

The Bible says, *"God's temple is sacred, and you are that temple."* God wants to live in you, and He wants a place free of harmful substances. Decide today to keep His temple (yourself) in good shape.

MISSION: Find pictures of what smoking does to lungs.

343

Those Sneaky Tentacles

Remember how Satan sneaked up on Jesus in the wilderness? He pretended to be helpful and generous, yet he tried to catch Jesus off guard and turn Him away from God.

But because Jesus clung to God, He wasn't trapped. He told Satan, *"Go away from me, Satan! It is written in the Scriptures, 'You must worship the Lord your God. Serve only him!'"* (ICB).

On a nature program I saw a six-foot octopus in a tank. The program host put his fingertip into the water to see if he could get the octopus's attention.

Gently a pinkish tentacle came up and felt the man's finger, then attached to it. Soon another tentacle wrapped around the man's fingers, and a third around his wrist.

The tentacles began drawing the man's hand into the water. He laughed and with his free hand tried to loosen the suction cups. But a fourth tentacle grasped his other wrist.

Each time the man nearly got free, more tentacles would reach out from a different direction. With help he finally peeled off the tentacles, but he had red marks where the disks had sucked onto him.

When Satan's sneaky tentacles try to capture you, don't get fooled by thinking you can manage alone. You might get free for a minute, but another "tentacle" will surely grasp you. You need someone to help you. In the case of fighting sin, that someone is Jesus.

CONTACT: Dear God, help me always to remember that Jesus is my only safety against Satan's temptations.

344

Hoarfrost

During chilly nights pine needles, tree branches, and spears of grass become frozen. Then, if the air temperature remains below freezing and there's a lot of moisture in the air, the moisture forms ice crystals, or hoarfrost. These crystals can grow to be as much as an inch long. They stand straight out and look spiky or feathery.

The first time I saw hoarfrost, I wanted to take pictures of it. But I waited until daylight, which was a bad idea. Just as the frost on your front lawn disappears when sunlight touches it, so does hoarfrost. The stuff is deceiving! It looks solid enough to last forever, but you just can't trust it to stay.

That's like hypocrisy. When you pretend to be something you're not, you're acting hypocritical. Saying nice things to someone's face but cutting them down behind their back is hypocritical. So is acting obedient, then disobeying when no one's watching.

Once people see someone else's hypocrisy, they have a hard time trusting that person. The Bible says, *"For what is the hope of the hypocrite, though he hath gained, when God taketh away his soul?" (KJV)*. Only Jesus can help you have the courage to always be truthful.

TRY IT: The next time you start acting a lie, ask God to help you be honest and not put on an act.

345

The Borrower

Home: Eastern Australia
Size: To 13 inches

Satin bowerbirds live in forested areas but spend much of their time on the ground. In the springtime the male works hard to attract a female.

First he clears an area of ground. Then he lays a foundation of twigs for his bower, the structure he builds to lure a mate. On both ends he piles twigs to support an archway of vines and stems that he's weaved. Then he decorates his "front yard" with brightly colored moss, feathers, berries, leaves, shells, and even glass and coins.

Never totally satisfied with the items he's collected, the bowerbird might "borrow" from a neighbor's bower. If he sees a particularly attractive item, he snatches it when the other bird isn't watching. At the same time he must defend his own place from borrowers.

The Bible explains, *"The borrower is servant to the lender."* When you borrow from someone, you suddenly become a debtor. That means you owe the other person something in return, and an uncomfortable pressure may grow between you until you can repay your debt.

Borrowing also has risks. If you use a friend's bike and accidentally wreck it, you must not only replace the bike but apologize to your friend, who may be angry. It's better to manage with what you have than to put yourself in a position of owing.

TALK BACK: Why and when do you borrow things? lend things? How do you feel at those times?

Reindeer

Home: Frigid northern areas
Size: To 600 pounds

Reindeer live in the frozen arctic tundra. In order to withstand subzero temperatures, they have a thick underlayer of fur covered with stiff guard hairs that waterproof it. Even a reindeer's nose is covered with fur to protect it from frostbite.

Reindeer eat lichen, grass, moss, and even twigs when other food is scarce. Both males and females grow antlers, which they use for defense and to dig into the snow to find grass.

Reindeer calves are born in the spring. When they're 1 day old they can already run faster than humans! They live with their parents in a large herd that migrates to find food. Sometimes they must swim lakes or channels, but they're strong swimmers.

Reindeer are the only deer that can be domesticated. Laplanders and other people in the north depend on reindeer for clothing, cheese, meat, and transportation. They even use a reindeer's shed antlers to make tools and utensils. Though domesticated reindeer must obey their owners, they don't go hungry like wild reindeer sometimes do.

While growing up, you may sometimes resent other people making choices for you. You may wish you had more freedom. But in order to grow up safely, you need care and direction from more experienced people. The Bible says, *"Children, obey your parents in everything, for this pleases the Lord."*

TALK BACK: At what age were your parents allowed to make all their own decisions? Did they always make good ones?

A Tough Nut to Crack

Home: Asia, Africa, South America
Size: Tree to 40 feet

The cashew tree, a tropical evergreen, has fragrant reddish flowers. It also produces pear-shaped fruit called cashew apples. Sticking out of the end of each apple is an ovary that's shaped like a kidney bean. That's the cashew.

Cashew nuts have to be plucked by hand from the cashew apples. But then the nuts are surrounded by two very tough shells. So harvesters spread the nuts in the sun to dry. Then they surround them with burning logs until the heat bursts the outer shell.

When this happens a caustic brown oil between the two layers sprays out. The poisonous fumes can injure eyes and blister skin.

The second shell, which is even harder than the first, must be cracked and removed by hand. Next the nuts are heated to remove their skin. Finally they're dried. Can you see why cashew nuts are so expensive?

The cashew is well fortified against most things that would try to eat it. You need to be fortified against evil in the same way. The Bible says, *"Therefore put on the full armor of God, so that when the day of evil comes, you may be able to stand your ground, and after you have done everything, to stand."*

If you take care of your relationship with Jesus, surround yourself with Christian friends, and let God help you make the right choices, you'll be well fortified.

MISSION: Prayerfully write out a plan to fortify yourself against the evils Satan may tempt you with. Monitor your progress.

348

Molly and the Toy Fire Engine

One day I sat on the bedroom floor wrapping Christmas presents. Molly, my springer spaniel, lay on the rug beside me.

When I set a little fire engine on the floor to wrap it, Molly sniffed it. Then she eagerly explored its nooks and crannies.

I pushed one of its buttons, and a siren went off. I pushed another, and a gruff voice said, "Fire! Let's go!"

Molly's eyes widened as she backed away.

I pushed another button, and the next voice scared her even more. "It's OK," I told her.

But she didn't believe me. She wanted to go outside.

Animals and humans tend to fear what they don't understand. So they might panic, run away, or even act hateful or violent.

You might feel fear when you find yourself with people of other races or beliefs, or even those who do things in a different way than you do. But the Bible says, *"Be careful in what you do because the Lord our God wants people to be fair. He wants all people to be treated the same"* (ICB).

If someone tries to get you to do something wrong, you must avoid them. But you shouldn't avoid people just because they're different from you. God wants you to try to understand and even appreciate differences. Each person, no matter who they are or how they act, is a child of God. And it's your responsibility to treat them as brothers or sisters.

TALK BACK: What kinds of people or situations frighten you? Why? What can you do to overcome those fears?

The Ambush Master

Home: Coastal waters of Europe, Africa
Size: To 6 feet

The angler, an ugly ocean-bottom fish, captures food by arousing curiosity. It has a long fin that resembles a fishing rod. At the tip of this fin is a flap of skin that looks like a small fish.

When a large fish swims by, the angler waves its fin over its head to catch the large fish's attention. The angler stays partially buried in sand, and its body is camouflaged with bits of skin that float like seaweed. So the larger fish doesn't see the angler and checks out the fin, thinking it's a fish.

That's when the angler quickly opens its huge mouth, sucking the curious fish inside. The angler earns its dinner—not through hard work but by ambush.

Sometimes curiosity makes animals and people investigate things they should stay away from. Satan preys on people's curiosity about harmful substances such as drugs. He makes them look exciting and convinces people that's it's no problem to try them "just once." He even pushes the idea that adults who talk against drugs are trying to keep kids from having fun.

But the Bible says, *"The teaching of the wise is a fountain of life, turning a man from the snares of death."* With God's help you can learn the truth and stay away from the dangerous lures Satan waves at you.

MISSION: Find a book at the library that explains how drugs affect your body and fool your mind.

Beekeeping

I have some friends who are beekeepers. Each year they take care of their hives, then harvest honey from them.

One day I asked them how bees survive through the cold winter months. Obviously, these insects can't collect nectar then. My friends told me that the beehives contain enough nectar for the winter.

They also explained how bees survive the cold by working as a community. During cold weather they surround their queen, forming a living ball around her. The bees on the outside of the ball gradually press toward the middle of the ball, and the bees on the inside move toward the outside. By constantly trading places, all the bees remain warm.

When the queen bee begins to get old, the worker bees raise new queens. These queens fight for control.

When the old queen finally leaves the hive, many of the workers leave with her. This leaves fewer workers to make honey the next season. So some beekeepers clip the queen's wings so she can't fly away.

Isn't it nice how bees work together to keep each other warm? The Bible says, *"How good and pleasant it is when brothers live together in unity!"* When everyone helps care for those around them, it makes life so much happier. And doing so honors God.

MISSION: Read Matthew 25: 34–40. Write it in your own words, explaining what you think Jesus meant. Then decide how you can put it into practice.

Desert Hedgehog

Home: Africa, Arabia, Iraq
Size: To 1.5 pounds

The desert hedgehog is covered with short, flexible quills. By tensing its muscles, it raises the quills, then rolls into a prickly ball.

Safe from most predators, the hedgehog goes about its business of catching insects, scorpions, or poisonous snakes. To catch a snake, it raises the spines on its head, approaches slowly, then rushes the snake. Since its head spines are usually longer than a snake's fangs, most snakes can't bite it. Instead, the hedgehog bites the snake's spinal cord, leaving it helpless.

Desert hedgehogs don't like water, so they live in very dry areas. They thrive in temperatures from 104 to 108 degrees Fahrenheit. When it gets too hot, they burrow into the ground or hide in rock crevices. When the temperature falls below 68 degrees, they hibernate.

When a baby hedgehog is born, its spines are covered by a thin layer of skin. Once it's a week old, the baby begins butting its siblings to compete for its mother's milk. After only six weeks, a baby hedgehog becomes independent.

The hedgehog's quills are its protective armor. You also can have an armor. Paul advised, *"Put on the full armor of God so that you can take your stand against the devil's schemes."* Without God's armor, you become easy prey for Satan and his followers. But with God's armor, you can fight Satan's temptations.

GOAL: Read Ephesians 6: 14-17 to discover what God's armor is. Plan how to get it.

December 10

"Bird," the Parakeet

Home: Australian grasslands
Size: To 7 inches, including tail

God must have chuckled when He created parakeets, also called budgies. Originally natives to Australia, these cheery birds are now bred in captivity.

My parakeet, named Bird, enjoyed sitting on her cage while I worked in the kitchen. When I talked to her, she'd ruffle her blue wings and chirp in response. Sometimes she'd fly to my shoulder to snuggle under my hair. She'd nibble my nose and try to kiss me, or she'd hop down my arm to bathe under the faucet's water.

Then one day she began putting seeds in my ear! She was taking care of me. Another time I called to her from the living room. Instantly her wings whirred as she maneuvered around a corner, then landed on my shoulder. That started a game of hide-and-seek. From then on, I could call her from any place in the house, and she would hunt until she found me!

Bird loved my husband, Bob, too—especially his bald head. She'd swoop above him, dragging her feet across his scalp. Eventually she'd land on his head, then reach down to preen his eyebrows!

"God also made every bird that flies" for us to enjoy. And *"God saw that this was good" (ICB)*. Though sin has caused most creatures to fear humans, God will someday destroy sin and re-create the earth. Until then our pets can help us better understand God's great, unselfish love for us.

TALK BACK: If you have one, what do you like best about having a pet? How are you responsible for its welfare? Does God feel responsible for yours?

353

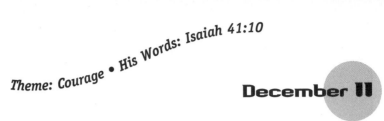

Swamp Beaver

Home: South American swamps
Size: 11-22 pounds

The nutria, also known as a swamp beaver, looks like a beaver with a rat's tail. This mammal is clumsy on land but has webbed back feet that help it swim well. It can even stay submerged for five minutes. But because its nose and eyes sit high on its head, it can keep most of its body underwater all the time.

The nutria has a thick undercoat of soft fur. This is topped by long fawn-colored "guard hairs" that shed water. Because it spends most of its time in water, it must regularly groom itself with oil from glands near its mouth. Using its front paws, it combs the oil through its hair to waterproof itself.

The nutria uses its long, ever-growing, orange-colored incisors to gnaw off tough water plants. Special bacteria in its stomach help it digest things many other animals can't eat.

Though native to South American countries, the nutria now lives in other areas, including North America. In very cold climates its long, bare tail may freeze and break off, but it doesn't seem to harm it. This animal has learned to adapt to harsh, unfavorable conditions.

During your lifetime you may also have to adapt to unfavorable conditions. Maybe you'll attend an unfriendly school or have a job around unhealthy influences. Your family might experience financial difficulties. But no matter what, God promises, *"I will make you strong and will help you"* (NCV).

GOAL: I will develop the courage to trust God and face life with a smile, even when things go wrong.

354

Jaguarundi

Home: Southwestern United States into South America
Size: To 22 pounds and 12 inches high

The jaguarundi looks like a large weasel. Smaller than a jaguar, this wildcat has short legs, a very long tail, a narrow body, and low-set ears on a wedge-shaped head. Secretive, it prefers brushy or jungle areas. Its build allows it to move easily through thick underbrush or into trees to catch small animals and birds.

The jaguarundi doesn't stalk other animals, as do most cats. Instead, it enthusiastically chases them for up to a mile, tiring them out. Then it can easily catch them. It makes up to 40 catches a day.

A good swimmer, the jaguarundi always lives near water and often catches fish. It breeds twice a year and produces up to three kittens in each litter.

If you're enthusiastic, you eagerly pursue your goals. Some people choose to pursue worldly interests. Some get involved in hobbies that take all their time. But your main goal should be to work for God, developing your talents so you can serve Him better.

"The backslider in heart shall be filled with his own ways" *(KJV),* said King Solomon. You won't be a backslider in heart if you dedicate yourself and your activities to Jesus and show your enthusiasm in becoming more like Him.

TALK BACK: What things are you most enthusiastic about? Name two ways you can work for God right where you are.

355

Those New Green Leaves

Most forest trees in Tennessee are deciduous. That means that in the winter they lose their leaves. But black oaks don't seem to notice when cold weather arrives. Though their leaves become crispy brown, they cling to the branches so tightly that even icy winds can't blow them off.

When springtime comes, new leaf buds begin to swell. As the buds grow they eventually loosen and push off the old brown leaves, which then fall and nourish the earth.

Those firmly attached old leaves are like grown-ups who are running the world and doing God's work. The young new leaves are like you. As you mature you'll gradually take over. You'll be the parents, the wage earners, the world leaders, the inventors, and the ones who spread the gospel. The future is in your hands.

Young Samuel found himself needing to prepare for the priestly tasks that lay ahead of him. The Bible says, *"The boy Samuel continued to grow in stature and in favor with the Lord and with men."*

In the same way it's your responsibility to prepare carefully for the future. Many problems lie ahead that will require strong leaders. The way you do things today will affect the future. With God's help you'll do well when you're the new "leaf on the tree."

TALK BACK: What characteristics do safe leaders have? Which of those characteristics do you have? Which do you need to develop?

356

December 14

Black Glass

While hiking in Mexico, I noticed pieces of rock strewn along the side of a river. The rocks looked black and shiny and had very sharp edges.

Called obsidian, these rocks were a product of volcanic activity. They used to be part of the melted rock that erupted from a volcano, but they cooled off too quickly to crystallize. Obsidian is made of the same materials as granite, but it's more tightly compressed and smooth.

Native Americans used obsidian for arrowheads and to make knives and other tools. They carefully chipped at its surfaces until they formed a sharp cutting edge.

Obsidian is actually glass. And though it looks black, it's actually clear. So you can see through it if it's thin enough. Because it contains a mineral called magnetite, obsidian traps, instead of reflects, the light that hits it. Did you know that trapped light appears black?

Obsidian taught me an important lesson. I read my Bible every day to learn about how God cares for me and wants me to live. But if I keep those truths to myself, I'm like obsidian hiding the light it receives.

King David made it a practice to praise God and to tell others about Him. He wanted to share God's light. Each day you also should be able to say with him, *"I do not hide your goodness in my heart. I speak about your loyalty and salvation"* (ICB).

MISSION: Today tell someone something that God has done for you.

Shine as You Go

Home: New Zealand
Size: To 1 inch

The glowworm lives in New Zealand's Waitomo Caves. It starts as a sticky egg on the ceiling of the cave. After it hatches it glows.

To attract flying insects brought into the cave by the river, the glowworm drops dozens of weblike lines. When an insect sees the glowworm's light and flies toward it, the insect gets tangled in the sticky lines. Then the web-spinning glowworm draws the line up and eats the insect.

The glowworm requires darkness so its light is visible. It also needs a windless environment so its lines won't tangle. And the insect needs moisture so it doesn't dry out.

Toward the end of its 11-month life cycle the glowworm wraps itself in its own sticky lines and soon emerges with two wings. It then breeds and lays eggs, beginning a new life cycle.

The glowworm demonstrates two things. First, that light attracts. God needs you to reflect the light of His love to others. Second, the lines you hang—kind words, gentleness, unselfishness, and honesty—catch people's attention and make them want to know more about Him.

Jesus said, *"Let your light shine before men, that they may see your good deeds and praise your Father in heaven."* He meant that your behavior should cause others to want to know God better. Ask Him to help you shine for Him each day.

MISSION: Choose a Christian character trait and with God's help try to develop it.

December 16

Bathtub Float Toy?

Home: South American ponds and rivers
Size: To 6 inches

The first time I saw Surinam toads in an aquarium, I didn't think they were real. They looked like inflated brown plastic toys clinging together in the underwater weeds. As I checked out their flat bodies, triangular heads, and tiny eyes, I noticed one of their legs twitch. Then I realized that they were real!

Underwater dwellers, Surinam toads have no tongues to dart at passing prey. Instead, they feel along the muddy bottoms of ponds and rivers with their sensitive star-shaped feelers. These are located at the end of each toe of their front feet. When they sense a small creature, they suck it into their mouth and eat it.

After the female lays her eggs, the male fertilizes them, then presses them onto her spongy back. The mother's skin soon grows around the eggs. There she shelters and protects them from lurking predators for about 80 days, until they emerge as completely developed little froglets.

David said about God, *"For you are my refuge, a high tower where my enemies can never reach me" (TLB)*. Like the Surinam mother protects her eggs, God wants to keep you physically safe and also guard you against Satan's temptations. So He sends angels to help you and the Holy Spirit to impress and warn you. Don't you want to accept His refuge?

TALK BACK: God has promised to protect you if you're willing. What methods does He use to do this?

A Broken Branch?

Home: Australia, Tasmania
Size: To 1.5 feet

While walking through the forest just after sunset, you notice something moving in a tree. Glancing again, you realize that it's only a broken branch. But after you leave, the "branch" continues to eat its supper.

What you saw was actually a tawny frogmouth. This nocturnal bird with mottled feathers looks like shaggy tree bark. And when in danger it can make itself look like a frayed branch. It creates this camouflage by stretching out its neck, squinting its eyes, making its body rigid, and showing the bristly fringe around its beak. It mimics its surroundings so it won't be noticeable to predators.

It's probably more comfortable for you to blend in with those around you, too. But if they do questionable activities such as watching violent programs, using unclean language, reading impure materials, and being unkind or disrespectful, it's unwise to adopt their lifestyle.

God warns that such conforming leads to eternal loss. He says, *"Do not . . . be like the people of this world. But be changed within by a new way of thinking. Then you will be able to decide what God wants for you"* (ICB).

It's time to stand out and be different in a Christlike way. Ask God for that courage.

CONTACT: Father, sometimes it's hard to be different from others, but I know You'll give me the courage to do it when I need to. Thank You for Your help.

360

It Just Sits Down

Home: South American highlands
Size: 150-350 pounds

The llama looks like a hairy camel with flattened humps. Its stomach is divided into different compartments, and it's a cud chewer. So it chews its food, swallows it, then brings it up and rechews it in order to prepare it for digestion.

The llama is an important animal to Peruvian Indian families. The female llama is bred for her long, soft wool. This provides yarn for warm clothing and strong ropes. And the llama's dung is burned for firewood.

The male llama can carry heavy loads, sometimes weighing 100 pounds or more. He can climb narrow, hazardous trails in the Andes Mountains at altitudes so high it makes horses sick. Heavy fleece keeps him warm, and long double eyelashes protect his eyes from blowing grit. His two-toed feet have thick, padded soles that give him good footing.

But a llama knows when to say "No!" If its burden is too heavy, it sits down and refuses to budge. If the owner tries to force it, it spits foul-smelling, half-digested food into the owner's face. Owners quickly learn how much their animals can carry.

How about you? You probably have schoolwork, chores, and devotions to do. And you want some time for fun. But can you say no to fun when you have other work to do?

"He that handleth a matter wisely shall find good" (KJV). Go ahead and have fun, but remember to put first things first!

TALK BACK: What can I do now to learn to make decisions that will help me grow into a godly, useful adult?

361

Games on the Ledge

Home: Northwestern North America
Size: To 20 pounds

With a group of tourists I sat in a bus at the top of a rocky cliff. Our nature guide pointed out a hoary marmot across the ravine, and we began to watch it.

Fat with pale hair, it perched on a boulder. First it looked into the valley far below, and then it eyed the sky. A moment later another marmot of about the same size climbed onto the same rock. Nudging the first marmot with its nose, it signaled that it wanted to play.

The two faced each other, sitting on their haunches. Then they began playing what looked like patty-cake with their front feet. Next they played a little war game, rolling and tussling. Finally they faced each other, noses nearly touching, and did patty-cake again. They became so busy with play that they forgot to watch the rocks below and the sky above.

"This is a prime time for an eagle to swoop down and knock one of those marmots to the valley floor," our nature guide told us.

We could see eagles circling overhead as the guide continued. "When smaller animals forget to pay attention, they often lose their lives. They need to keep watch at all times."

Satan tries to divert your attention from the important things in life, too. That's why Jesus warned, *"Watch and pray so that you will not fall into temptation."*

FOCUS: You have an enemy who wants to destroy you. But God is greater. Remember to dedicate your life to Him each day.

Frizzy the Squirrel

I have a bird feeder that fits inside my office window. It has one-way glass that lets me watch birds up close.

But a squirrel I've named Frizzy has decided that the feeder is hers. She spends hours in it, eating the black sunflower seeds I put there. When Frizzy leaves, the birds come. But soon Frizzy returns, chasing them off.

In the late afternoon the sun slants through the trees onto the feeder, making it a cozy place to dine. Frizzy then lies down and stretches out in the seed trough, trying to cover all the food. Even though she can't eat everything there, she wants it all for herself.

Animals live in a "me-first" world. They fight for food sources so they can feed themselves and their babies, not caring that others might go hungry.

A "me-first" attitude is called selfishness. It was started by Satan and has caused a lot of pain.

God knew selfishness would destroy people, so He unselfishly gave His Son Jesus to save us from it. He didn't give grudgingly but with His whole heart. When you follow His example of putting others before yourself and giving wholeheartedly, you'll experience a special kind of joy.

"Freely you have received, freely give," Jesus said. Only God can give you the ability to be truly unselfish. Ask Him for that gift today.

MISSION: With your parents' permission, give something you still want to someone less fortunate. How did you feel deep inside?

Pig-tailed Macaque

Home: India and Malaysia
Size: To 18 pounds

Pig-tailed macaques are very intelligent members of the monkey family. They got this name because their short tails curl over their backs, like a pig's tail does.

These monkeys live together in small groups ruled by one male. In the daytime they forage through the forest for tubers, fruit, and leaves. At night they sleep in trees.

Sometimes they raid farmers' fields, quietly working together to gather the best potatoes or corn. If the monkey standing watch warns of the farmer's approach, the group silently slips away.

Shy, macaques will run away or hide when disturbed. But if they're pursued, they'll first stare angrily at the enemy. If that doesn't work, they'll show their teeth, and finally they'll crouch and rush at the pursuer.

Intelligent, macaques seem to be able to learn and reason. Once some macaques washed their potatoes in ocean water. Other macaques watched them and then tried the same thing. They discovered that salty potatoes taste better! Also, when mother macaques want to wean their babies at about six months, they'll often pull the nipple from the baby's mouth and offer it a finger to suck instead!

God has given you intelligence too. As you use your mind to grasp new ideas, you become able to learn even more. You master things you thought you'd never be able to do. Proverbs says, *"A wise man will hear, and will increase learning" (KJV)*.

CONTACT: Dear God, thank You for giving me a good mind. Help me use it to learn only good things.

364

Sea Otter

Home: North Pacific coasts
Size: To 100 pounds

As I rode on a ferry I noticed a gnarled log floating beside the boat. Suddenly it sprayed water in all directions. Looking again, I realized that it was a sea otter floating on its back.

The otter carried a flat rock on its chest. Whacking a shell against the rock, it broke open the shell and gnawed out the meat. Then it rolled in the water, washing away the shell pieces.

Sea otters need to eat a quarter of their weight every day in fish, mollusks, and crustaceans. They dive to find their food, then usually carry it to the surface in their paws.

Clumsy on land, they spend most of their lives in water, sleeping on their backs with their paws over their eyes. They even give birth as they float. The mother nurses the new pup on her chest as she swims.

With no body fat for warmth, otters use air trapped in their heavy fur as insulation. If oil has spilled in the water, it mats their fur so it no longer protects them from the cold.

When God created humans He said, *"Let them have dominion over . . . every creeping thing" (KJV).* Having dominion means being in charge of something and protecting it.

Animals must live in the environment that humans leave. If people ruin their habitat, they suffer. So do your part to keep the earth in good shape.

MISSION: Trash harms wildlife. Take a garbage sack on your next hike and clean up debris left behind.

Sticky Spit

Home: North America, Europe, Asia
Size: To 1 inch

Building comes naturally to the female leafcutter bee. God has implanted within her the blueprint for her nest.

She builds a cigar-shaped nest out of rose leaves and petals, clover leaves, and saliva. It has many partitions, with a separate cell for each egg. The nest is attached to a tree trunk or placed in a small hole in the ground.

It might not sound as if these materials would make a strong home. But with her scissor-like jaws, the female cuts pieces of leaves and petals and glues them together with her saliva. Up to 20 oblong leaf pieces make up the sides of each cell, and round pieces close the ends. If a piece doesn't fit exactly, the bee makes another.

Finally she lays one egg per cell and places pollen and nectar there to feed each baby until it's grown. The nest is sturdy enough to discourage predators and warm enough to keep the babies safe over the winter.

After laying the eggs, the female dies. The following spring her babies hatch, then later build nests for their own eggs.

Don't you sometimes wish that God had programmed your mind to know everything you need to know? Instead, He's given you the ability to reason and choose what to do. He says, *"Diligent hands will rule."* That means you should eagerly pursue the joy of learning, discovery, and creativity.

TALK BACK: God actually did program your mind in some ways. Name them. Why do you think He did this?

366

Golden Jackal

Home: Europe, Africa, Asia
Size: Average 24 pounds

When I worked in Canada, I liked to go to a large country animal park to watch five golden jackal pups. Jackals are wild dogs that live in the grasslands and bush. They scavenge for carcasses but also hunt live prey. Quick-moving and illusive, they work together to support their family.

At the zoo the largest jackal always pushed his nose through the wire cage. He'd look me right in the eye, wag his tail, and beg for attention.

Once I foolishly stepped across the "No Trespassing" sign and squatted in front of him. Reaching out my mittened hand, I let him sniff.

"He's tame," I said to myself.

Just then he chomped on my leather mitten and started pulling it through the cage! Luckily my hand slipped out of the mitten.

But I learned three important lessons. "No Trespassing" means *keep out*. What looks tame might not be. I'm no match for something as quick as a jackal!

What about you? Do you ignore warning signs and think you'll beat the odds? Are you tempted to try forbidden activities "just once"? If so, remember one thing. Wild is wild. Without God's protection, you're no match for anything.

The Bible says, *"The thought of foolishness is sin" (KJV)*. Don't take a chance on doing things you know you shouldn't just because it looks as if no harm will come from it.

TALK BACK: When others want me to secretly do something "harmless," how can I refuse politely?

Keeper of His Flock

Shepherd dogs have been bred to look after sheep and other animals. They seem to like doing it just for the joy of pleasing their masters.

Buzzer, a shepherd mix, thought the boys in his master's family were his "flock." Each day he walked little Tommy to school. Then he'd walk back home to keep 4-year-old Carl out of mischief. After school Buzzer would hurry back down the road to walk Tommy home.

One afternoon Tommy and Buzzer were walking on the roadside when Buzzer stopped to sniff something. Suddenly he noticed an oncoming car veering toward his precious Tommy. Instantly he bounded to his young master. Jumping against Tommy's right side, he knocked the boy into the ditch.

The car missed Tommy, but Buzzer wasn't as fortunate. As he died, he licked Tommy's hand in a final show of affection.

Devotion like that comes from pure, unselfish love. God has that kind of love for you. In fact, He cherishes you as if you were the only one in His creation. And because of His boundless love, He's provided a way for you to spend eternity with Him.

Jesus said, *"I am the way and the truth and the life. No one comes to the Father except through me."* God sent Jesus into the world to bring you safely home. Won't you let Him do that?

CONTACT: Thank You, Father, for sending Jesus to die for me. Help me accept the gift of life He offers.

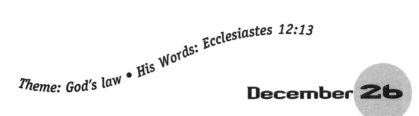

The Longest Neck

Home: Africa
Size: To 17 feet tall, or more

The giraffe is the tallest land mammal. It has only seven vertebrae in its long neck—the same number that humans do.

It rips acacia leaves from trees with its 18-inch tongue and its long muscular upper lip. The foliage provides most of the giraffe's water, but when it does drink it must spread its front legs apart in order to get its mouth to the ground. In this position the giraffe becomes easy prey for its main predator, the lion.

God created the giraffe's long neck and heart to work together in a special way. The animal's large heart generates double the normal blood pressure in order to pump blood up its long neck to its brain. But when the giraffe has its head lowered, the extra pressure could ruin its brain. So God created one-way check valves in its jugular veins to hold the extra blood back. That way the blood can't rush to the giraffe's head.

God's physical laws help creatures survive and also keep our planet rotating as it should. If these laws could be bypassed, disaster would result. God also gave humans the Ten Commandments —*our* laws to live by.

The Bible says, *"Honor God and obey his commands. This is the most important thing people can do" (ICB)*. Obeying the commandments will help you live a happier, safer life.

TRY IT: Prop your feet up above your head. How long does it take to feel the blood pressure throbbing in your head?

Snowshoe Hare

Home: Northern, arctic regions
Size: 5-10 pounds

Snowshoe hares are perfectly adapted to survive in the coldest weather. Their small black-tipped ears conserve body heat. Their long, furry toes spread wide to keep them from sinking into the snow as they run. They have excellent vision and eat whatever vegetation they can find, including the bark from young trees.

Unlike other rabbits, snowshoe hares are born with open eyes and thick fur. Within three days they can hop. As the snow melts they molt and get earth-colored coats, so they're camouflaged in each season.

One frigid night in Canada I took a walk to admire the newly fallen snow. Deep and soft, it covered the fields and lawns and muffled my footsteps. Suddenly I saw something white streak across the field. Fascinated, I stopped to watch.

It ran, it leaped, it did a flip in the air, and it came down running in the other direction. It was a snowshoe hare, and it looked so happy. I decided it was leaping for joy!

Life on earth sometimes gets difficult, but when I think about someday living in heaven with Jesus, it makes me happy. Luke said, *"Be glad in that day and leap for joy, for behold, your reward is great in heaven" (NASB).* Let's thank Jesus for what He has in store for us!

MISSION: Just as sneezes are "contagious," so are smiles. Today share Jesus' love by passing a smile to everyone you meet. Watch the ripple effect.

December 28

Humpback Whale

Home: Seas
Size: To 72 tons

While writing this I'm in Alaska watching for humpback whales. They've traveled here from Hawaii to feed on krill and fish.

Just above the waves I spot a blow—the mist humpbacks spray into the air to clear their blowhole before surfacing. A moment later the dark hump appears. Then a T-shaped tail rises high above the water for an instant before the creature dives in search of more food.

As the humpback lunges toward its prey, its expandable mouth fills with water. The animal then forces the water through its baleen. The baleen is made of thick plates that look like wide ribs edged with stiff wirelike hairs.

As the water goes through the baleen, fish get caught in this "strainer." The whale then wipes its enormous tongue across the baleen, then swallows the catch. In this way an adult manages to eat at least 1,000 pounds a day.

When humpbacks return to Hawaii for the winter, they no longer eat but find mates, breed, and bear the former year's babies. Since they must live off fat they stored during their summer feast, those who neglect their hunting don't survive this time.

David said, *"Taste and see that the Lord is good."* He knew that people must "feed" on spiritual food while it's available and store it in their memories. So be sure to spend time with God each day. It's like gathering up strength for difficult times.

TALK BACK: What would happen if you went without food for a week? What about if you neglected worship for a week?

Your Company's Showing

Home: Canada to Caribbean
Size: Robin-sized

Mockingbirds are lively gray birds. They have white patches on their wings and tail that show when they fly.

Though they have their own song, they habitually mimic other birds' calls. Singing tirelessly, they mark and defend their territorial boundaries.

Each morning I hear a mockingbird singing. Sometimes it gives off 25 different calls! But today's song was completely different. It was the cry of a seagull. I guess the mockingbird has been keeping new company.

Remember Samson? God set him apart to do a special job. But against his parents' wishes he began making close friends with godless people. Then he heard about a pretty Philistine girl. *"So he went down and talked to the woman; and she looked good to Samson" (NASB).* It wasn't long before he married her and basically put aside God's mission for him. In the end those associations ruined his life.

Just as with Samson or the mockingbird, it soon becomes obvious who your close friends are. Their vocabulary creeps into your speech, and their thoughts, actions, and interests become yours. If they aren't Christians, it's easy to start making excuses for doing things you once felt were wrong.

Whom you choose for close friends really matters. So be wise! Ask God to help you make careful choices.

TALK BACK: What characteristics should you look for in a close friend?

Solid Mud

Near Anchorage, Alaska, sits a waterway called Turnagain Arm. Extending about 50 miles, this low area between some mountains allows seawater to enter. During full tide it looks like a deep and placid lake.

But twice every 24 hours the tide goes out. Then the water rushes away, leaving a wide area that appears to be solid mud. Eagles strut across it, hunting for stranded fish to eat. Even small mammals wander onto the mudflats to hunt.

But the mud isn't what it appears to be. It's really rock that's been pulverized by grinding glaciers. The tiny pieces of rock trap and hold water. So though it looks firm enough to walk on, the waterlogged rock actually acts like quicksand!

If you step onto it, you begin to sink. At knee level you can't pull your feet out. Unless someone rescues you, you'll get trapped by the incoming tide, a wall of water up to six feet high.

As earth's history nears its end, some leaders will appear to be good Christians. But because they've let the silt and grime of a sinful world rule their lives, they won't be safe to follow. That's why it's important to study your Bible for yourself and know what's right and wrong.

The Bible instructs, *"Do not believe every spirit, but test the spirits to see whether they are from God."* You must also test what humans tell you.

TALK BACK: How can you test leaders and others who tell you new things?

Still Growing!

Home: State of Alaska
Size: Approximately 20,320 feet tall

Denali, which means "The High One," is also known as Mount McKinley. It's the tallest mountain in North America. Though it towers above the other mountains, it's often hard to see. That's because warm fronts coming from the Pacific Ocean collide with the frigid mountain air. The two fronts produce new weather, often wrapping Denali in a cloud layer.

Composed of granite, Denali covers more than 8,000 square miles. Temperatures to minus 50 degrees Fahrenheit have been recorded at its peak. The mountain lies on an earthquake fault above two tectonic plate shelves. As these shelves push against each other deep in the earth, Denali gets squeezed upward in the same way a watermelon seed pinched between your fingers moves upward. So this famous mountain is still growing about three fourths of an inch every year.

Just as Denali is still growing, you need to continue growing. You need to grow physically and mentally. But you also need to continue to grow in your spiritual life—to continually become more like Jesus.

The Bible says, *"You should want the pure and simple teaching [of God]. By it you can grow up and be saved"* (ICB). As you enter the new year, keep in mind that growth is a necessary part of living. So learn all you can, do all you're able to do, and above all, remember to accept the daily gifts Jesus offers you.

CONTACT: Thank You, Jesus, for all You've done for me this year. Help me to continue growing for You.

Resources

A Field Guide to Animal Tracks (Peterson Field Guide)

A Field Guide to Insects America: North of Mexico   Borror and White

A Field Guide to Reptiles and Amphibians
   of Eastern NA (Peterson FG)   Conant

A Golden Guide—Weeds

A Guide to Field Identification Wildflowers
   of NA (Golden Press)   Venning

Animals of the Seashore   Guberlet

Audubon Soc Field Guide to NA Insects and Spiders

Audubon Soc Field Guide to NA Birds Eastern Reg

Butterflies and Moths, Dorling Kindersley Handbooks

Complete Field Guide to Americal Wildlife   Collins, Jr.

Cooking with Natural Foods   Beltz

Earth Facts, Pocket Full of Knowledge

Field Book of Natural History   Palmer

Field Guide to the Birds of NA, Nat'l Geo.

Foxfire 3

Illus Encyc of Animal Life, The (20 volumes)

Kingfisher Illus. Encyc. of Animals, The   Chinery, Ed.

Life of the Marsh, The   Niering

Life of the Pond, The   Amos

Life of the Seashore, The   Amos

Life of the Desert, The   Sutton

Life of the Jungle, The   Richards

Living Lanterns, Luminescence in Animals   Simon

Mammal Guide, The   Palmer

Nat'l Audubon Soc Field Guide to the SE States

Nat'l Audubon Soc Field Guide to the Night Sky

Nat'l Audubon Soc Field Guide to NA Butterflies

Nat'l Audubon Soc Field Guide to NA Reptiles and Amphibians, The

New York Public Library Desk Reference, The 1989

Pond Life, A Guide to Common Plants and Animals
   of NA Ponds and Lakes   Reid

Rocks and Minerals	Pearl
Seventh-day Adventists Believe	
Simon and Schuster's Guide to Mammals	Boitani and Bartoli
Spiders of the World	Preston-Mafham
Spotter's Guide to Trees of North America	Mitchell and Ruggiero
Stars and Planets, A Barron's Nature Guide	Ekrutt
Stars, A Guide to the Constellations, Sun, Moon, Planets	Golden Press
Tidepool & Reef, Marinelife Guide to the Pacific NW Coast	Harbo
Trees of North America—Golden Press	Brockman
Wild Technology, Inventions Inspired by Nature	Gates
Wildlife Fact Files	

Theme Index

Theme	Date
Advantages, using your	9-21
Advice, seeking	6-28
Ambition	5-12
Angels	3-24
Anger management	1-9; 3-28
Animal heroes	1-15; 2-15; 3-1; 5-9; 7-4; 8-27; 9-6; 10-25; 12-25
Annoyance, coping with	8-11
Apology	8-16
Backsliders, welcoming	10-29
Balance in nature and life	3-22
Behavior	9-4
Belonging	5-18
Bible	
guidance	8-5
reliability	7-23
study	1-30; 11-23; 12-28
Blame, shifting	1-26
Borrowing	12-3
Calamity	9-29
Care for others	12-8
Change, willingness to	11-28
Character, developing	1-11
Cheerfulness	2-29
Chicken, being	7-14
Choices	1-12; 2-17
Christlikeness	5-13
Cleanliness	4-28
Clothing	8-8
Commandments, Ten	7-9; 10-18; 11-4; 12-26
Communication	5-23
Conforming	12-17
Conscience	4-15; 5-25; 9-8
Conservation	
environmental	3-15
mental	3-16
Contentment	10-17
Conversation, useful	11-19
Cooperation	9-2; 10-31; 11-11
Cope, learning to	6-14
Courage	1-31; 12-11
Creation versus evolution	11-7

Theme	Date
Curiosity	12-7
Decisiveness	1-13; 6-24; 12-18
Determination	2-10; 9-25; 11-25
Development, spiritual	5-5; 7-31
Diet	2-18
Diligence	7-19; 8-22; 9-9
Disaster readiness	11-15; 11-16
Discernment	1-16; 4-2; 5-2; 5-3; 8-19; 12-30
Discipline	
accepting	10-1
self-	4-26; 11-10
Discretion, obedient	2-26
Doing your best	1-24
Drugs, avoiding	7-10
Empathy	9-22
Encouraging others	6-2
End-times	3-27; 10-12; 11-1
Enthusiasm	10-16; 12-12
Environmental responsibility	12-22
Evolution versus creation	11-7
Example	8-30; 12-15
Fairness	9-14
Faithfulness to God	11-24
Favoritism	9-23
Fear	12-6
Feelings, unreliable	2-19
Flexibility	1-6
Foolishness	10-19; 12-24
Forgiveness	1-7; 4-17; 5-1; 10-30
Friends, choosing	6-10
Giving, in secret	5-29
God/God's	
armor, putting on	5-17
blessings	5-28
care	6-13; 8-12
discipline	3-30
forgives	5-27
gifts	12-10; 12-23
greatness	1-28
hearing	8-18

Theme	Date
instructions, hearing	4-30
knowledge about us	11-20
law, accepting	3-31
light, sharing	7-21
love	7-6; 10-15; 10-21
plan	8-6
power	3-5
presence	6-6
promises/guidance	2-11; 2-14; 2-22; 3-11
protection	1-15; 1-18; 2-15; 3-18; 3-26; 6-17; 12-16
provisions	1-19; 2-12; 3-6; 6-1
purpose for us	6-23
shaped by	11-26
staying close to	6-7
trusting	6-25; 7-7
truth, "hearing"	2-20
understanding	9-16
voice, knowing	9-13
work in our lives	5-10
your importance to	6-22
Good, reaping from bad	8-24; 10-6
Gospel, sharing	2-13; 4-25; 5-14; 6-9; 6-11; 12-14
Gossip	1-5; 7-3
Grief, dealing with	9-30
Growth	
Christian	2-16; 5-19; 12-31
physical	2-24
Grumbling	11-14
Habitat, creating favorable	2-1
Habits	
defeating bad	10-27
management	3-9
Health	11-30
Heaven	11-5
Help, requesting	9-15
Holy Spirit	2-8; 3-8; 5-10; 5-21; 10-7
Honesty	1-27; 2-3, 2-4; 10-2
Humility	4-20
Hypocrisy	12-2
Ideals, developing	3-13

Theme	Date
Independence, spiritual	5-31
Individuality	4-23
Industriousness	6-19
Influence	2-25; 2-27; 3-29; 12-29
Ingenuity	9-5; 11-18
Instruction, accepting	9-19
Intelligence	12-21
Jesus	
building on	9-10
example, following	4-16
focusing on	10-26
is at the door	1-17
Lord of everything	11-17
sacrifice	6-15
safe with	7-16
Joy	2-21; 6-5; 9-20; 12-27
Judging others	8-23
Judgment, trusting own	3-19
Kindness	3-10; 8-26
Laziness	6-19
Leadership, preparing for	11-2; 12-13
Listening	2-23; 11-9
Looks versus personality	2-28
Miracles	8-31
Missionary spirit	5-30: 8-13
Mood	6-18
Needs, physical	4-12
New Jerusalem	1-10
Obedience	2-7; 3-20; 7-20; 8-21; 10-20
Occult	
danger of	4-7
escaping	4-10
guarding against	4-8
recognizing	4-9
Orderliness	4-14
Ordinances, foot washing	10-7
Outer Space	
Milky Way	8-2
stars	8-1

Theme	Date	Theme	Date
Patience . . .4-3; 5-15; 6-3; 11-6; 11-12		Sin	
Peacemaker. 1-8; 2-5		hiding 7-18	
Peer pressure 9-27		result of 1-14; 6-30	
Perceptions, accurate 5-16		Size, physical. 7-26	
Persistence . . .3-4; 3-12; 4-21; 5-4; 6-4;		Speech, pure 5-20; 10-9	
7-29; 8-4; 9-3; 9-11; 11-25		Spirit of Prophecy, importance. . . . 1-30	
Personality versus looks 2-28		Steadfastness. 8-14; 10-28	
Pitfalls, avoiding 5-6		Sticking together 1-23	
Play, importance of 9-28		Stubbornness. 1-25; 4-24	
Praise to God. 3-7; 11-3		Submission 12-4	
Prayer 3-25; 4-22; 8-3; 8-10			
Pride 2-6; 4-13; 6-8; 10-10		Talents, using 4-11	
Procrastination. 10-4		Teamwork 9-18	
Prophecy. 8-28		Teasing 7-30	
Protection		Temperament. 7-22	
God's 1-15		Temperance. 7-25; 8-29	
spiritual. . . . 1-22; 4-4; 8-15; 10-22;		Temptation, avoiding. . . 1-21; 3-2; 6-21	
12-5; 12-9		Tenderheartedness 3-17	
Purity 3-21; 5-22; 9-17; 10-2		Thankfulness 6-20	
Purpose, all creatures 6-26		Thoroughness 4-5	
		Tithing 1-4	
Redemption. 5-8		Tongue, controlling 1-2; 3-3; 7-13;	
Reflecting our Maker 4-1		8-25	
Regeneration 6-12		Transformation 4-18; 8-20	
Relationship with God 1-1		Trinity, the 2-9	
Reliability. 1-29; 7-2		Troubles, facing 5-24	
Repentance 3-14		Trust	
Reputation 2-2		encouraging . 1-20; 5-7; 10-11; 10-23	
Responsibility 7-1; 7-24; 8-7; 8-27; 11-11		in God 4-6; 11-27	
		Trustworthiness 5-11; 7-15	
Safety, physical 11-21		Trying again 8-9	
Salvation 3-1; 4-27; 7-5; 7-8; 7-28; 9-12			
Satan		Unity. 10-13	
being used by 5-8		Unselfishness 9-1; 10-3; 10-24;	
counterfeit 10-14		10-25; 12-20	
persistence 6-29			
repelling. 7-12		Watchfulness 3-23; 9-24; 10-5;	
Second Coming 1-3; 11-22		12-1; 12-19	
Secret, nothing is. 4-29		Wisdom. 4-19; 6-16; 11-8	
Self-control. 6-27; 9-26		Witnessing, patience in. 7-27	
Selfishness. 7-11		Worship, personal 9-7	
Shaking, the 7-17			

Animal/Object Index

Animal/Object	Date
AMPHIBIANS	
Frog	
African clawed	9-16
bullfrog	6-4
paradoxical	8-23
Salamander	10-14
Toad, Surinam	12-16
BIRDS	
Blackbird, redwing	6-9
Bowerbird, satin	12-3
Budgie	12-10
Chicken	7-22
hero	9-12
Chuck-will's-widow	11-29
Coot	6-5
Cormorants	11-10
Crane, sandhill	3-11
sandhill/whooping	10-29
Crossbill, white-winged	10-13
Crow	10-5
Duck	9-15; 9-27
Eagle, bald	5-31; 6-30
harpy	10-23
Feathers	2-9
Finch, woodpecker	9-11
Flamingo	2-25, 2-26
Frogmouth, tawny	12-17
Fulmar, northern	8-25
Hammerkop	8-14
Hawk, red-tailed	8-9
Hero, feathered	3-1
Hoatzin	7-19
Humming, ruby-throated	9-1, 9-2
Jay, blue	3-19
Kingfisher	7-29
Mandrill	4-17
Mockingbird	10-5; 12-29
Nests	7-17
Ostrich	3-29; 8-19
Ovenbird	4-21
Owl	
barred	8-18
burrowing	10-24
Parakeet	12-10

Animal/Object	Date
Parrot, African gray	3-25
Peacock	4-13
Puffbird, swallow-winged	3-13
Raven, common	3-7
Robin story	5-16
Sparrow	1-24
Stork, shoebill	1-8
Swallow, cliff	11-21
Tern, least	6-14, 6-15
Waxwing, cedar	8-29
HEAVENS	
Constellation	8-5
Orion	1-10
Earth	8-6
Eclipse	10-20; 10-21
Electromagnetic waves	8-31
Light-year	8-3
Meteor showers	11-1
Milky Way	8-2
Moon	8-4
Northern Lights (Aurora)	1-28
Pulsars	8-30
Star	8-1
INSECTS	
Ant, black	4-30
Ant lion	4-18
Bee, honey	12-8
leafcutter	12-23
Beetle, click	9-3
dung	9-23
whirligig	10-18
Butterflies	
Bird-wing	10-10
Blue, common	11-20
Large	10-31
Red admiral	6-16
Swallowtail, tiger	5-5
Butterfly/Moth comparison	5-3
Caterpillar	8-28
Cicada, seventeen-year	7-31
Earwig	8-21
Fly	
fire	7-21

Animal/Object	Date
horse	8-11
house	4-28
Mantis, praying	7-25
Mosquito	6-29
Moth/Butterfly comparison	5-3
Moth	
lobster	5-20
luna	5-4
zale	3-22
Spider	
angler	4-9
black	10-12
black widow	3-14
defense	4-10
funnelweb	4-5
jumping	11-4
netcasting	4-7
tarantula	2-16
trap-door	1-17
web-spitting	4-8
webs, orb	4-6
Springtail	3-5
Stinkbug	2-29
Termite, Formosan subterranean	9-9
Tick	7-10
Walkingstick	4-1
Wasp, potter	1-4
Worm	
earth	6-22, 6-23
glow (New Zealand)	12-15
ice	2-12
Water Strider	6-8

MAMMALS

Animal/Object	Date
Aardvark	8-7
Anteater	
silky	10-23
spiny	6-20
Armadillo, giant	5-11
Baby Animals	10-15
Badger, American	10-28
Bat	
brown, big	7-7
little	7-5
mouse-eared	7-8

Animal/Object	Date
yellow-eared	7-9
similarities	7-6
Bear	
black	4-16; 10-1
hero	1-15
sun	7-15
Bilby, greater	3-27
Binturong	2-21
Bushbuck	1-11
Camel, double-humped	1-7
Cat	
cheetah	3-20
cougar	11-5
domesticated	
kittens	1-26
story, hero	7-4
story, Synjee	2-23; 6-21; 10-11
leopard	7-16
lion	9-14
ocelot	10-26
tiger, Siberian	5-12
Coatimundi	3-12
Deer	
Chinese water	3-17
mouse	10-17
musk	2-27
Dog	
African wild	10-3
noses	8-27
sled	11-2
story	
Belle	10-19
Brandy	4-26
Bruce	7-1; 8-16
Buck	2-2 to 2-8
dachshund	7-30
hero	5-9; 9-6; 12-25
Itsy	3-10
Lady	5-21
Molly	1-1; 1-20; 1-21; 4-2; 10-4; 12-6
Yellow	6-10
Zannie	11-14
Zero	6-25
Dolphin	9-28

Animal/Object	Date	Animal/Object	Date
hero	2-15	giant	5-1
Donkey	2-10	sea	2-22
Dormouse	8-12	Pig	9-19
Elephant	1-18; 11-22	Platypus, duck-billed	9-22
Ferret	1-6	Polecat	1-31
Fossa	1-16	Porcupine, African	9-26
Fox		Rabbit	
bat-eared	1-13	cottontail	2-18
gray	4-19	jack	11-12
Giraffe	12-26	Raccoon	10-7
Goat		Rat	
domestic	4-24	giggling	9-20
wild	1-12	naked mole	10-9
Gopher, pocket	4-14	pack	4-29
Hare		Ratel	9-18
spring	3-2	Reindeer	12-4
snowshoe	12-27	Saiga	9-25
Hedgehog, desert	12-9	Seal	
Hog, feral	8-17	crabeater	5-2
Honeyguide	9-18	hooded	3-28
Horse		Serval	10-16
brumby	1-25	Sheep	
story, hero	10-25	bighorn	9-17
Hyrax, tree	11-27	domestic	5-10; 9-13
Ibex, alpine	5-15	wild	1-12
Impala	11-28	Shrew	
Jackal, golden	12-24	elephant	7-3
Jaguarundi	12-12	european	4-22
Lemming	1-3	Sloth, two-toed	6-19
Llama	12-18	Squirrel story	3-6; 12-20
Macaque, pig-tailed	12-21	Sugar glider	11-8; 11-9
Marmot		Tapir, Brazilian	6-24
alpine	8-22	Tarsier	7-26
hoary	12-19	Tasmanian devil	7-13
Meerkat	11-11	Viscacha	8-15
Monkey		Warthog	8-10
red howler	5-23	Weasel, least	9-4
squirrel	11-6	Whale	
story	7-30	beluga	11-3
Moose	11-25	humpback	12-28
Muskrat	6-6	Wombat, common	7-18
Nutria	12-11	Yak	11-23
Okapi	10-30	Zebra, Grevy's	4-23
Opossum, Virginia	3-18	Zorilla	9-5
Otter			

MINERALS

Animal/Object	Date
Brimstone	7-23
Chalk	3-31
Crystals	5-19
Dirt	6-12
Marble/Clay	11-26
Mica	1-30
Obsidian (black glass)	12-14
Tuff	9-10

MISCELLANEOUS

Animal/Object	Date
Animal watching	1-19
Group names	5-18
Habitats	
arctic tundra	1-2
backyard	2-1
Mount McKinley (Denali)	12-31
pond	6-1; 6-2; 6-3; 6-4; 6-5; 6-6; 6-7; 6-8; 6-9
Hearing	2-20
Killing	1-14
Litter, environmental	3-15
mental	3-16
Pet sources	8-26
Slivers	5-25
Stapes (bone)	2-19
Surface film, water	6-7
Teeth	4-11
Tongue	3-3
Traps	5-6
Water/Creek	2-17

MOLLUSKS

(also see *Water Creatures*)

	Date
Snail, Garden	5-17

OUR WORLD

Animal/Object	Date
Air pressure	11-13
Black smokers	11-30
Brook	10-8
Doldrums	6-18
Erosion	6-13
Fault	9-29
Fire, forest	5-24
Glacier	2-11

Animal/Object	Date
Gravity	11-13
Hoodoos	8-13
Mud	6-3; 12-30
Regeneration	4-27

PLANTS

Animal/Object	Date
Cactus, prickly-pear	6-27
Cashew	12-5
Century	2-13
Cocklebur	11-18
Cordgrass	11-7
Corpse lily	10-2
Cucumber, squirting	1-9
Emergent plants	6-2
Fig, strangler	10-27
Mayapples	5-29
Mistletoe	7-11
Oats	6-11
Photosynthesis	4-12
Rice	7-27
Tomato	5-8
Tree	
bark	4-4
mimosa	9-8
oak, Black	12-13
pine	8-24
tulip magnolia	2-28
Twigs	2-24
Vines	1-27; 3-30; 7-20
Weeds	3-9

REPTILES

Animal/Object	Date
Alligator	3-23, 3-24
Gecko	3-4
Iguana, Green	6-28
Lizard, Australian Frilled	7-14
Skink, Crocodile	11-19
Snake	
constrictor, boa	1-5; 4-3; 9-24
hognose, eastern	7-12
python, ball	5-7
Toad, horned	4-20
Turtle, snake-necked	9-21

WATER CREATURES

(except mammals)

Animal/Object	Date
Anemone, giant sea	10-22
Barnacle, ivory	11-24
Cone Shell	10-6
Crab	
ghost	6-17
hermit	8-8
purple shore	3-26
Fish	
angler	12-7
clownfish	10-22
cuttlefish/cuttlebone	3-21
eel, electric	9-7
flounder	8-20
John Dory	7-24
mudskipper	5-30
paddlefish	5-22
tuna, bluefin	2-22
Jelly Fish, moon	6-26

Animal/Object	Date
Limpets	7-2
Octopus	5-13; 5-14; 7-28; 12-1
Sand Dollar	3-8
Scallops, blue-eyed	4-15
Sea Horse	2-14
Snail, Moon	1-22, 1-23
Zooplankton	4-25

WEATHER/NATURAL DISASTERS

	Date
Clouds	5-26
Drought	1-29
Earthquake	9-29
Hoarfrost	12-2
Hurricane	11-17
Precipitation	5-27
Rain	5-28
Tornado	11-15; 11-16
Tsunami	9-30